What About Advertising?

WHAT ABOUT ADVERTISING?

BY

KENNETH M. GOODE

AND

HARFORD POWEL, Jr.

Publishers

HARPER & BROTHERS

NEW YORK *and* LONDON

1928

To the Unknown

Advertising Man:

THE COPY WRITER, THE SALESMAN, THE ACCOUNT
EXECUTIVE, THE PRODUCTION MAN—THOU-
SANDS OF THEM—WHOSE LOYAL, ENTHUSIASTIC
AND UNSELFISH WORK HAS MADE FAME AND
FORTUNES FOR MANY AND LIFE MORE PLEASANT
FOR ALL.

CONTENTS

A WORD IN PERSON

THERE are many good books on advertising. We add our word not because other writers have not done well, but because they may have done too well. Most of them make an ambitious attempt to reduce advertising principles into scientific formulæ to which human action shall be forced to conform. We suggest quite the opposite course. Reduce the principles of human action to a formula. Advertising has then only to follow politics, diplomacy, and all ordinary business practice in conforming politely and profitably to these humanities. Advertising spreads a field of infinite complexity. By a simpler approach we hope, within these covers, to reverse the telescope—to bring vast objectives down to a tiny cross-section in easy focus for an ordinary business man.

Our combined experience with advertising adds around thirty-seven years. It touches *Collier's* and the *Saturday Evening Post, Vogue* and *Harper's Bazar, Vanity Fair* and *Hearst's Magazine, The Youth's Companion* and the *New York American.* Sometimes as editors, sometimes as sellers. But always as students of a single subject, the way of the public mind.

More practically, we have been, fortunately, behind scenes in New York's greatest two department stores and one of Boston's. Seven of our thirty-seven years were in advertising agencies. We have done many miles of copy for others. And for ourselves. We have bought space and sold it. We have written about advertising a little and read about it much. Most of all, we have watched advertising work. Besides general impressions gained in these thirty-seven years, the pages that follow have the more solid authority of a searching study of recorded results.

Our activity happens to have been much with publisher's selling: advertising and circulation. And books. We have, however, *sold* mineral water, cigarettes, and candy; antiques, insurance, and burial vaults; furniture, golf shoes, and gas masks; radio and real estate; canned goods, correspondence courses, Chinese games.

This range of experience may protect our reader against inflexible formulæ and the often irritating over-assurance of those whose gnarled and knotted tree of knowledge has never been transplanted. And, because we have seen so much of advertising and know so little about it, we hope for a certain sympathetic response from our fellow non-experts to whom we have the honor of submitting this small book.

K. M. G.

H. P., JR.

What About Advertising?

What About Advertising?

CHAPTER I

Man Proposes

One cold December night a policeman on a lonely beat was accosted by a bedraggled stranger. He was starving. He wished to go to jail. The more he argued, the more he pleaded, the more firmly the policeman refused. Finally the tramp picked up a rock and shattered the nearest window.

The policeman locked him up.

So far the story is true. But for sake of argument, imagine the tramp a broken-down actor who had studied law—in short, a man skilled in logic and elocution. Suppose that, inspired by his need, he made the perfect plea; something between Lincoln's speech at Gettysburg and Mark Antony's oration over Cæsar's bleeding body.

Would it have moved the policeman to action?

Suppose, further, the frozen tramp had repeated his perfect appeal over and over again, with every attractive variation. Could he, do you think, have got his food and lodging as quickly as by smashing the window?

Advertising is said to employ, one way or another, 600,000 people. It ranges from a perfumery label to an electric billboard, from a slogan to a circus parade, from a form letter to a world's fair at Wembley. No single rule can apply to all. But any advertiser who minds this little story of the tramp and the policeman can never go astray on one great fundamental: the psychology of advertising is a *buying* psychology, not a selling psychology.

It is not even selling as reversed in the mirror.

It is buying, studied from the rear!

The tramp's appeal was sincere and honest. Theoretically, the policeman had no chance against such perfect "copy." Nevertheless, it took the rock through the window to do the business, because that business had to be done in the policeman's mind! And in his mind nothing short of window-smashing meant jail.

The success of any advertisement, in the same way, exists only in the mind of its readers. Until some one—like our policeman—has actually been influenced toward action, an advertisement remains, like our tramp's speech, only a group of words some one has taken the trouble to put together.

Advertisers carelessly picture themselves in the fortunate position of a regimental chaplain who can preach regularly to his thousand men, whether they like it or not. Advertisers in real life are more like trappers who must, by their own ingenuity, attract and catch singly every elusive prospect.

For every advertisement has two *active* sides:
1. You write what you want;
2. I read what I want.

Once in a while the twain meet. But not nearly so often as is generally supposed, *because I am as selfishly interested in what I will read as you are in what you will write.*

A successful advertisement, like a successful contract, depends on the meeting of minds. Millions of men have made hundreds of dollars by attracting public attention. But hundreds of men have made millions of dollars by letting the public guide them. The distinction between the two will richly repay careful study. Human nature flows in strong currents; human action runs in channels centuries deep. Plenty of advertisers have successfully turned the consumer's mind toward their product. But the millionaires are those who have turned their products toward the consumer's mind.

And there you have one of the real difficulties in appraising advertising as a practical aid to business. When anything is about ripe for the public—or, looking at it more exactly, when the public is about ripe for that thing—good advertising will tremendously speed up its distribution and sale. At a less favorable moment even better advertising may fall quite flat.

In that triumphant psychological frame-up, the Carpentier-Dempsey fight, the Frenchman's first trip was a whole year too early. He had to be sent home to let the idea ripen with the American public.

In Mayor Hylan's first election every New York newspaper, except two, devoted thousands of dollars a day of best editorial space to the campaign against him. Nevertheless, Hylan ran up an astounding vote. Naturally, the supporting papers claimed credit for his triumph, just as the others would most gladly have claimed it for his defeat. With the newspaper line-up exactly the same four years later, the results were completely and overwhelmingly reversed.

Applied too soon, advertising is like watering a tiny seedling; too late, like watering an old stump.

Then again, things like bobbed hair, smocks, Fords, radios, chain stores and crossword puzzles spread so fast of themselves that even when advertising does catch up with the band wagon, skeptics won't always grant it credit. Economists are fond of pointing out how the sale of certain black chocolate in the United States improved the sale of pianos in Ecuador. Presumably, piano advertising in Ecuador was as innocent, in this instance, as any paid advertising of Eskimo Pie here. As a newer example read this clipping from a trade note of the *New York Times:*

EYE-SHADES IN GREAT DEMAND

Manufacturers producing the celluloid sport eye-shades, which are now having widespread sale, report that in many cases they are unable to fill one-third of the orders they receive from retailers. . . . Meanwhile, however, jobbers of novelty goods who are able to supply the eye-shade are opening many desirable accounts among retailers.

Here the manufacturers cannot fill one-third of their orders. Yet no advertiser claims credit. Advertising will eventually aid Florida to get established as that splendid state deserves; but no friend would admit, much less claim, that advertising, in any proper professional sense, was responsible for the great 1925 boom. Nor, we believe, would any enthusiast wager great amounts that Florida wouldn't grow rich although never spending another nickel on advertising.

Lorin F. Deland, in his wonderful little book *Imagination in Business,* tells an amusing story of a campaign to restore the wearing of Congress Gaiter shoes by giving a life insurance policy to every wearer. Here in our own day is the $1,000,000 advertising campaign announced by the Associated Milliners to make American women "hat conscious." After long, lean seasons of untrimmed, unprofitable hats, the milliners propose to force their customers into something more elaborate. Let us hasten to record that a sort of floppy, bigger hat is noted on the summer streets the very week of the announcement. This may indicate fashion conditions ripe for a style change in hats. If so, the proposed advertising will prove a well-timed piece of business and well deserve its success. Otherwise, it may meet the sad fate of the well-planned propaganda to repopularize ostrich feathers. Four hundred ostriches a day die in South Africa because it failed. Corset manufacturers, also, attempted for a while to bring women back into whalebones by advertising the physical and moral dangers of loose-waisted living. Then they redesigned their line to meet modern woman's needs—and quickly regained their lost trade.

Our interest, therefore, lies not so much in the success of the proposed milliners' campaign, as in the certainty that if it *does* succeed it will be celebrated as an example of the power of advertising. Written up in magazines, orated at conventions, it will be quoted for years as a profitable lesson to languishing trades.

Helen Wills, quite unconsciously, started the green eye-shade as a smart August mode for taxicab drivers. If, working the same trick backward, a half hundred society leaders, actresses, and film favorites happen to hang on to the comforts of the present plain little round hat, they may unconsciously nullify the whole $1,000,000 campaign for bigger and better hats.

In that event, it would profit nobody to praise the milliners' million-dollar campaign, no matter how perfect the advertising, any more than it pays anybody to exult over the success of the unadvertised eye-shade. But in no case would anybody have the bad taste to mention the big-hat campaign as a failure. Advertising publications naturally don't emphasize Cluett Peabody's reorganization on account of soft collars, nor Park and Tilford's being thrown by prohibition into the hands of Schulte, nor the taciturn Gotham Hosiery taking over Onyx, for twenty-nine years a conspicuous advertiser. Cuticura and California Oranges are cited in every textbook. Few, however, dwell on the spectacular expenditure of E. M. F. automobiles or Sterling

Chewing Gum. Advertising history is built by advertising advertising's successes, forgetting its failures. From the business viewpoint this constructive course is natural and proper. But the kindly tradition of allowing each advertiser—without autopsy—to bury his own dead, has done much to delay progress. As Mr. S. Roland Hall puts it:[1]

A conspicuous fault . . . is a reluctance . . . to point out the misuses, the over-uses, and business catastrophes that may rightfully be laid at the door of advertising. . . . In business, as in surgery, some of the most valuable lessons are learned through dissection and autopsy. It is unfortunate there should be so much dread of the disapproval of those who have space or other advertising material to sell.

Taken today in its broadest sweep, advertising can hardly claim to be even an experimental science. In fact, to call it an "industry" is probably stretching a point. Through $1,500,000,000 expenditure yearly it should rank, industrially, not far behind lumber and timber, boots and shoes, flour and milling, and somewhat ahead of butter and cheese, copper and cane sugar and canning. One may not forget, however, that, unlike these other products, advertising is not itself a tangible commodity. As an industry, advertising would represent primary selling which, without *any* secondary selling, could turn out 99 44/100 per cent loss. In leather and shoes, timber and lumber, vegetables and cans, the waste in converting raw material into finished product is both known and negligible. The most known about adver-

[1] S. Roland Hall in *Theory and Practice of Advertising.*

tising waste is that it is far from negligible. Even in the minds of foremost authorities, the relation of advertising to sales seems various and vague. Not all selling successes are due to advertising. Not all advertising is a selling success. That much, anyway, is universally admitted. So, unlike those simpler one-track industries involving leather and lumber, the really active speculation in advertising begins when its own sale is completed.

Advertising, then, resembles that type of suburban architecture described as a "Queen Anne front and Mary Anne behind." Viewed as an industry in its own right, selling its own products—space, circulation, ideas, ink, paper, paint—advertising boasts one of the most highly organized and effective of all our business machines. Coolly reviewed by one trying to utilize its services for his own profit, advertising is, at times, apt to assume a sadly unindustrial aspect.

For the benefit of those who may be perplexed by this anomaly, we propose to show that

1. The value of advertising varies widely.
2. This variation is due:
    (a) To elements within the reader.
    (b) To elements within the copy.
    (c) To elements within the circulation.
3. The variation in all three elements is due to fixed laws, and is, therefore, ascertainable.
4. Advertising will some day discover these laws and scientifically utilize them. It will then become even greater than its present claims. Until then, new trade conditions constantly threaten its security.

So we shall, in turn, take up people—the man who issues the advertisement and the man who receives it; and copy, the point at which their minds may meet; and circulation, the force that makes this meeting possible. Any reader who honors us with an hour will, we fear, find little encouragement to a blind trust in an irresistible power. He may, however, discover instead a basis for an even firmer faith in advertising and, we sincerely hope, a practical thought directly helpful in his own problems.

CHAPTER II

DR. JEKYLLS AND MR. HYDES

WHEN the King of Siam visited France, he was invited out to Auteuil. He declined with polite surprise. "Everybody knows," he explained, "that one horse can run faster than another!" *Which* horse, to him, was a matter of complete indifference.

The King of Siam's lack of curiosity about racecourses resembles surprisingly the attitude of the American business man toward his own advertising. Everybody knows one advertisement is better than another. Only a few revolutionary souls, however, seem to feel any determined interest in knowing *which* is better. Or how much better. Born as a short cut to sure results, advertising has gradually aggrandized itself into an art loftily disdainful of all results.

Much is heard about successful advertising. Little is heard about failures. People naturally assume that since many advertisements are so very good, any advertisement is good enough. And that all advertisements are more or less alike.

Not one business man in ten thousand—not one advertising man in twenty—realizes how sensitive even a good advertisement can be. Few can believe how little a thing, inside or out, will upset results. And conversely, what slight changes will turn ap-

10

parent failure into triumphant success. A headline changed from "Cold Feet" to "Warm Feet" is said immediately to have doubled returns. Chapter XIV speculates a bit on the cause of some of these variations. Meantime, we stop here long enough to prove from actual records how astoundingly apart apparently similar advertisements may run.

First, compare the results of different copy in the same publication: Here are real advertisements at work. All belong, of course, to the same series of the same advertiser, and all are identical in everything but copy.

Issue		Cost Per Reply
	In A B Monthly	
July	Copy X	$ .85
August	" Y	3.47
	In C Magazine	
November	Copy Z	.20
June	" W	1.03
	In D Magazine	
February	Copy Z	.66
May	" U	7.50
	In E Magazine	
January	Copy T	.31
March	" S	1.22
	In F Magazine	
January	Copy R	.68
May	" P	4.57

In G Weekly

| April | Copy I | .42 |
| May | "   II | 14.20 |

In Medium H

| October | Copy A | 12.35 |
| November | "   D | 18.22 |

In M Magazine

January	Copy S	.36
February	" T	.49
March	" U	1.03

In L Weekly

March	Copy IT	.29
February	" TT	.97
April	" XT	1.29

All these comparisons, so far, have been of advertisements

In the same series
In the same size space
In the same publication

In other words, identical advertisements *except for copy.*

Now reverse the experiment and see what can happen to the *same* copy in different circumstances. The results that follow are from identical advertisements; word for word as to copy; exactly the same size; from the same plates, or set as nearly alike as different compositors could make them.

COPY—*"Why XXX is Different"*

			Cost Per Reply
In Magazine A	April		$ .32
" " B	April		.43
" " C	January		.68
" " D	May		1.43
" " E [1]	June		2.00
" " F	June		2.14

COPY AR

	Cost Per Reply
Medium A	$ 8.38
Medium D	40.00
	Selling Cost
In Magazine A	$ 1.06
" " F	2.10
" " F	3.08
" " O	4.67
" " Q	6.94
Newspaper E	$ .26
" J	$ .42

COPY CR

Medium	K	$22.22
"	J	54.58

COPY KGC

In Magazine G	$ .05
" " T	.31
" " M	.59
" " A	.65
" " C	1.29

[1] Magazine E shown here at the prohibitive cost of $2 a reply had, just one month earlier, *with another piece of copy,* brought in leads at 54 cents apiece.

Copy CHF

In Magazine B	$ .07
" " M	.49
" " C	.51

Copy CT

In Magazine AG	$ .13
" " T	.35
" " EC	1.05

We could easily fill this book' with such comparisons. Those given are from a dozen different independent sources. They are conservative as well as reliable. These records naturally represent keyed advertising. But keyed advertising simply reflects the combined effect of prevailing influences. All general publicity comes under those same influences. This concerns every man who spends a dollar for advertising. No matter how little he cares for direct returns, he cannot ignore his advertising dollar's buying ten dollars one day and a thin dime the next. That he may be satisfied in either case is beside the point. Always there is an implied obligation to spend business money to the best known advantage.

One advertising agency, after studying results on $30,000,000 worth of keyed publicity, tells us a sales variation of 300 per cent among different appeals is not unusual. Figured on a thousand sales of a twelve-dollar article, that variation would make a difference of $24,000 in the value of a single advertisement. Dr. Daniel A. Starch points out a certain shoe manufacturer who would have had $96,000 worth of advertising for a $72,000 expenditure, if all his advertisements were as good as his best.

These facts lend color to an expert opinion quoted by Mr. James H. Picken,[1] that business letters, taking good and bad together, could, without a penny additional expense, be made to produce from 50 per cent to 100 per cent better selling. He cites a circular sent out by a public utility corporation to get "leads" for stock salesmen. The first effort proved a miserable failure, pulling only one-tenth of 1 per cent. Properly rewritten, the same letter pulled 3 per cent regularly, and in some cases as high as 7 per cent—thirty to seventy times the original result. The able president of a successful New York company had 1,100 names on an important list. His letter to the first hundred got eight answers. Rewritten by his advertising adviser, the same letter got nineteen. So, instead of 88 replies from the whole list, he had 209. A mail-order house sent, in quick succession, four different letters making the same offer. All four flopped. The fifth struck the right appeal. It pulled 47 per cent sales and made magnificent profits. Another two-page letter, as improved by an expert, increased a firm's sales 33⅓ per cent, giving an increased profit of $12,000.

Hundreds of such letters are on record among direct-mail men. And, since letter writing as a business seems to be gaining over copy writing as an

[1] James H. Picken, *Business Correspondence Handbook*, p. 24.

art, might not Mr. Picken's proposition prove equally true of all advertising? In a most important article [1] Dr. Starch has demonstrated exactly that possibility:

Of a series of fifteen advertisements for a player-piano (he writes) the best one brought 258 replies, while the poorest one brought one reply. The other thirteen advertisements brought returns scattered all the way between these two extremes. If all fifteen advertisements had been as effective as the best one, they would have produced 3,870 replies instead of only 796.

Of a series of five lathe advertisements, the best one brought forty times as many inquiries as the poorest one.

Of a series of eight advertisements of a book sold entirely by mail, the best advertisement sold three times as many copies as the poorest one, differences in seasons and mediums being considered.

Of a series of seven insurance advertisements, the best one sold three times as much insurance as the poorest. If all seven had been as effective as the best one, the resulting sales would have been $105,000 instead of $74,000, a difference of $31,000.

Of a series of fifteen typewriter advertisements, the best one was twice as effective as the poorest one.

Of a series of seven encyclopedia advertisements, the best one was over twice as effective as the poorest one.

Of eight advertisements for a calculating machine, the best one brought 380 inquiries and the poorest brought 92; of eight advertisements for a filing device, one brought 174 inquiries while the poorest brought 62. In both cases allowance was made for differences in seasons. All advertisements were of the same size and appeared in the same mediums.

Then, by an interesting coincidence, Dr. Starch

[1] Daniel A. Starch, "Testing the Effectiveness of Advertising," *Harvard Business Review*.

goes on to suggest for all advertising precisely what
Mr. Picken proposes for business letters—the possibility of a 50 per cent to 100 per cent improvement
in selling power:

The average advertisement (he continues) even in high-
grade mediums, *has only about half the effectiveness* of the
top 10 per cent of advertisements of other makers of products
advertising in the same mediums.

Think how American business would be stimulated
by a 50 per cent increase in the selling power of its
billion-and-a-half-dollar advertising expenditure!
The worst thing about reading a poor book is the
chance lost to read a good book. That states exactly
the case against weak advertising. If its present
wastes were cut in half, business could easily afford
to spend two billions on advertising where it now
spends one.

Imagine, if you will, one football team beating a
rival 142 to 4. One baseball team trimming another
75 to 6. One tennis player leading 6-0, 6-1, 6-0.
One bridge expert winning 24 rubbers to his oppo-
nent's 8. One golfer 10 up and 8 to go. Suppose, as
equals, they fought seriously for high stakes. Advertising contests just as unequal take place every
day. The best dozen advertisements in any hundred
you see anywhere, are demonstrably ten, and even
twenty times, better than the last dozen. Do the
owners of these beaten advertisements turn green
in the gills? Would they believe bad news of a
favorite piece of copy? Few advertisers are like
the famous client described by an agency friend:

"Mr. L——," he said, "is remorseless about using copy on its record. He will keep a wonderful ad. out of a magnificent medium *without trusting common sense at all!* But he's a grand client. He goes by results. And, barring earthquakes or act of God, he will keep going forever."

Remorseless advertisers like Mr. L—— are few and far between. Most advertisers lose interest the day the advertisement appears. That is like leaving the grandstand just as the game starts. Viewed as an ice-cold business proposition, this interest in the advertisement rather than its results is hard to explain. Viewed as a purely human quality it is easy to understand. "Handsome is as handsome does" rings true in the children's copybook. But the Tired Business Man in the front row of the Follies never seem to be taking that maxim too literally. And, as the next chapter will suggest, advertising— like a visit to the Follies—is seldom an ice-cold business proposition.

CHAPTER III

ROOSTER CROWS AND RESULTS

EVERY now and then somebody explains, almost pridefully, that advertising is not an exact science. This is one of the points on which, to borrow Mr. Frank Fletcher's apt phrase, there should be less resignation and more resigning! Advertising will never be even an experimental science until every advertiser is compelled by public sentiment

(1) To know what he is trying to do.
(2) To know what results.

There are almost as many reasons for advertising as advertisements. There are department-store pages that have paid for themselves before the last newspaper is off the press. There are indirect ricochets as intricate as one of Hoppe's masterly caroms. Only the advertiser knows his shot. He need not tell it. But he ought to *know* it! And know its effect!

So long as the man with the right to spend knows precisely what he is after—and knows he is getting it—he might, beyond criticism, spend $10,000,000. But if he spends even $10,000 without knowing exactly what he is trying to do, his stockholders have at least a moral right to an explanation. There are hundreds of ways to spend advertising money. Each is legitimate so long as clearly recognized and courageously identified. If advertising men were as careful as investment bankers, much copy might include the words so familiar to readers of the financial section:

The goods described in this advertisement have already been merchandised by other methods. This advertisement is for the purpose of record only.

The next chapter devotes itself to indirect benefits held to be derived from advertising. Before considering this imposing list, take half a minute on direct benefits. Start with a clear perspective on what advertising—rightly handled—can do. Take the case of a Boston investment house selling $130,000 worth of stock through mailing 1,000 folders. Take the Youngstown realty company that won the Multigraph Company's 1926 cup by selling $250,000 worth of real estate at an advertising cost of 3 per cent. Take the valve manufacturer who increased his business 500 per cent in five years of magazine advertising. Or the curtain rod that increased its volume 900 per cent in eight years' advertising, mostly in magazines. Or the dental-cream maker who got 125,000 answers in a prize contest so important that the winner wrote a ten-thousand-word essay. Or the Hartford Insurance Company, that developed $10,-119,010 sales from leads got mostly by mailings. Or the oil-burning furnace that utilized a Chicago newspaper to jump its sales 175 per cent the first year and 230 per cent the second year. Or the radio offer that made 14,000 people call on tire dealers within four days. Or take even the little lumber company that made a profit of $125 on $1 by sending out a hundred government postal cards.

With equal chance to turn their advertising into cash and a wide choice among indirect objectives, we find, nevertheless, a lot of advertisers pleasantly spending with no definite goal in sight. Professional advisers cannot control this blithe self-expression any more than doctors can decline wealthy hypochondriacs, or lawyers avoid spite litigation. But to his doctor or lawyer, if never else, every intelligent man tells the truth. So should every man, before putting any considerable sum into advertising, dig deep in his conscience for the real motive.

Back in Philosophy I at college, Professor Armstrong used a fishing trip to illustrate the difference between motives. The fish we catch never repay the trouble they cost us. The pleasure of fishing is, obviously, our real motive. Dynamically, we go for fish; teleologically, we go for the day in the open air. An advertiser might do well so to straighten out in his own mind any similar confusion of motives. Then, whatever may be his real ambitions, he can always determine how well his advertising is doing.

He may not seek direct sales. He may prefer repayment in advertising's more intangible advantages listed in the next chapter. Nevertheless, so long as he is spending any dollar that any other department of his business might use elsewhere, he owes himself, his company, and the advertising industry the courtesy of a clear decision as to exactly what he is buy-

ing. If he finds his motive purely business, let him
estimate in advance about what results—how much
—when—and where—he expects from each dollar.
He need tell nobody. He should by no means quit
advertising if he falls short. But never should he
draw a check without reasonably close calculation
as to when and how that money is coming back to
him. Or, if he prefers to consider advertising a long-
time investment, let him know how he is going to
assure permanent profitable interest on every dollar.

A newspaper man was asked point-blank why he
used valuable space for the hoary old agate-line
comparison with other newspapers. Apparently he
followed custom. Reasons came slowly. "Oh," he
said, finally, *"it stirs up our competitors!"* There
spoke Sam Hecht, shrewd rule-of-thumb analyst.
Frankly he recognized the rooster-crow, second
strongest of advertising motives. Scarcely a day
passes without some prospering publisher, naïve as
Goliath with his giant spear, hiring a page in the
New York newspapers to crow at his competitors.

"What's the most interesting thing anyone can
find in any photograph?" once asked a noted psychologist of his college classroom. "Your own like-
ness," he told them after an hour's wide discussion.
The class agreed. "The whole world," observed a
great editor, making the same point, "is divided into
two parts—those who want to get into print and
those who want to keep out!" The urge to see ourselves in print is universal. And so powerful that
the chief anxiety of those themselves not thus dis-

tinguished is to shine in the reflected glory of some
one who is. Every year President Coolidge gets
1,500 gifts, mostly from people he never heard of.
The Rumaniacs that swarmed around Queen Marie
proved the world's desire to sneak into the limelight.

This is particularly true in business. Employees
like working for a famous concern as naturally as
they dislike living in an unknown suburb, or driving
an unknown car. To officers and stockholders, of
course, the fame of their company is a distinct financial asset. These facts not infrequently influence
expensive institutional advertising. Theoretically
dedicated to the glory of the company, such advertising radiates a genial glow to many important individuals. Salesmen are particularly pampered. Some
organizations that wouldn't increase commissions 10
per cent to save their salesmen's souls, will put
$100,000 into advertising as a genial gesture of
encouragement.

This vanity advertising, when independent and
aggressive, has distinct merits, much as a Sunday silk
hat. Unfortunately for advertising originality, fear
of staying out is often more potent than faith in
going in. Too many advertise as they subscribe to
the Christmas fund. They ask what the others are
doing. And put themselves down for about the same
amount. This accounts for the otherwise quite inexplicable anxiety of each man to have his advertisement right alongside his competitor's. And not
too different!

Vanity advertising thus loses by not having the courage of its convictions. Unspoiled originality and an honestly personal message might do wonders in redeeming pages now wasted. At any rate, the difference between a man's seeing his own advertisements snugly alongside his competitor's, and the discomfort of seeing his rival's in print without having them see him, can safely be set down as the most powerful influence for advertising.

These, then, are three great advertising motives:

The Go-with-the-Gang motive
The See-Ourselves-in-Print motive
The Rooster-Crow motive

Though seldom recognized and never admitted these motives are entirely legitimate. Preparing this advertising, and often enough the advertising itself, does good. But vanity advertising should not be taken too seriously *commercially*. Selfish conversation about our own affairs seldom enthuses even our best friends. Advertising in the same spirit can scarcely count on cordiality from strangers. Therefore, advertising written to please ourselves can hardly be expected to bring in business profits. Any piece of copy that thoroughly satisfies two or three heads of a business has already accomplished much. It is entitled to rest on its laurels.

"Henry Ford," said Edward S. Jordan, "is the most successful automobile manufacturer because he was the first man to build an automobile for the other fellow. All of the other early manufacturers built cars in which they liked to ride themselves."

Some business man may, with a little introspection, detect traces of a similar fault in his advertising. So long as he makes due allowances for the personal, and so, most likely, anti-commercial element, no harm can arise. On the contrary, that man may find advertising brings him one of life's greatest gratifications—the opportunity for self-expression. You may, perhaps, have noticed that the passenger on the back seat always feels that he, and especially she, could drive better than the person at the wheel. Everyone also has the inherent conviction that he could write a good play or novel if he only had time and real inclination. Add these two convictions together, multiply them at will, and you won't exaggerate greatly the feeling of 90 out of every 100 business men toward their advertising. Undertakers escape entirely their clients' competition. Lawyers generally. Doctors sometimes. Advertising men never!

Universal and compelling as is the pleasure of seeing one's picture in the public prints, it dwindles to nothing compared with the joy of seeing one's own words in clear black type. My sentences! my semicolons!! flashing in every home in the country, state, nation! Men who will never find time to write the Great American Novel can still thrill the bursting joys of authorship. With deadly seriousness, therefore, they correct advertising copy and revise layouts. With just pride and clear conscience they spend thousands of dollars to place this masterpiece before multitudes of perfect strangers, who for some never-explained reason they feel will read it. As every young mother honestly thinks her first-born the only baby worth serious consideration, just so enthusiastically does every new advertiser parade as universal facts his own peculiar preferences and his distinctly personal experiences. And we repeat once again that this is a natural and quite harmless pastime, provided its business results are not taken overseriously. The danger is only to other advertisers and to the younger generation of advertising men. The public may be relied upon to sidestep with the speed and precision that comes with long practice.

Publishers and advertising agencies are interesting examples of the reverse side of this urge for expression. Although they live by the sword, so to speak, their own copy is scarcely overwhelming. This Achilles heel is not, as some cynic suggested, due to the fact that advertising agents and publishers don't believe in advertising. Nor even because their high-pressure young men don't solicit one another. It is rather that their creative complex—the urge for public expression—is so thoroughly satisfied in the ordinary conduct of their business. A traffic cop on a Sunday stroll through the streets, a 'bus conductor at a burlesque show, a manicure holding hands, and a publisher paying for his own advertising, all get about the same thrill. So, where others rush into print regardless of expense, the advertising men themselves seldom bother to tread.

Regardless of the apathy of these hardened professionals, however, advertising always has been and always will be a perfectly proper means of self-expression. So long as others spend fortunes on privately printed books and on more or less privately produced plays, there can be no possible objection to any advertiser supporting those who, at an appropriate price, measure off a neat plot of space and dedicate it to his literary and artistic creations.

Eliminate absolutely this element of personal and commercial vanity, and perhaps a third of your highest-priced advertising would gradually fade from sight. Require, further, every advertiser to state exactly what he expects to accomplish—or even hopes to accomplish—through a given advertisement, and a good deal more would follow it. Incidentally this shrinkage might eliminate at least 90 per cent of our most brilliant copy, for the less there is to say about a product the greater is the skill required to say anything.

CHAPTER IV

The Devil's Ad-vocate

When there was less advertising there were more saints. At every Canonization ceremony—which our readers will recollect as the exact reverse of an ordinary trial—the custom was to have the devil represented by his own advocate. The gentleman chosen for this flattering position was bound to bring forward, in polite effort to prevent a favorable verdict, every discreditable detail he could gather in the saintly candidate's earthly career.

Trying frankly to examine forces that sell each year a billion-and-a-half dollars' worth of futures, this book may reflect, here and there, no vast respect for some cherished traditions. This will scarcely disturb any advertiser who knows what he wants. And gets it. To the advertiser who isn't sure he gets anything, we proffer no apology. Coming competition will soon require every advertising manager to show something definite for his dollar. He can't count hits until he knows his aim. The last chapter glimpsed advertising's ability to bring in cold cash. Now, with a bow to the stately old custom, let us turn to the broad claims as to advertising's indirect benefits:

1. *Society Generally*

Advertising educates public as to efficient buying and cheapest and best markets.

Advertising is responsible, in a way, for the entire welfare movement.

Advertising brings the newspaper an honorable source of revenue without which it might be subject to grave temptations from illegitimate special interests.

Advertising increases knowledge by wide sale of books and periodicals.

Advertising makes possible magazines with trained expert editorial staffs.

Advertising makes us rich in comforts and conveniences.

Advertising makes people dress better, eat better, sleep better.

Advertising is chiefly responsible for the increase in savings and investments.

Advertising contributes to health through sanitary packages.

Advertising makes a seasonal product an all-the-year-round one.

Advertising has gone far in raising the standard of living.

Advertising as a continuing body has produced a receptive state of mind—a willingness to go ahead and a determination not to be left behind.

Advertising creates new habits and stimulates new thinking.

2. *The Nation*

Advertising helps fortify prosperity by raising the standards of living.

Advertising creates employment for thousands, and adds millions to the wealth of the country.

Advertising creates a rapid interchange of commodities and money to produce good times.

Advertising changes eating habits of country.

Advertising multiplies human wants and thereby is a vital factor in progress.

Advertising makes the general run of people more open-minded.

3. *The Individual*

Advertising makes a more competent customer— a better-informed buyer.

Advertising helps keep the customer from cheating himself on prices.

Advertising makes the struggle for existence a little easier and lighter.

Advertising is a machine for making it easier to live.

Advertising eliminates drudgery in housework through labor-saving devices.

Advertising saves time, money, and effort, eliminating useless shopping around.

Advertising has enabled consumers to buy from producers in practically all parts of the country and all parts of the world.

Advertising spreads information about commodities that bring about progress, that add to comfort, convenience, economy, and personal satisfaction in the consumer's own circle.

Advertising informs the interested reader of what worth while is happening in consuming fields outside of his own circle.

Advertising, by building up desire for many things, spurs ambition.

Advertising educates the consumer to a proper and full use of commodities, thereby increasing the consumer's benefit.

Advertising lifts our living to a higher plane, and thereby makes us work a little harder.

Advertising enables the consumer to escape the dictation and the narrow stocks of local dealers.

Advertising builds a saner and better standard of living.

4. *The Arts*

Advertising makes a greater public appreciation of art by the quality of illustration and hand lettering it uses.

Advertising brings into millions of American homes a better appreciation of the fine arts.

Advertising is largely responsible for recent progress in the art of printing.

5. *Industry*

Advertising is a spiritual force in commerce.

Advertising is a practical form of business insurance. It stabilizes production by eliminating big fluctuations in sales.

Advertising has brought about cooperation among competitors.

Advertising helps create new fashions and greatly helps the introduction of a fashion for women, provided it works with the grain.

Advertising enables inventors to enjoy the fruits of their genius during their lifetime.

Advertising is the intelligence arm of all our distributing system.

Advertising has improved trade practices.

Advertising brings business propositions to advertisers.

Advertising enables a company to budget its entire business by controlling sales.

Advertising is a factor in improving the quality of goods and reducing their cost.

Advertising is a powerful instrument in raising the standards of business practice and thought. Modern business could neither have been created nor maintained without advertising.

6. *The Advertiser*

Advertising improves the *esprit de corps* of great corporations.

Advertising protects against sharp competition.

Advertising art sets standards the goods must live up to.

Advertising makes it easier to sell the securities of a manufacturer who has made his name widely known.

Advertising builds up good-will reserves.

Advertising is the only possible way to national market.

Advertising helps raise standards of company cooperation.

Advertising will stiffen up company morale for outside competition.

Advertising cuts down bad debts, and makes collecting easier.

Nobody can quarrel with any man who deliberately dedicates his advertising to these ends. But even an advertiser for indirect benefits can hardly be harmed by knowing in advance the object of his advertising, or the purpose of each advertisement. Or—since indirect results fluctuate as widely as direct—by investigating its success within a reasonable time after publication. When the chief object is found achieved, all incidental extra benefits may be graciously and gratefully accepted as a bonus for the risk.

In all its varying mixtures of direct and indirect returns—vanity, ambition, imitation, and commercial utility—advertising has developed through four ages. First, the age of Novelty. The typewriter advertised in *The Nation* in 1876 must have attracted wide and profitable attention. Space rates were low; people had lots of time. Dealers stayed put. Customers bought what stores offered. Good advertising paid well indeed.

Then came the age of Exploitation. Enterprising advertisers learned to sell results "short," as our Wall Street friends would say. With advance proofs and circulation millions to talk about, any good salesman could sell merchants, months in advance, the effect of coming advertising. As Mr. John Benson sketched this activity in his Bok Award Speech: [1]

In past years merchants would stock goods because of being nationally advertised, even on the mere promise of a campaign. They took an active interest in it, by cooperating locally. They tied in their own newspaper advertising with the national appeal; they put in window displays, hung out signs, displayed merchandise, demonstrated in the store, enthused their clerks. Of course such activity was bound to sell goods.

Growing interest in quick turnover, however, replaced dealers' faith in somebody else's advertising. Then, by the most brilliant coup in advertising history, was quietly substituted for an always problem-

[1] Address at Bok Award Dinner, Cambridge, Mass., February 15, 1927.

atical, public demand, that really magnificent
conception of consumer *"acceptance,"* at which both
merchant and manufacturer might smash eternally
to their hearts' content.[1]

Third came the age of Excess Profits—a short and
feverish war-boom period. A painting of a beautiful
blonde exercising a bulldog, or a tall thin man on a
polo pony, was supposed to get people so excited
about So-and-so's special brand of shoelaces that
crowds would not only refuse to accept any substitute, but would ostracize their old family shoe store
for not specifying these laces. When war taxes went
out, this—mostly—went with them.

Then came the age of Merchandising. It relegates
advertising to the position of a father with a débutante daughter or sophomore son. Advertising pages
show up on schedule, are respectfully admired, and
pay the bills; but the keen zest is for markets, purchasing power, merchandising, window displays, and
retail salesmen. Ambitious agency men find themselves running not only the manufacturer's factory
and the merchant's store, but rapidly extending their
activities to personal contact with the customer himself. They compete one another into making
elaborate questionnaires, surveys and researches,
mostly on their none too ample 15 per cent space
commission. Advertising's enterprise along these
merchandising lines has been costly, but exceedingly
effective. Merchandising has, in fact, so short-cir-

---

[1] "How Consumer Acceptance Made Advertising Practical," Paul E.
Faust. *Printers' Ink Monthly*, August, 1926.

cuited advertising's own broad circulation activities
that Mr. Benson was moved to record:

> The fact that advertising is and has been an effective force
> in moving merchandise is not *prima facie* proof that it appeals
> to the consumer. Its secondary effect upon the trade, in many
> cases, is far greater than its primary effect upon the consumer.

Or as the Editor of the "Mailbag" states it a bit
more strongly:

> "A hundred persuasive salesmen have told ten thousand
> easily persuaded dealers that twenty-six pages, reaching
> 3,000,000 people, a total of 78,000,000 impressions, are to run.
> The dealers buy, display and suggest the product. It sells.
> Is this a triumph of advertising? No, it is a triumph of the
> medicine bundle, a triumph of faith in advertising—and faith
> works wonders."

Today, yielding to newer trade conditions and
perhaps completing a normal cycle, advertising appears to enter a fifth age. Advertising, *as* Advertising, seems about to return. The statistical urge,
after exhausting less pertinent objects, turns at last
to advertising returns. Having researched everything in sight, some one has thought of researching
advertising results. After interviewing the public
about everything else, experts begin to ask them
which advertisement might lead them to buy. And
as advertising thus gets down to solid ground, many
a distributor who used in hard times to cancel his
whole schedule will find a way to make his fighting
advertising twice as effective. And double his
appropriation.

Advertising has passed its high point of waste.

Its peak of expenditure is not yet in sight. Gorgeous self-assurance is still advertising's great weakness. Dazzling cocksureness that advertising benefits everybody in general has, to be sure, drawn in its multitude of golden butterflies. But the accompanying carefree uncertainty as to specific benefits has been equally effective in preventing adequate advertising by those who could—and should—use it most profitably. As competition tightens up, we shall see a squeezing out of those who have no really vital idea to advertise. On the other hand, that competition will force an even greater influx of those who use advertising neither as trumpet nor as weapon, but as a profitable tool.

With sincere admiration for all its splendid selling of itself we still suggest advertising has not yet been properly introduced to the right people. As soon as its standards of exactness approximate those of successful chain stores and mail-order houses, advertising will find itself closer to many giant organizations now cold to its seductive glory. As soon as advertising learns really to help these business behemoths, competition will compel them to use it. Even today, the gesture of independence by chains, syndicates, and leaders in many lines come from an intelligence too keen to accept advertising as now offered. Yet not quite keen enough to penetrate its greater possibilities!

CHAPTER V

SPARKS WITH FIRE

OUT near Douglaston the Long Island Railroad trestles across a broad salt-water swamp. Each August lush grass and cat-o'-nine-tails crackle, dry and yellow, in the sultry sun. Along comes a freight locomotive, dropping sparks.

One tiny red-hot coal sets ablaze the whole ten acres!

Twice a day for a whole year the engine has gone back and forth, dropping those same sparks. While the grass was green and wet, the whole fire box might have been spilled without spreading a six-foot fire. Along all the rest of the right-of-way that engine might drop those same sparks through eternity without hope of successful conflagration. Or a whole procession of engines might pass that same spot every minute strewing enough ineffectual ashes to prevent ever a chance of a real fire. Only on that one August day, dry and yellow in the sultry sun, can that one red spark set off that ten-acre fire.

Any small boy can see this in terms of dried grass and engines. Yet, when the same situation comes about in advertising, our most practical men go off on tangents. They glorify some little sales spark that successfully sets afire some great consumer field, quite forgetting that, if all advertising were

37

equally effective, the whole world would be one vast Pompeii!

We should have a Chicago fire every Thursday.

Those sparks do exist. Advertising *can* enable *any* business to do things it could hardly otherwise. Somewhere along your own right-of-way, perhaps, is a field advertising can set ablaze. Your field may be a thousand acres. Or ten square feet. The accuracy with which you estimate its area; the pains with which you test its readiness; the skill with which you work its profits, will tell whether you are an advertiser doing business—or only another business doing advertising.

It pays to advertise—just about as it pays to collect. Or pays to sell. Or to manufacture. Or, in a word, as it pays to do business. In 1923, for example, we find in 298,933 business corporations only 179,360 that made any profit at all. The advertisers and non-advertisers among them split presumably in about the same proportion. A successful business is one that doesn't fail. Enterprise and capital enough to make a business success practically always result, sooner or later, in some sort of advertising. To ascribe to advertising the success of any business that advertises is only natural, and, in many cases, wholly justifiable. One finds difficulty, however, in believing that—with or without advertising—the genius of Eastman and Patterson wouldn't have dominated the camera and cash register fields. P. T. Barnum and John Wanamaker were their own best advertisements! Wrigley is bigger than his little

Spearmint man. Jordan's clever sex appeal automobile copy is far from the only trick in his bag. Advertising, after all, is the advertiser! When he is a definite personality like Marshall Field or Cyrus H. K. Curtis—a man who would certainly succeed without it—his advertising flourishes. As Mr. Edward L. Bernays puts it:

> He creates events so interesting and important they inevitably get talked about, in the smoking car, the clubhouse, the radio, the press, the lecture platform, or just in the particular trade world concerned . . . the important thing is what a person is and does. What he says is merely the echo of these vital facts!

When such a character flattens into a corporation and advertising tries to mirror an elusive corporate personality, its power wanes. Because advertising, *on the way up,* so vividly radiates the strong personality responsible for its success, advertising often gets a lot of credit that belongs to the man.

In fifty years no vital relation between advertising and business success has ever been found. Or if it has, a sorely needed formula has been kept secret far too long.

"The trouble with advertising," suggested Mr. Edward S. Jordan, "is that there are too many clever people connected with the business trying to make it complicated instead of trying to make it simple." The result of this cleverness, as we have already observed, is to keep advertising a sort of business Peter Pan. Grown to the size of an industry, it still remains a game. Regardless of ability, every man still

spends his appropriation largely according to his
own fancy. Most haven't the slightest idea what
they get for their advertising money. And many
don't care.

Practically anybody who wants really to work at
it can advertise at a profit. Yet it is entirely probable
that six out of every ten advertisements never repay, directly or indirectly, the time and money invested in them. Many that fail individually might
still be redeemed as a part of a long-term campaign.
But the average advertiser's mind doesn't work that
way.

If the average golfer played golf as ineffectually
as many of our most highly respected advertisers
advertise, he might be laughed off the public links.
If, on the other hand, the average advertiser advertised as well as the good golfer golfs, he might reasonably hope some day to enjoy the country's most
exclusive courses. There are plenty of golfers who
drive automatically off the first tee, with only a vague
consciousness of eighteen holes somewhere ahead
and a whole afternoon full of strokes. Also there
are a few advertisers who play each advertisement
like a golf shot, solely for the purpose of arriving at
some fixed point. In the main, however, each game
sticks to its own characteristics: Golfers depressingly
businesslike. Advertisers delightfully casual.

Imagine, for example, the advertising manager
of the Uno Gas Company, grouching home to his
patient Griselda: "I'm through with advertising
forever. Been off form for a whole month. Messed

up my trade-paper campaign so it took three insertions for what I should have done easily in one. My results are a joke. I'm going to resign before the office boy recommends it." Or two wealthy advertising agents lunching at the Biltmore: "You know that dealer-inquiries cost we bet on last week? Well, I got 'em for forty cents in yesterday's *Times*. The position was just right. I—" "You poor fish," interrupts the other, "I made a 38 in the *Herald-Tribune*—twice. Say, did you ever try moving your display a little farther toward the top? It seems to carry at least 3 per cent better. Got the idea from watching Sears-Roebuck!"

On the other hand, imagine yourself down at Pinehurst for the semi-finals of the Advertising Men's golf tournament. "That was a fine drive of yours, Bill. How far did it go?" "Oh, I didn't notice particularly. I'm not interested in direct results."

"Expensive set of clubs you swing, Henry. Isn't that solid gold in your brassie?" "Yes, sir, that's my goldie. Our directors feel an organization as large as ours can't afford to play cheap golf." "But does it carry farther than your old one?" "Oh, I couldn't say as to that. It's the *class* atmosphere we're really after!"

"What was your score, Bobby?" "I didn't keep any score. It's a dreadful nuisance to count all the time—and besides, there are a lot of bankers and influential men around today. I'm shooting mostly to interest them."

"For Heaven's sake, is Arthur going crazy? Look

at him! He drove from the first tee to the fourth green and now he's starting cross country from the fifth tee to the eighteenth hole!" "No, Arthur's all right; he's just playing a little general golf."

Fantastic, yes. But not so silly as it sounds. Nobody will deny that most men keep meticulous score of golf strokes. Or that many advertising men study statistical reports of baseball, football, or tennis played hundreds of miles away. Is it not equally true that these same men don't attempt to measure the *results* of their own *work* with half the interest, let alone accuracy, that they watch the effects of other people's *play?*

"Dramatic art on Broadway," wrote some critic in the far more conservative past, "won't make much progress until certain producers realize the female kneecap is a joint and not an amusement!"

Advertising, similarly, in our opinion, will never earn the solid economic esteem it so enthusiastically claims, and so patently lacks, until it becomes a serious business. As the first step, we believe it must decline to be exploited as a term of artistic self-expression.

Before us is a $100 advertisement that brought in 341 direct orders for a three dollar book. And another for $100 that sold $710 worth of Shakespeares. A summer hotel we know of stays open all winter by mailing 18,000 letters. A letter to 14,000 physicians cost $2,550, and in less than a year brings orders for more than $124,000. Fifteen thousand circulars, costing $635, bring another man $8,000 worth of business. A fountain-pen manufacturer opens 24,000 new accounts at a cost of 58 cents each. A magazine page advertisement at $600 brought orders for 111 sets of $24 books—$2,640 worth of direct sales. A department store spends $311 to sell $11,508 worth of Oriental rugs. A tire company acquires 21,000 new customers at an average cost of $2.40 apiece. A full page in four New York newspapers brings personal calls by 4,180 prospects for oil-burning furnaces.

There are thousands of these cases. Not romances of iron-jawed millionaires starting barefoot with a couple of postage stamps, but everyday business of ordinary men like ourselves.

Every day, on the other hand, millions of circulars are mailed that never repay their postage. Tons of expensive advertising pages, that might just as well have remained virgin white, go each week to waste. A printing expert once estimated for us—from actual examples—that advertising agencies alone throw away every day a ton of unread, unlooked-at, circular matter costing somebody at least $500,000 a year.

So much glaringly unprofitable spending greets us everywhere, we find it hard to remember that from the first crude sign on the hot baths at Pompeii, advertising was designed solely for *the advertiser*. In the language of Wall Street, the selling of advertising has grown so much better than its buying that control of the industry has gradually passed into the hands of those whose profits come from the advertising itself. Advertising's *own* goods are space, circulation, copy, paper, and paint. Generously baited with valuable ideas, adorned with unselfish service, these commodities—paint, paper, copy, circulation, and space—are what seven out of ten of our best advertising men sell.

Naturally enough, therefore, advertising suffers from auto-intoxication. The traditions behind our present practices are pieced together, not out of the experiences of those who profit by using advertising, but out of the selling arguments of those who profit by its sale.

In these days of keen competition, none would ask sellers of advertising to withdraw any legitimate pressure. In advertising, then, as in other lines these days, the logical place for improvement is in the buying.

The only object of any business—as this book uses the term—is to make money. Strangely, few people appreciate this. Most of us dramatize business as a background for our own personalities. One man thinks the XYZ Electric Company exists for him to make mechanical drawings; another thinks of it as a place to improve office routine. The welfare worker sees the XYZ Electric Company only as her opportunity to improve the working girl; the office boy as his chance to improve his typewriting.

And, by training and temperament, the advertising staff, least of all, is likely to escape the strife for self-expression!

As Percival White states it: [1]

The old type of advertising manager is not likely to fit into the new organization. He was concerned too much with the advertising itself and not enough with what the advertising accomplished for the company. (Only in the department stores and mail-order houses has advertising been more consistently coordinate with sales.) He was, furthermore, without adequate conception of objectivity of demand; his idea was that it was by advertising alone that goods were sold.

Therefore, every business should keep in control of advertising one man who knows the *object* of that business. He, at least, will always remember that his main job is to make money, and only incidentally to get delightful pictures from Norman Rockwell, or devise ingenious new combination color plates. On the other hand, he won't forget a single instant that, big or little, every company policy, every company purchase—from letterhead to motor truck—must be carefully studied by him with a single eye to its selling effect on the public.

So far as this ideal publicity executive can, for his company's welfare, profitably utilize organized outside advertising, he will invest without stint. But he will feel no obligation to support advertising as a great general economic force. He will remember the only reason for any business putting *business* money into advertising is to sell more goods at more profit and so earn more money for its stockholders.

If, beyond this strict business requirement, there is, in the name of advertising, to be any incidental

[1] Percival White, *Scientific Marketing Management*, p. 234.

benefaction to social welfare, belles-lettres, or con-
temporary art, he will, no doubt, prefer to pay out
the money in extra dividends, giving stockholders
themselves the pleasure of making that donation entirely absolved of any business obligation.

We, the writers, hasten to volunteer our enthusiastic conviction that the one class above all others that
least needs our kindly protection is stockholders in
business corporations. Other classes notably able to
carry on without our stout-hearted intervention are
business in general, advertising in general, and big
advertisers. This book, then, for better or for worse,
is in behalf of the smaller business man who still
takes his advertising seriously, for the man who has
been led to believe that advertising ought to help
him. And for the host of smaller magazines and
trade papers now grievously undervalued. Also, for
a lot of straight-thinking advertising managers and
straight-shooting agency men, whose honest and intelligent work must thrust them far ahead in their
profession as soon as even a few of its basic principles are more generally understood.

The day is not so distant when the a b c's of advertising will be not only as clearly defined, but as uniformly used by all competent workers, as are today
the axioms of architecture, engineering, meteorology,
and navigation.

As Mr. George C. Miller, president of the Dodge
Manufacturing Company, puts it:[1]

[1] George C. Miller, "Today's Competition Demands Advertising Program Based on Facts," *Class & Industrial Marketing*, June, 1927, p. 23.

Our works superintendent came to me and said, "I want to spend $30,000 for a tool. Here is what it will do. It will cut the price of this product 25 per cent. We sold $100,000 worth of the product last year, and we can make more money or cut the price this year."

He gives me speeds, cutting power, and handling facilities. There is no question in the world about that fellow's getting $30,000, because he is telling you things you can't dispute.

Because advertising hasn't yet so standardized its tactics, half the time that should go into important sales strategy is now wasted in unscientific debate over purely personal preferences. There are too many manuals, too well done, for us to try to tell anybody *how* to advertise. Our hope is lightly to review the strategy, leaving tactics to more able masters. But before any reader rashly decides there is no compelling need of better advertising strategy, we beg a moment for the next two chapters.

CHAPTER VI

SLEEPING DOGS ASTIR

AN EMPTY barrel tosses on the high seas. White-caps burst into foam. Towering crests topple into terrifying troughs and sweep endlessly, irresistibly, over the horizon. But the empty barrel just bobs up and down! That barrel is in closest contact with colossal forces. It shares in majestic magnificent action. Millions of tons of water toss it to and fro. But what does the barrel do?

Substitute now for that empty barrel some notably impressive, but not very compelling, advertisement in any armful of Sunday newspaper or bulging magazine. Take, almost at random, copy that reads:

The larger pocketbook demands economy of quality—to the limited purse it is essential.

* * *

In these facts, too, is found justification of the painstaking methods employed by ———— in perpetuation of ———— quality.

These are good sentences from excellent living advertisements. With your most generous allowance for their loss through removal from context, try to figure out what impression a statement of this sort can be expected to make on the minds of a million people. Suppose the man in the seat next to you looked up from his newspaper and said, earnestly:

"The larger pocketbook demands economy of quality."

Would you answer: "To the limited purse it is essential"?

Or suppose your wife, speaking kindly of the superintendent of the apartment building, said:

"In these facts is found justification of the painstaking methods employed by Mr. Petersen in perpetuation of this building's quality." Would you rush the maid down to Petersen with a five dollar bill?

Printed by the million million, words such as these —good words in well arranged sentences—fill fast mail trains. Sweep across 3,000,000 miles of territory. Burden armies of postmen. Jog through snow and dust of 45,000 far-flung R. F. D.'s. Pile and flash on innumerable newsstands. Search out scattered cottages and towering apartments in 15,000 towns and cities. Amid all this magnificent activity, what part do these words play?

When gentlemen buy wide circulation for messages which they wouldn't themselves deliver by any chance at their own bridge or dinner table, what effect do they imagine this investment is having on the public mind? And why? Are they satisfied to contribute blindly to advertising as a great economic force? Or do they expect "advertising" in some unseen way, to reinforce their own ineffectiveness with some supernatural power they can't even attempt to calculate?

If this seems unreasonable to any advertiser, let him make his own tests. Let him memorize a dozen lines from his own copy. Then try them on his wife, his partner, or even his office boy.

Let him repeat those lines in a quiet conversational tone.

See if he can detect any quick glint of response in his listener's eye, an attentive flash of the ear, an exclamation: "That's true! I'm certainly glad you mentioned it!"

Why does anyone spend thousands of dollars printing for distribution among millions of miscellaneous people a bunch of words that he can, in five minutes, prove definitely won't hold the interest of the first three friends he meets on the street?

The answer is, of course, the words interest *him!*

He is fascinated by his own advertisement. As he views his gleaming white proof and pronounces it "O. K." he honestly believes that this advertisement is going to look to a vast number of people the same as it does to him.

This subjective element—this very natural idea that because he is greatly interested, a lot of other people are going to be a little interested, costs the business men of the United States more money each year than the nation's standing army.

Nothing but years of professional training in advertising enables a man to regard copy and layouts simply as a sort of photographic negative. And so to disregard pretty completely what he wants to *say* for the sake of what he wants his readers to *do.*

We are not hard-boiled. Much as any men, we appreciate an attractive advertisement for its own sake. Well-written copy has been our life interest. We don't suggest that every advertisement should carry a coupon. We realize that much advertising isn't easy to keep track of, and that some selling can best be done indirectly.

Even so, the astounding unconcern of advertising men about actual results is harder to believe than a fairy tale. Everybody's calm lack of interest as to what *happens* when any given advertisement is published is perhaps the most extraordinary spectacle in American business. Able bankers who know the worth of a bond down to the fourth decimal, and engineers who calculate the coefficients of all sorts of strange forces, seem alike to slide off into a hypnotic doze when it comes to the simple question of exactly what they buy with their advertising dollar.

Take, for example, the automobile industry. Who would approve an expenditure for a new type of engine without calculating closely the proposed horsepower, and approximating the engine cost per unit? But vast sums are spent for advertising by automobile engineers—experts on power—aided by automobile bankers—experts on investment. These expenditures are, in turn, checked by many of our keenest sales managers and advertising men. Somewhere down the line, surely, somebody must calculate in advance what each advertising unit—as a unit —is expected to accomplish. We mention the automobile advertising merely because it is so dazzling.

Turning in another direction, let us quote verbatim the printed remarks of the head of a large radio company:

We spent approximately $500,000 on advertising which was pretty broadly scattered in newspapers, magazines, trade papers, etc., and its quality as advertising was quite unusual and, I am certain, of at least average competency.

This advertising pulled in no greater or less ratio than radio advertising did for other companies in 1925, and to hint that our whole advertising program was a failure is entirely wrong.

Most abuses in modern advertising, strangely enough, can be traced to this calm faith in its unfailing efficacy. Your neighbor will agree his city is poorly governed. He may lose faith in trial by jury. Or in college education. Or feel religion is a waning force. But where can you find any literate American, without a rockbound, fundamental, fatalistic faith in advertising? [1]

Advertising has a brilliant present. None doubts its brilliant future. Yet even its most enthusiastic friends must sometimes wish spectacular success rested more on science and less on salesmanship. A publisher of several famous magazines once remarked: "We won't advertise this January number. It's out Christmas day—the deadest time of the year." As he spoke he had a dozen solicitors bringing advertisers into that same January number. Paradoxically, he was right. He knew that

[1] "Advertising is the religion of business. He who questions its unlimited sway must be prepared to answer the charges of commercial heresy and industrial apostasy." GORDON B. HANCOCK, *Social Forces,* June, 1926, p. 813.

out of the 12,000 national advertisers some are always to be had for every number of every publication. Nevertheless, one can't help feeling that some who used that January number might have done better with more of that publisher's force of character.

When business is good and money is plenty, every advertiser loves to be persuaded into a flyer. But as soon as sales fall until he sorely needs orders, he begins to slash expenses. Four times out of five, advertising is the first thing thrown overboard. Good, bad, or indifferent, beginning, middle, or climax of a campaign—it goes like snow on a hot stove. In 1920, when everybody was already oversold, every reputable magazine was deluged with advertising; a year later, when nobody could sell anything to speak of, the magazines fell away to skeletons and a number of them were buried. The figures published for 72 magazines are revealing:

1920	1921	Loss
$132,414,799	$95,439,236	$36,975,563

In general business, panic loss seldom averages more than 6 or 8 per cent. The advertising loss in these 72 publications this one year was 28 per cent. Thus, in hard times, do advertisers get even—to their own detriment—with the system that allows them to waste when money is plenty. The panicky advertiser doesn't try to salvage what he has already spent. He doesn't even stop to see what severed arteries are left bleeding. He might well slash his pay roll and put everything into selling. But he doesn't. Red ink in eye, he rushes at the very advertising he lauded six months ago as an "investment" and, with ferocious joy, rids himself of an "expense."

This is scarcely strange. So long as advertising is not taken seriously as a definite factor in the immediate sale of goods, it must remain on the defensive—no matter how aggressive it may manage to make that defense appear. This is unfortunate for those who buy, as well as those who sell. The truth, as usual, lies between. No advertising is good enough to justify more money than one knows how to get back. And practically no advertising is bad enough to justify an advertiser, once well started, giving it up. Advertising's future lies in a rapid perfection of agreement as to what is good even in times of panic. And what is waste, even in prodigal prosperity.

According to the "depth bomb" or cumulative theory of advertising, hundreds, if not thousands, of grand old accounts started a decade or two ago should now be at the very fullness of fruition. Take an issue of *Cosmopolitan* or the *Saturday Evening Post* of ten years ago and count how many of its advertisers are active today.

Or right at hand is the *National Geographic Magazine's* circular showing exceptional longevity of its own advertisers. The *National Geographic,* remember, is a substantial magazine famous for its profitable returns. Of the 270 different advertisers that used the *National Geographic* during the year 1926,

64 were new to the magazine that year. The other 196 had, in the previous twenty years, used it at least once before. Forty of that 270 had been in as many as ten different years. Six out of 270 had been in fifteen years. And one veteran alone had been in all twenty years. Or, from a slightly different angle, the *National Geographic* figures for 1925 show still active ten advertisers that started with it in the year 1920, eight that started in 1917, five that started in 1914, and none that started in the year 1909. From a full-page advertisement praising its own stability as an advertising medium, we learn that the *Ladies' Home Journal* retains in 1926 about thirty-five advertisers who started in the eleven years from 1897 to 1907. If a leading magazine like the *National Geographic,* as proof of longevity, shows only 38 per cent using its excellent columns as many as five out of a possible twenty years; and if a great institution like the *Ladies' Home Journal* saves, in the long run, an average of only three advertisers a year, the fatalities among third- and fourth-rate advertisers in third- and fourth-rate media must be discouraging.

Without dwelling a moment more than necessary on this uninspiring side of our subject, one sample paragraph may indicate the sort of unfriendly evidence that lurks in the shadows of advertising's golden effulgence.

Says Robert Ruxton: [1]

[1] *The Printing Art,* 1922, p. 585.

Some time back I had an analysis made of the advertising of one great publication, the analyst reporting that: "There were 997 concerns listed; 943 of these concerns advertised *before* January 1, 1921; 55 advertised *after* January 1, 1921; 664 concerns out of a total of 943 stopped full-page advertising before January 1, 1921. *This is equivalent to a death rate of 70.41 per cent.*

Our interest is scientific. We see nothing tragic in giant automobile or radio concerns spending advertising money with amiable unconcern. Their big, bright, double-page spreads and posters cheer the office forces, encourage salesmen, stiffen up retail agents, make billboard companies prosperous, pay the wages of paper-mill tree choppers, and do much for general morale. A couple of cents out of every dollar, less even than the stockholder gets, can damage no advertiser; and a small appropriation by a great company radiates benefits in a wide circle. Harm is done only when empty-barrel advertising— whether of automobiles, of soap, or soup—is swallowed whole and presented to the public as an example of the *practical* genius of the American business man.

To quote Mr. Robert K. Leavitt, speaking as secretary of the Association of National Advertisers:

Too many of us are as ready as I was——to justify advertised goods simply because they are advertised. Too many of us are so sure of the real economies advertising *can* effect we forget it doesn't always effect them.

Such frankness is noteworthy. Many brilliant leaders waste their skill in *a priori* justification of all advertising. If each would devote equal time to making every advertisement within his control justify itself, day by day in dollars and cents, to the man who pays for it, advertising would need no defense.

Æsop tells of the monkey who tried to dip a handful of nuts from a narrow-necked vase. Unable to pull out his overloaded paw, and unwilling to lighten its load, he sat to see what would happen. This may suggest somewhat the present status of advertising. We suffer from an attempt to emulate the hospitality of Noah and still enjoy the reputation of Caesar's wife. Anybody with an idea to sell to anybody else is, *per se*, an "advertising man." Conversely, anybody with an idea he never could sell to anybody else may himself print it in a magazine, stick it on a billboard, send it out by mail, and call it an "advertisement." With all so considerate of the other man's failures, and each silent about his own, advertising can hardly be blamed for accumulating unsound traditions and uneconomic practices.

No industry can afford indefinitely a Pyrrhic success. The flood of incoming, almost voluntary, advertising has spent itself. Every advertisement you see in a magazine nowadays is fought for. Behind the scenes, so far as the reader is concerned, a splendidly organized war is waged for every advertising account, and a battle fought for every advertising appropriation. Just as agents struggle with one another for clients, so do magazines and newspapers and billboards and radios struggle with one another for the advertising dollars of those clients. This is another reason why advertising has assumed an overt importance. It has vast intrinsic value. No longer content to be the humble handmaid of the trades it serves, advertising has proudly set itself up as an independent trade whose first and chief concern, naturally, must be its own support.

Against this well-organized competition for the advertiser's money comes, in light relief, the advertiser's own attitude as to what benefit he receives. For nine out of ten failures the advertiser has only himself to blame. Coming fresh to a new toy, he forgets that, little as our industry has done to organize essential knowledge, no intelligent man could work as hard as most of us do without learning individually something of his trade. Yet this experience has to bow a humble head to each advertiser's personal prejudices. One experienced copy writer claims:[1] that inexpert interference by high officials makes the most costly pages far less effective than minor space in the *New Yorker* or *The American Boy*. Also, that first-class advertising agencies refuse to sacrifice their best brains to this *ex officio* onslaught. Mr. W. R. Hotchkin, a veteran famous for his practical selling, expresses the expert's viewpoint with more truth than politeness:

If some of the blacksmiths, butchers, and fodder packers who have done this world a lot of good and themselves much credit would only have the horse sense to tie up their own

[1] Paul S. Dennison, "Super-censorship and Second-rate Advertisements," *Advertising and Selling*, February 24, 1926.

hands and tongues when they go into an advertising "conference" about their advertising campaign, and let the experts do the work for which they were chosen and for which they are being paid, they would be amazed to see how much greater results would pull.

Nevertheless, right or wrong, the man who pays the piper calls the tune. He submits copy and ideas to casual friends for criticism. Preliminary tests bore him. Nor will he always spend time to check up even those results available for his guidance. In fact, it may not be too rash to guess that out of every hundred people connected with advertising, eighty are quite content never to know the final results. The advertisements *look* the way they want them to look; they read the way they want them to read. The necessary compromises in the board of directors have all been smoothed out. Schedules have been neatly typed. Proofs have been sent the salesmen. The dealers have all been notified of a campaign about to sweep the goods off their shelves. Why worry? Let sleeping dogs lie!

Old Æsop forgot to say one important thing: Sleeping dogs come home to roost! Presumably the only reason for letting a sleeping dog slumber is to gain time to reason with him awake. The sleeping-dogs policy as applied to advertising doesn't seem working any too well. Every so often some critic, supposed to be safely sleeping, bobs up like Mr. Percy S. Straus before the Federal Trade Commission. Some watchdog like Mr. Thorstein Veblen barks viciously that advertising is "to an alarming degree

parasitic and uneconomic." Mr. Lew Hahn, director of the National Retail Drygoods Association,
snarls:

> The retailer who hooks himself on to the national adver-
> tiser's scheme is betraying his public's trust and selling his own
> birthright for considerably less than a mess of pottage.

Mr. Ralph Borsodi echoes:

> When an article is nationally advertised . . . stop, look,
> and listen!

Some Harvard authority snaps out "advertising
has no place in economics"; articles sniff that
"bankers are not sold on advertising men." Books
bite on the "tragedy of waste," or "national advertising vs. national prosperity." We even hear deep
official baying from the U. S. Department of Commerce. As an excellent statement of the opposition
view of advertising, take these words of Mr. Stuart
Chase:[1]

> . . . it is a blind game; fascinating and romantic if you
> please with its millions to be made from a happy slogan, but
> untouched with any science or utility in satisfying human
> wants.
>
> A wiser social order would not tolerate such frantic egotism
> —even as the professions do not tolerate advertising today.
>
> To determine technical merit on the basis of who can shout
> loudest and longest is a Neanderthalic survival which civilized
> society will some day outgrow.

Openly flouted by these unbelievers and over-

[1] Stuart Chase, "The Wastefulness of Advertising," *The New Republic*,
September 30, 1926.

advertised by its too loving friends, our business has ahead no road of roses. Hear once more Robert K. Leavitt:[1]

With the public, advertising can afford, I think, to rest its case upon the general merits of its goods. But with the legislators it has got to improve its case by logical argument and citation of specific cases. It has got to justify its existence by demonstrating in no uncertain terms the fact it is a producer of real economies. And this proof it has got to make—if the proof is to be effective—in the startlingly near future.

There is plenty of such affirmative proof. In these few pages we mention at least fifty instances of highly profitable advertising. The difficulty is to get anyone calmly to assemble the whole case. The temptation to spread-eagle seems irresistible. Mr. Guy Emerson, vice-president of the National Bank of Commerce in New York, cautions:

If it is right to spend money for advertising in a given case, even where it is impossible actually to prove that commensurate results will be obtained, it certainly should be possible to make a straightforward showing, *based upon business experience in analogous cases*. When this is done the banker will be found responsive.

Nevertheless, advertising leaders seem as reluctant scientifically to organize the known facts about advertising in general as the average advertiser is to discover them about his own pet masterpiece. Circulation, yes; markets, yes; but advertising, yes-and-no!

Meanwhile, some say advertising pays; some say

[1] *Printers' Ink,* This Business of Taxing Advertising, July 1.

it doesn't; some say it doesn't matter whether it pays or not. Some are making money; some are losing. Some don't care which, so long as everybody's happy. This has lasted a long time. For reasons suggested in the next chapter, we feel it can't last a great deal longer. When selling gets caught up with manufacturing, advertising has got to catch up with selling. Or lose the greatest opportunity in the world's history.

Faith in advertising is an excellent thing; but, like faith in America, it imposes a certain responsibility. If you believe in advertising, you must believe in good advertising; for its history is littered with sepulchral failures. Weakly managed companies have thought advertising would be cheaper than good salesmen. Vacillating advertisers have turned their copy on and off spasmodically like a small boy fooling with the hose. Big, comfortable companies have thought a tiny dribble of advertising would fool their own salesmen and the public too. Tricksters, too, a shady company, with fake rheumatism cures and dirty novelties and swindling stocks and cheap corn whisky to make ailing women happily drunk at home.

This crude period has passed. The boom days are over. As Mr. A. C. Pearson pointed out in his London speech, even the public is becoming "distribution conscious." The man on the street is beginning to realize his cost of living is still 60 per cent above 1914, in spite of the 60 per cent more goods being turned out for him. The next chapter suggests that all selling has heavy work ahead. Already advertising begins to be characterized by less fluff and fuzz. Many people of intelligence are, for the first time, beginning to study it with a critical eye. For example, Mr. C. F. Kettering, president of the General Motors Research Corporation, who said to the A. N. A. at Detroit:

In my opinion advertising men must not be too inclined to accept as established acts of nature anything which prevents them from reducing the present 60-per-cent cost of distributing merchandise.

The great advertising men of tomorrow may turn out business-sportsmen, as keenly unwilling to waste an advertising dollar as to waste a stroke at golf. There is every indication that the brains and energy which have made advertising so brilliant a game will make it an even better business.

Advertising can—if it will—make good on a strictly business basis. There is no longer necessity for letting sleeping dogs lie. Even now, any man who will take the trouble can make his advertising pay. But first, he must determine honestly and precisely his real motives for running it. Whatever these motives, direct or indirect, personal or business, there is no reason why intelligent advertising should not achieve them.

None need fail at advertising!

Any man with a business that deserves to succeed can definitely improve that success through proper advertising.

But he must take his advertising seriously. He cannot dash off a few great thoughts on the back of an old envelope. He must plan with the canniness of a Scotch engineer and test with the patience of a German analytical chemist.

CHAPTER VII

Advertising's Golden Chance

Thirteen hundred million dollars was the total revenue of newspapers and magazines in 1925. Of this the public paid $325,000,000 for their periodicals. Advertisers paid $975,000,000, or 70 per cent of the entire income. It took rare courage, therefore, for a publisher of ripe judgment to testify at the anniversary dinner of one of the world's great newspapers that his experience convinced him half the money put into advertising goes to waste through lack of proper preparation. Another man of his business generation, after thirty-five years in large-scale experiment on actual campaigns, has just reiterated an opinion that advertising waste runs as high as eighty cents out of every dollar. A dozen advertising managers, at cigarettes between speeches of a recent meeting of the Association of National Advertisers, are said—startlingly—to have agreed that competitive use of constantly larger space had hoisted advertising waste nearer ninety cents out of every dollar.

This, of course, represents the view of a small minority. Distinguished speakers are still too inspired by advertising's contribution to America's high standards of living to concern themselves with the colossal tax society contributes in return. The

nation pays more to support advertising workers
than to maintain its army and navy. Much of that
expenditure is profitable. Rid of unnecessary waste,
practically all could be profitable. The nearest advertising itself has come to any public admission of
clay feet was, perhaps, in the address of Dr. Julius
Klein, director of the Bureau of Foreign and Domestic Commerce of the U. S. Department of Commerce, made before the Associated Advertising
Clubs of the World at Philadelphia. Dr. Klein said:

The campaign for the elimination of waste in industry and
trade being waged by the Department of Commerce under
Secretary Hoover's leadership has been concentrated against
fifteen major types of avoidable losses. The thirteenth of
these is described as waste due to the enormous expenditure
of effort and money in advertising and sales promotion without adequate information on which to base such campaigns.

When fifty cents out of each dollar profit used to
go into war taxes, everybody built a new factory to
let the Government pay half. Production is still
walking home from that joy ride! For the same
reason, many a million slid easily into "institutional"
advertising. The tendency today is to take profits
when you have them! Therefore arises a new interest in results. Lower taxes, business and personal,
will mop up selling waste as surely as they created
a new efficiency in factories and railroads. Advertising is rapidly aligning itself with new conditions.
Outside elements merely hasten an internal evolu-
tion already under way. For, when closer competition forces less tolerance, only those who have

demonstrated marked ability to use an advertiser's dollar profitably will have an opportunity to use it at all.

In general business, meanwhile, the new conditions are here. The past five years established a new trade rhythm. To begin with, a flood of money. The United States today holds half of all the world's gold. Skillful handling releases vast millions of capital formerly tied up in slow merchandise. Life insurance premiums on 100,000,000 policies are constantly reinvested. Installment selling adds six or eight billion dollars to resources for commercial credit. On top of all this, Europe pours in an extra $200,-000,000 every year.

Also ample spending. We live more than prosperously. The whole nation lives prodigally. Anybody can buy anything. For a teaset or a taxicab, a $5 book or a $50,000 house, only a nominal cash payment and a reasonable reputation is required. Union wages have increased 180 per cent in the past twenty years. Each month during five whole years the average American's capacity to buy has increased steadily at a rate better than one-half of 1 per cent. Not only has each American 11,000,000 more neighbors than he had five years ago, but every man, woman, and child among them is able to buy today nearly one-third as much again.

Even so, factories have worked faster than the U. S. Mint. Great as is money inflation, goods inflation more than offsets it. In spite of prodigious wealth, there are still too many goods. Industry

has outgrown population. Science has definitely out-
stripped consumption. Power increases even faster
than factories—nearly 250 per cent since 1899. Machinery has grown fastest of all.

"The cumulation of these forces," says Herbert Hoover, "has
increased our national efficiency to a degree which I hesitate
to express statistically lest we appear to exaggerate. But I
might observe that, by and large, while we have increased our
population 17 or 18 per cent in a dozen years, we have swelled
productivity of the nation something like 30 or 35 per cent.
Our farmer produces 13 per cent more, off the same number
of farms, as twelve years ago; our railways carry 22 per cent
more traffic with about the same number of men. We have
tamed the kilowatt to be the friend of man. We have now
domesticated some 68,000,000 kilowatt hours annually where
we used 23,000,000 kilowatts twelve years ago. They increase
output and decrease sweat. Even such old industries as flour
milling and boot and shoe manufacturing have advanced handsomely, while newer industries, such as the automobile and
rubber, have gained more than 300 per cent." [1]

Some of us can remember the "hill horse" used on
street cars to help the regular team upgrade. Today,
every American factory worker has at least four such
hill horses always at his service. Electric motors
furnish each man his individual four horsepower,
indefatigable and ingeniously hitched to jobs his
grandfather had to tackle single-handed. Mr. J. E.
Davidson calculated last May that electrical power
alone does today the work of 170,000,000 men. The
General Electric Company has been at work on a
machine with the muscular energy of 2,000,000 men.

[1] *Magazine of Wall Street*, December 18, 1926.

With more brains in office and less indifference in shop, modern machinery has wrought a miracle. Between 1914 and 1925, ten industries showed increases in labor efficiency ranging from 90 per cent to 210 per cent. One textile mill, after cutting down to 775 a pay roll of 1,150 workers, reports, nevertheless, a greatly increased output. Bethlehem Steel dropped 2,300 men, between 1923 and 1925, and increased production.

Were this new efficiency absent, were our increased output merely the result of more men on the pay roll at higher wages, as in the prosperous days of President McKinley, everything would be serene. My extra workmen making rush-order radios would, in that case, be earning more money to buy your washing machines; and your washing-machine over-time wages would, by way of reciprocity, flow back to buy my radios. But, in the thirty years since that simple era of balanced production, the output of manufactured goods has grown twice as fast as the number of people at work making them. And, roughly speaking, physical production is still growing at least three times as fast as population. All over the nation, factory workers are giving away to machines. Each year since 1923 two out of every hundred workers have been laid off.

So, instead of each workman turning out about enough goods to barter against his own needs—with, of course, a fair share for nonproducers—our super-mechanicalized factory hands are able to pile up a threatening surplus. Even back in 1925 the aver-

age worker who earned only $1,279 to *spend himself*
turned out $7,479 of goods for others to buy. A
shirt manufacturer who today makes, at the same
cost, three shirts for every two he made in 1925,
says:

> If we attempt to market this surplus through salesmen,
> the cost of developing new territories would absorb a consid-
> erable portion of the saving effected by decreasing burden per
> unit through increased production. So the easiest immediate
> solution is to sell this surplus to big users at cost.

This is fine for the "big users." But it makes the
little fellows pay all the factory profits. Naturally
enough, merchants are demanding that factories be
slowed down to keep step with consumption. And
rightly. For were the trends of the past five years
to continue unchanged, 1930 would find us with a
population of 125,000,000 turning out goods for
170,000,000.

Paul M. Mazur points out [1] the grave significance
of our present trend:

> Mass production has rendered a great service to the Ameri-
> can purchaser. But the establishment of mass production as
> an idol, to which there must be sacrificed the recognition of
> a variation in consumption demands, is bound to create in-
> dustrial depressions.

Distribution has never been so delicately—and
dangerously—adjusted. Returning high prices in
any line will soon bring a new flood of goods from
eager, underworked factories.

[1] Paul M. Mazur, *Principles of Organization Applied to Modern Retailing*, p. 3.

Chain stores in 1926 sold $272,000,000 of goods at actual loss and another $884,000,000 at cost plus overhead. The first topic discussed by the 8,000 accountants at the International Cost Conference at Chicago this summer was the effect of selling goods below cost of manufacture. Even the conservative economists warn us that the problem of today is no longer one of making cheaper goods, but of getting them more cheaply distributed.

Capital used to be ultraconservative. Today, capital itself continually forces expansion. The banker can no longer be content to finance production. He must regulate—and stimulate—organized consumption. As Bernard M. Baruch puts it:[1]

The big question before us now is whether we can solve the problem of overproduction. We have learned how to create wealth, but we have not learned how to keep that wealth from choking us and from bringing on widespread poverty to the producers in the midst of their abundance.

Manufacturers will, of course, cut prices to meet competition. (The two big mail order houses announce cuts from 3 to 6 per cent for Fall 1927.) And cut costs to keep profits.[2] They must simplify selling.

And above all, they will wipe out waste. Increas-

[1] *Forbes' Magazine* for April, 1927.

[2] "The explanation of the smaller net profits," says Montgomery Ward's statement, "lies in the fact that 1926 was a year of declining commodity prices, resulting in a recession in the margin of gross profits per dollar of sales. Moreover, there was a greater demand than usual for merchandise carrying a relatively low margin of gross profit."— *New York World*, January 21, 1927.

ing density in population will tend to decentralize national distribution into convenient territories. Manufacturers are becoming their own wholesalers through strategically located warehouses. A modern chain of vast warehouses now lends local money on goods in their keeping. City-bound automobiles will sweep the little country store off the crossroads corner. The small independent units—whether retail, jobbing, or manufacturing—will have to get together or get out.

Local merchants agile enough to keep on the band wagon will become more and more powerful. Already the chain idea spreads into every line from soft drinks to garages. "Within a few years," writes Mr. William J. Baxter, of the Wool and Clothing Research Bureau of America, "the entire business of supplying clothing to the nation will be controlled by nation-wide chains of retail clothing and department stores."

Every hour, day and night, throughout the year, a new chain store is born—with two an hour on Sundays. So far only 8% of the nation's retail trade is by chain stores. And another 5%, perhaps, by mail-order houses. Yet their simple direct method is revolutionizing the whole distribution system. Department stores themselves are organizing chains. The great mail-order houses are fast extending their retail outlets. Sears Roebuck now has fourteen. House-to-house competition becomes a serious threat to the orthodox distributor—already there is one firm selling $5,000,000 a year in picture frames!

Automatic stores everywhere will be backed by cash-and-carry jobbers; five-and-ten-cent grocery stores, with three eggs for a dime, and butter packed ready for your coat pocket, are here already. So are up-to-date motor peddlers—veritable little department stores on wheels!

Ten years ago the factories found merchants to sell their goods. Ten years hence merchants will find factories to make their goods. Men who control markets will either own factories, as the Liggett-Rexall stores do now, or dictate their own terms, as does Woolworth. This will gravely inconvenience "dealer influence" advertising. Private brands will return more and more to resist manufacturers' dictation as to quotas. Sooner or later, advertising will be forced to add to its old job of getting goods into stores the real work of actually moving them out.

Markets, meantime, have flown off on their own tangents. Women buy three times as many dresses with three and one-half instead of twelve yards for a dress. Lower prices and easy payments make yesterday's luxuries today's necessities. Electrical washing machines, in the last decade, jumped from 20,000 a year to 620,000 a year; bathtubs from 500,000 a year to 1,500,000 a year. With $500,-000,000-a-year radio, $100,000,000-a-year country clubs, and $90,000,000-a-year cigarette expenditures thrown against them, staple products have had to yield to new and more necessary luxuries. While automobiles cost every man, woman, and child in the United States around ten dollars a month, millinery, clothes, sugar, leather, stand almost stagnant. The average life of an automobile has crept up to seven years. And tires run 12,000 miles! As many pins as ever are lost, but, in spite of three years' growth in population, shoe factories in the first half of 1926 were making some 200,000 pairs a day fewer than 1923. To stimulate the lagging, lopsided consumer, manufacturers in nearly every line have had either to ease their terms or reduce prices. Installment buying has helped some of them. But this new competition has made life still more difficult for those who can't easily sell on time.

"Back of it all," explained the late Ralph Van Vechten, president of the State Bank of Chicago, "is the nation-wide trend toward economy!"

People want to buy better merchandise on the basis of real value, without having to pay the penalty of uneconomic practices anywhere along the line. There is an unrelenting fight being waged on waste, wherever waste may be. If there is any factor or any practice in the whole process of manufacture and distribution that is wasteful and unessential, simply business prudence demands that it be eliminated."

Mr. Van Vechten has named one powerful influence. The other is the absolute physical inability of American people to absorb everything they can make for each other. The General Electric Company cleverly advertises that an automobile workman today, backed by his 19-horsepower auxiliary, turns out five times as many cars as he used to. That is an achievement: A source of pleasure and prosper-

ity. The fact remains, nevertheless, that one workman can still drive only one car.

Machinery can build these four extra cars. It can
run them. But it cannot drive them. Neither can
machinery consume its other products. Great masses
of people come into that picture. And people, in the
mass, change very slowly. Even during the World
War, when high-pressure propaganda made it un-
patriotic to eat a roll awaiting a waiter, the reduc-
tion in food was, we are told, less than 10 per cent.
And that was mostly through studied avoidance of
ordinary waste! To make the average American
family today eat even 6 per cent more would probably be impossible. Certainly they show no signs
of wearing 6 per cent more!

Eight per cent variation from normal, one way or
the other, is a liberal estimate of the buying difference between piping prosperity and deep de-
pression. What can 6, 8, 10, or even 12 per cent
increase in consumption do with the potential factory output as given by Mr. Ralph Borsodi? [1]

Our steel plants are now equipped to produce 80 per cent
more steel than the normal requirements of the market.

Our shoe factories have an excess of capacity of 80 per cent.

Our copper smelters an excess capacity of over 100 per cent.

Our lumber mills have an excess capacity of over 300 per
cent.

Our automobile industry has a capacity of 80 per cent
greater than the ability of the market to absorb automobiles.

With this crush of production towering high above

[1] Ralph Borsodi, *The Distribution Age*, p. 43.

any possible speeding up in consumption—with prices of steel products dropping 23 per cent in four years—everyone can now see plainly what Roger Babson suggested several years ago:

. . . . Merchandise has become a free-for-all scramble for a place on the family budget—a fight to see whether the consumer will spend his money on an automobile, phonograph, clothes, a house, or something else. . . .

Distribution is at last clearly recognized as the narrow neck of the bottle.

The train begins to crowd the engine.

As selling spurts to catch up with production, advertising must catch up with selling. Any advertising that cannot, immediately and definitely, shoulder its share of the large-scale production already upon us, may have to be content to concede itself simply the silk hat of commerce.

If Mr. Coolidge's cordial estimate of advertising as a cause of all this large-scale production were only half as exact as it was complimentary, the solution would be obvious. As befits a delightful guest, however, the President's speech at the banquet of the American Association of Advertising Agencies was more tactful than scientific; with more, perhaps, of political effectiveness than political economy. At least a dozen men in his audience could have shown Mr. Coolidge that mass advertising is an *effect* of mass production. Rarely a cause. Certainly no man in that distinguished audience could forget the fact advertising, his industry, had extended itself companionably along with all the others. As surely as the manufacturer of pencils or pig iron must find customers to keep his machines at work, so advertising must market each month the product of huge presses and meet pay rolls for thousands of highly specialized workers.

Two years ago Mr. S. W. Reyburn pointed out that one of advertising's most cherished corner stones was beginning to crumble. The local merchant, observed Mr. Reyburn, could no longer be counted a manufacturer's selling agent. Increased knowledge among millions of women today keeps local merchants busy as buyers for their own customers. Increased skill among purchasing agents makes quantity selling equally difficult. Of a representative group of 116 professional buyers, 68 were found to be university graduates, 47 with engineering degrees. Ninety-two were technically, or practically, trained. These experts coldly scrutinize the old-fashioned inspirational salesman into a state of exhausted silence.

In these conditions, salesmen and advertising able actually to move goods will naturally command higher rewards than ever before. But the new trade rhythm promises little for indirect influence. Or for prices much above the market. More and more the liberal advertiser may find himself fighting the temptation to use his appropriation as a bonus to some large distributor. Or directly to cut prices.

Friends of advertising have for years offered the sweeping justification—touched on by President Coolidge—that, by bringing about mass production, advertising has lowered prices. Any advertising man assuming responsibility for the present pressure of low-priced goods would be as popular as a rainmaker down in Louisiana claiming the original shower that brought on the Mississippi flood.

Be that as it may, here is advertising's golden opportunity to make good the classic claim. Present prosperity is based on more people having more things than ever in history. Future prosperity clearly depends on still more people having still more things. That means lower, lower, lower, and still lower prices. To place itself forever beyond criticism, advertising has only to demonstrate what has always been claimed for it—ability to bring about these lower prices! In doing this it will have the help of the most deadly commercial competition the world has ever seen. War waste ran prices up; war intensity will bring them down. Synthetic processes, new methods, and foreign competition will reduce raw materials. Competition between distributors will keep them low. Trading-up campaigns, price maintenance propaganda, money inflation, and legalized trade combinations will show a staying influence, here and there, now and then. But, in the long run, each consumer is out to get the greatest value for his own dollar. And, recovered from the war, the whole world is studying how to give him that extra value. Two-pants suits, three-to-the-pair stockings, remade cars, reprinted novels—are all surface bubbles from a struggle deep below.

As keener competition and more efficient production slowly grind down the margin between cost and selling price,[1] inefficient, wasteful advertising can hardly hope to thrive. He whose advertising adds real driving power will forge ahead faster than ever. But the power will have to do more than simply blow the whistle.

<u>It must turn sales wheels</u>.

Even driving forward, however, few men can afford to spend an advertising dollar without some idea of how far it takes them. In Chapters IX, X, and XI will be found a method of approach that may, perhaps, help some advertiser. Used rather generally, it might even safeguard the $1,500,000,000-a-year structure the last half century has erected on faith in advertising's ability to live up to high expectations.

Self-supporting advertising, in fact, becomes more than an individual problem. It approaches an industrial necessity. Advertisers can, and do, start and stop without serious immediate harm. The New York department stores proved that during the newspaper strike. What really matters is the vast capital and employment invested in publishing and publicity establishments on the assumption that any advertiser who drops out can always be promptly replaced.

---

[1] "The producers of cotton piece goods have had about all they could do to keep the mills sold up. They have done, and are still doing, most unusual things, such as one hundred sample cards for fifty pieces of goods, packing goods in half-cases; half pieces; parcel post and express shipments; making allowances; taking goods *back;* all involving extra costs, but without charge."—Martin A. Downes, of Cannon Mills, Inc., in the *New York Journal of Commerce,* January 18, 1927.

So far this has been easy. Too easy, possibly. It may always be easy. Nevertheless, the only advertiser safe for an agent or publication to tie to is our combination Scotch engineer and German chemist. Like the remorseless Mr. L——, this man sees clearly his advertising target. He studies his own aim as carefully as the other man's ammunition. He tests each step and appraises his success as he goes. He will stick. He will increase his appropriation. He is anxious to spend. He can afford to pay. Most of all, he doesn't have to be replaced. And for this type of man, advertising has most fortunately at hand the very showing demanded by Mr. Emerson in behalf of the bankers. The next chapter will introduce this newer advertising method, and the proof of its success!

CHAPTER VIII

The Money Players

HUMAN nature loves to do war dances and to express itself in print. In even the dullest business, advertising offers man a legitimate field, consciously or unconsciously, to enjoy these primitive impulses.

Man, therefore, takes to advertising as a duck to water. For fifty years brilliant minds have been rationalizing into a business an impulse that otherwise might have gone to waste as an inarticulate Barnum-and-Bailey complex. The world's most skillful salesmen, also, have done their share.

All this time, slowly developing in outer darkness like the Jews in Egypt or early Christians in the catacombs, has been a despised race who go at advertising completely backward. Adhering to traditions of their primitive ancestors, they persist in thinking of advertising as of any other branch of business, only in terms of net profit. And now, like trick photography of a moving-picture farce, slide in these unorthodox advertising men, not altogether welcome yet able to show advertising how to make good in dollars and cents almost every claim uttered by its less practical enthusiasts.

These ink-stained gentlemen with their strong-lens glasses, the go-getters of advertising, don't buy white space on speculation. Or even two-cent postage stamps. Advertising to them is a methodical business, like raising potatoes or mining coal. They have no picturesque controversies as to the genteel way to sell Kipling. Their annual conventions are simple comparisons of decimal points! Aggressively led, always ably, and often brilliantly, by men like Robert Ruxton, Robert Ramsey, J. Howie Wright, Homer J. Buckley, Otto Guenther, Walter Ostrander, E. T. Gundlach, W. B. Ruthrauff, F. B. Ryan, G. Lynn Sumner, Charles Austin Bates, and S. Roland Hall, this long-submerged school of pragmatists is slowly but surely thrusting its direct mailed fist through our politely polished dancing floor. They, too, have their axes to grind, their own commodities to sell. Neither in achievement nor ability do they outmeasure the better men in the more ambitious branches of advertising. But they have two tremendous advantages:

They keep their eyes on results.

They prefer facts, not fancies.

No advertiser these days is big enough to ignore them. The American Wholesale Corporation of Baltimore, without a single salesman, sells $10,000,000 a year through two catalogues, at a total selling cost of 1.98 per cent. Butler Brothers, wholesalers, sell upward of $110,000,000 to dealers through the mail. Nor is any advertiser too small. A Detroit butcher shop increased business 700 per cent in a year by sending a hundred postal cards a day. A jeweler in Seattle made $1,325 sales by mailing 600 one-cent cards to inactive accounts. They will tell you how one Maryland firm with letter and follow-up to a carefully picked list of fifty names—total cost around $11—brought seven inquiries of which the first three yielded sales amounting to $5,525. Or, how a Brooklyn store used 5,000 letters, costing $147, to sell 279 mattresses—the sales amounting to $4,450. Or, how, by mailing out an advance "proof" of a newspaper announcement, a San Francisco store got a pre-opening sale of $10,000 on units averaging less than one dollar. Or, how one letter three years ago sold $33,000 worth of kitchen cabinets to dealers at a net sales cost of 2 per cent. Or, how an automatic-sprinkler firm up in Canada sent out a sales letter to 1,016 prospects, costing $256 complete, which brought installations totaling $21,213. Selling cost about $1\frac{1}{4}$! Or, how the Syracuse Trust Company sent out 2,000 letters and got 228 replies, with fifteen orders for service in wills disposing of $750,000. Or, how, by mailing out 9,000 postal cards, at a cost of $110, a San Francisco store gave its dress department the largest single day on record.

In our opening chapter we promised a basis for a firm faith in advertising. Later we suggested that there is no real excuse for any man willing to work failing in advertising. Here we kill both these birds with one barrel: Take four magnificent department stores, landmarks of America's greatest four cities, household words throughout the nation. Marshall Field, Chicago; Macy's, New York; Hudson's, Detroit; and John Wanamaker's, Philadelphia. Each uses full-page advertisements every day in a broad list of great newspapers. If there is anything to be known about merchandising, if there is anything to be known about selling through print, paint, or plate glass, surely these splendid stores know it. They are the acme of high institutionalism!

Now leave these four great cities. Turn south a moment to Atlanta. Sears Roebuck celebrates its fortieth birthday by opening a southern branch office. Two hundred and fifty carloads of merchandise roll into town in one long succession of freight trains. Six at a time, these freight cars unload into the new $3,000,000 storehouse. Incidentally, postage saved the first year will pay for the site of that great building. Just as Sears marches into Georgia, comes a similar invasion of Kansas. Six thousand people, some from as far as fifty miles, attend the opening of Montgomery Ward's new establishment in Marysville, a village of some 4,000 souls. Inspired by the wide after effect of their exhibits at local fairs, this is the first unit of a proposed chain-store-sample-room system with one thousand branches. With regular chain-store front, each will exhibit in rotation about 3,000 items out of the 33,000 articles in the regular catalogue.[1] This, the newspapers say, is an experiment in "super-mail-order salesmanship." Even without the "super," Montgomery Ward's ordinary mail-order salesmanship had proved reasonably effective. It averages well over $3,000,000 a week. More than $500,000 in small orders slide its mail

[1] After a year's experiment, this store now functions as a retail establishment, selling about half its goods directly over the counter.

chutes every day—half a million of merchandise to be shipped before tomorrow's breakfast. Sears Roebuck, even larger, sells to 11,000,000 different customers—more than one out of every three families in the United States.

Now turn back an instant to our four great department stores—Marshall Field, Macy, Hudson, Wanamaker; put their business all together in one vast volume. Then try to realize that a single Chicago house does as big a business as these four great stores. So if advertising means in any degree moving goods through printed matter, mail order must be ushered to a place very near its head.

In 1928, not less than $450,000,000 will be spent on direct mail. Strangely enough, a weekly magazine is probably the greatest user of direct mail in America. It is said to spend $8,000,000 a year. Nearly all 12,000 national advertisers use mail on their extension work. Wrigley sends out 70,000 mail pieces every business day, 18,000,000 a year. National Cash Register spends more than $40,000 a year on mailings. Burroughs Adding Machine, $50,000 a year. Mellen's Food so uses the major portion of its advertising appropriation. National Harvester Company spends over $500,000 on direct mail. Besides these national advertisers there are at least as many local advertisers again using mail for direct selling. A survey of Ohio retail stores found them so spending from 15 per cent to 30 per cent of their total advertising appropriations. And when all national and local advertisers using direct mail have been added together, there will still be as many again of miscellaneous businesses which, without any other kind of advertising, make at least one mailing a year. Both in universal popularity and in volume of business, this method demands the thoroughly respectful consideration of any advertiser.

Tiffany's and Altman's, neighbors on Fifth Avenue, have their orders by mail. Baby chickens and high pure-bred live stock are sold by circulars. A handsome book mailed to twenty-five people sold the $100,000 vase it advertised. A yacht designer sold nineteen boats at $500,000 by mail to a list of multimillionaires, at a sales cost of one-tenth of 1 per cent. Violets and automobile hearses are ordered with a two-cent stamp. Machinery of expensive types finds frequent mail customers. Banking, accident and life insurance, are conducted regularly by mail.

The International Correspondence School uses both circulars and magazines. Also a large personal selling organization. Selling costs are kept in Scranton as scientifically as other good businesses keep their manufacturing costs. These records are said to show orders closed by mail at less than half the average general sales cost. The Aladdin Company, of Bay City, Michigan, gets about 1,500,000 inquiries a year. Half their sales can be traced directly to the catalogue sent out in response to those inquiries. Although Aladdin units run from $350 to $1,500, they gave up show rooms, branch offices, and large forces of high-powered salesmen. Printed matter and postage stamps were found cheaper and more effective. The Hecht Company in Washington, D. C., after years of testing, decided to spend from 15 per cent to 20 per cent of its advertising money on direct mail. An Eastern rug manufacturer, a prominent magazine advertiser, after securing dealer representation in large towns by personal selling at a cost of $40 for each store, put on a mail campaign. He added nearly 10,000 outlets in smaller towns at a cost of less than $7 apiece. A Texas department store by mailing to a list of 35,000 increased its out-of-town sales $100,000. In the little town of Warren, Pennsylvania, one company mails out 20,000,000 pieces a year. It sells $2,500,000 of men's clothing and specialties. Daily letters bring in $500,-000 a week. Thousands and thousands of other companies are doing actual mail selling at a cost of from 5 per cent to 30 per cent—with the general publicity thrown in!

Within ten years direct-mail selling has increased probably 500 per cent. There is no god but results. And test is his profit! Here, perhaps, we may repeat this book is not direct-mail propaganda. We argue only for *resultful* advertising. We believe that no business man is in any position to judge modern advertising until he knows what the professional result-getters can do. We are interested in the businesslike department-store advertising. We admire the Bermuda system of throwing in by cable advertising in twenty-three cities the moment bookings begin to drop. Also the Miami Conservatory District selling $1,800,000 of contractor's equipment through little classified advertisements in industrial and trade papers. We admire the hundreds of thousands of perfectly ignorant people who consider a job from a four-line "Situation Wanted" ad. as natural as a stick of chewing gum from a penny-in-the-slot machine. Thirteen tons of rubber, for example, is a lot to send out in samples. The Gates Rubber people used that much in getting 21,000 new tire customers. Five thousand new accounts is a lot to open in two and a half months; one company did it with a single letter. Eighty-five per cent response would be quite high for anybody to get from any list; one company got 85 per cent answers out of a list of 2,100 jobbers!

In spite of this vast popularity and proved success, many able connoisseurs—more interested in advertisements than in advertising—still treat direct selling with the same patronizing admiration gentlemen amateurs bestow on Gene Tunney and Walter Hagen.

This is the more strange because the most sporting of all advertising is this keyed copy. It's like whipping for trout. Or shooting a grizzly bear. Other sorts of advertising demand 25 per cent to 100 per cent credit for fish that got away. Or for bears that left only a trail of blood. Keyed advertisements, on the other hand, can count only the fish in the creel. And hides nailed to the wall. They pay in full. Or flop. Although entitled, along with any other advertising, to certain credit for general publicity beyond actual traced results, mail order, nevertheless, asks no allowance for unreckoned benefits.

We dwell on this point so strongly here because men like Chase and Borsodi tend to ignore absolutely the astounding selling done every day by those who use advertising strictly for that purpose. Some advertisers cannot. Others will not. But the method is there nevertheless. One must beware, however, of the assumption that success with a simpler method necessarily indicates greater ability. To ascribe superior *selling* brains to chain stores or mail order houses is a common error. Their success comes from advantageous buying, ability to avoid waste, and economy of large operation. Their selling genius —with a few noteworthy exceptions—is below average. Many a Hannibal is lifting advertising elephants over the Alps of an impossible distributive system while his duller rival trots a sleek direct-sales donkey in the smooth valleys below.

Without here precipitating the controversy constantly crackling in the clouds, we merely suggest that any man about to spend money on large space, or any man wanting to make sure his selling policies are properly lined up with public fancy, can employ "keyed" advertisements as scouts and skirmishers as effectively as Noah used his dove.

Keyed circulars fly out in pairs, by dozens, scores, hundreds, thousands, millions; they can be mailed simultaneously in hundreds of direct comparisons. Any combination anybody thinks of can be given instant trial. The answer comes back like a serve to

Tilden's racket or a pitch to Babe Ruth's bat. Within four days keyed orders begin to arrive. Within ten days you know the verdict. Within two weeks you have 60 per cent of your orders shipped and billed. You may then speed to immediate profits by forcing strong factors. And you may throw out weak features as fast as they fail. Or, with more time, you can run a regular elimination contest like a golf tournament, trying out each variation of circular, or new combination, individually against all the others.

And just as a winning horse or successful play has an established value, so has any advertisement that wins out in a good stiff series of tests. This is the answer to those who dodge responsibility for advertising results because they are so hard to trace.

Adequate preliminary tests will so establish the value of a good advertisement that its owner may thereafter spend millions on it with perfect confidence.

Mr. Hopkins tells of advertising a five-dollar article. His replies were costing 85 cents. Another man brought in copy he thought better. Replies jumped to $14.20 each. Still another man suggested another approach which for two years brought replies at 41 cents each. That advertisement, on the hoof, was worth $100,000. So beware of compromise. Advertising copy is one place where two heads may be too many. Whenever ideas clash, the sporting as well as the businesslike method is to try out both, one directly against the other. This implies, of course, a definite aim for every advertisement. The artillery methods of our new advertising era are becoming exactly that exact. An entire chapter is next devoted to sighting your own advertising gun. Then we shall take a look at the target, the copy projectile, and the circulation power that hurls it.

CHAPTER IX

PANGOLINS FREE!

A RICH uncle dies in East Africa and leaves you a fine pair of pangolins. The "pangolin," your dictionary may tell, is an animal with oversized claws that lives exclusively on the larvæ of white ants. When disturbed, he rolls into a ball inside an armor of overlapping scales. Around Tanganyika these scales sell at a couple of shillings apiece as charms to keep off lions.

To give such rare and engaging animals to the zoo seems both ungrateful and pusillanimous. Therefore, you start a pangolin farm in Westchester to breed little pangolettes for all sorts of artistic and commercial purposes.

Even before the lease is signed, while your pangolins are still seasick, you decide to advertise. Somebody on the 8:33 from Bronxville suggests a double-page spread as a starter. But $15,000 seems quite an investment before you have even sample-line production, so you reluctantly postpone pangolizing the entire nation on the kick-off.

With an absolutely virgin industry, you approach an absolutely immaculate market with an absolutely open mind—an opportunity probably never before afforded any advertiser. Make the most of it. Take plenty of time to find out precisely what you want to do yourself. Then you can safely tell the public what it must do to help you.

What, exactly, do you expect to do with this pangolin business? And, as a corollary, just *why* are you going to advertise?

Have you any pet theory as to how an advertisement should read? Or are you willing to leave it to a competent advertising agent?

Do you care how your advertisements look? Or shall you be content simply to make money?

Will you use the publications that sell the most pangolins at least expense? Or have you a list of favorite magazines?

Would you insist on magazines? Or so long as you sold your annual output would you be willing merely to mail circulars? Or tack up tin signs?

Will you try for direct orders? Or do you seek more finesse in your publicity?

Suppose not a single one of your friends ever saw any of your advertisements; could you still be happy knowing that your customers saw them? Is there any business connection—bankers, supply houses, or mere acquaintances—you want your advertising particularly to impress? Or anybody's advertising you have in mind to imitate?

Even after you have thus wrestled your own motives into submission, the work has hardly begun. Let's assume you honestly find yourself advertising for the sole purpose of selling pangolins at the greatest profit with the least cost.

You are then at the great divide:

(a) Will you appropriate a fixed sum for advertising, and work from there to the details of space and copy? In other words, will you, today, bet your whole pile that you know what people in Peoria and Painted Post think about pangolins?

(b) Or, will you go about it the other way? Will you find out some sure-fire sales idea, build it gradually into profitable advertising, extending its operation as rapidly as circumstances allow?

By this time you will have searched out your motives for advertising. You have figured out also your selling approach. Now you are ready to make the even more important inquiries about other people's motives for buying.

What news is there about your new pets that will selfishly interest the greatest number of people? What is the most strikingly attractive way to present that news?

What in people's mind is the right price for a pangolin? What is the highest price people in large numbers will pay? Between that price and the lowest you can afford, what figure will give the greatest gross revenue?—*i.e.*, the largest number of sales at the highest price?

Is that price so high as to place your pangolin altogether beyond the reach of the average income— say a family with $75 a week. If so, what kind of installment offer can you make?

Must your advertising induce a new expenditure by the prospect's part? Or will it merely change the direction of expenditure to which he is already reconciled? Must he decide actually to spend *new* money for pangolins, or merely choose pangolins in place of something else?

Does there exist a natural desire for pangolins? (*The most important question of all.*)

How do you *know* there is this natural desire? How widely have you seen it expressed? Is the natural desire for pangolins the same in all classes of people? In all sections of the country?

Why will anybody buy pangolins? If there are many reasons, which of them is the most universal? Is it, at the same time, the strongest reason?

If there isn't a natural desire for the pangolin himself (as seems quite likely, there being few African white ants in cornfields of Iowa) is there an active demand for some unique service—other than safeguarding against lions—he can render? Or some service, more or less universally required, that your pangolin can render considerably better or less expensively than anything else now on the market?

Is the pangolin by nature something that "must be seen to be appreciated"? Can he be sold best by demonstration? There is, of course, no way of sending samples. Is your East African animal hardy enough to be sent out on trial offer?

If you were to stick up on your front door a sign saying

> PANGOLINS FREE

how many out of every hundred persons passing by would take the trouble to step in and take one home?

If you were to do the same thing in a store window in your nearest large city, how many of each hundred passing there would accept your free offer?

In practice this test is nearly always impossible. In theory, the answer you would get, which we here christen the *"Coefficient of Normal Demand,"* is about the most important thing in advertising. If for example, you could know the relative potential demand for pangolins as against three-cent newspapers or $100 washing machines, as quickly as Schulte, Liggett, and Woolworth know the exact sales value of one street corner as against another, your advertising problem would be vastly simplified. You could tell at once whether to stick to your old job or go out and borrow $100,000 to invest in advertising.

Since you can't get any such mathematical answer, what else can you do but go ahead asking questions and testing? Step by step you will develop a selling hypothesis. Although this method may, at first, insult your ambition as a national advertiser, it will as it goes be eminently practical. Extend it just as rapidly as your preliminary tests show safe.

Like an advancing army, keep a swarm of experimental skirmishers in advance and on both flanks. Have every employee, every friend, bringing captive into your Intelligence Department every sort of testimonial, suggestion, complaint, and comment. As these countless variations demonstrate their worth in actual tests, reject them or absorb them completely into your general plan.

But once you have found your main line of attack, stick to it. Follow U. S. Grant's one great principle: Don't maneuver your main army. Yield eagerly to circumstances; add here, cut there; bend and twist. Don't run off on tangents. And, above all, don't stop!

To have a main line of attack implies an objective clear and close enough to make an attack worth while. Vague objectives make vague advertising. To get real results you must know what you want. And when. Faith without works is only another way of saying advertising without visible results. Unless you feel your advertising should be definitely productive there is little use reading further in this book. If, on the other hand, you have read patiently thus far, we ask you next to consider how you will have your advertising results—direct or indirect? If indirect, go back to Chapter IV for a long list of possibilities as estimated by the leaders in the advertising profession. Choose among them.

Whether you choose direct sales or indirect, or both, your choice of objectives is, of course, your own. Your choice of methods may seem equally your own. But the path of experience may be better trod than you realize. Whether you care to profit by that experience, or blaze a new trail, is hardly our affair. If you consent to know at all times your goal and your progress, we shall feel our tiny mission so far successful. If, in addition, you will study the success of the professionals who live on their results, we shall be even more flattered. If, still further, you will engage—as one does in golf—the services of the best professional advertising man to be found, our success will have been complete.

To carry on meanwhile, we assume your pangolin venture to be an absolutely commercial enterprise. Artistic, sporting, eleemosynary and personal-expression advertising are, like virtue, their own reward. At best, only the commercially successful advertisement can be counted an investment. Since yours is strictly business, any advertising money, whether spent out of your capital or your earnings, must obviously —

> (a) Return itself within a short period through profitable sale of pangolins that would not otherwise have been sold;
>
> *or*
>
> (b) Return itself in a long period, plus ordinary interest on the balance outstanding each year of delay;
>
> *or*
>
> (c) Be written in as a capital investment, and, each year perpetually thereafter, bring, in the form of *extra* sales, a money yield as profitable as any other first rate investment.

Advertising, you will find, cannot be counted a basic charge against business, like office rent and clerk hire. It is generally called a selling cost. More often—and more strictly speaking—it is sales speculation. Every dollar spent in your advertising is, in effect, a bet on the part of somebody that he can—in the long run—sell more pangolins that way than anybody else in the shop could sell by any other use of the same dollar.

Incidentally—but importantly—it is a bet that each advertising dollar can be used so seductively in space and copy that it will prove more effective with the retailer than a correspondingly greater profit direct to him. Also more attractive to the consumer than a correspondingly lower price.

The original dollar for this advertising venture comes, of course, out of capital. How much more must follow depends, it seems to us, on how promptly each advertisement pays for itself. We know one man whose first advertisement returned both price and profit before the publisher's bill was due. So long as each insertion does this he need never touch his capital, except as a short-time loan to a given advertisement. Moreover, accumulating profit will serve as insurance against an occasional advertising failure. If he can continue even half as well as he started, all his advertisements will soon be financing themselves.

The circumstances in this case are exceptional, of course. The principle, nevertheless, is the same in all cases. In the long run, every advertising campaign must, directly or indirectly, return all the money invested. Or it must keep drawing somebody else's money to replace the waste.

Where the market allows the expense of unprofitable advertising is shoved on to the public through a higher price for the article. Where competition is too keen for that, the money must either be squeezed out of some other company operation or drawn from time to time out of capital or surplus. When the advertising, as a whole, is anywhere near good enough to pay for itself, this drain may be covered up. Where the business is prosperous anyway, it will never be discovered. In some cases the struggle elsewhere to pay for the advertising may help bring about a supremacy that will always be attributed to the advertising.

When, on the contrary, the advertising falls too far short of paying for itself, the question becomes one of financial strength. For the pleasure of printing the kind of advertising they prefer, big companies with small appropriations may be quite content with slightly shorter profits. Small companies with big appropriations may merely join a few months sooner that vast majority buried by Bradstreet under the epitaph "Not enough capital." The future of your great American pangolin industry is far too important to risk to any such untimely end! If the human tides seem set too unfavorably, you will save money by promptly giving your pangolins to the zoo. If, on the other hand, you find you can steer into favorable currents already flowing your way, you need not worry about the smallness of your first year's advertising appropriation.

One of the greatest documents ever written about advertising was the twenty-five word report of the Advertising and Special Effort Committee of the National Association of Booksellers. It read simply:

Any special effort on a worthwhile book will pay for itself *provided* that the book is one that will be carried by word of mouth.

Shamefully mixing metaphors of artillery and oceans, we will, in the next few chapters, try to show why a favorable attitude on the part of the public is worth more to an advertiser than anything his banker could offer.

CHAPTER X

The Sea of Humanity

IN THE United States are about 118,000,000 people. Dropping the 5,500,000 who can't read or are in jails or hospitals, we have 112,500,000 left. Subtracting 23,000,000 boys and girls under fourteen, we find, roundly, 90,000,000 people still within range of ordinary advertising artillery.

These 90,000,000 people comprise every able person over fourteen. Necessarily, therefore, they include the proprietors and clerks of all retail stores. Also all middlemen, salesmen, and advertisers. In fact, 11,000,000 of the 90,000,000 are supposed to live, one way or another, by helping distribute goods. So, concentrated in this 90,000,000 we find not only all customers, but America's whole army of wholesalers, jobbers, retailers, and store clerks. This 90,-000,000 contains, therefore, all the "sales resistance."

As customers of the 1,300,000 retail stores in the United States are 1,304,300 Smiths, 1,024,000 Johnsons, 730,500 Browns, 684,700 Williamses and 658,-300 Joneses. And Millers, Davises, Andersons, Wilsons, and Moores by the quarter million. Customers, on one hand, owners and clerks, jobbers and salesmen on the other, they twine and intertwine. No large advertiser need, therefore, consider any particular difference between his consumers and distributors. Where they are not actually identical, the law of averages makes them practically identical in all mental and social characteristics.

Admirable market surveys have sorted out the bank accounts of these Browns, Andersons, and Joneses. They have classified the 1,304,300 Smiths down to their last dime. Yet few advertisers seem to have any vivid picture of the John Smiths who own that dime. If every advertiser had to go to a town meeting at the little red schoolhouse and personally repeat his copy word for word, face to face, to a hundred Johnsons, Millers, and Williamses, there would be a lot of different advertisements in next month's magazines.

First, as to education. Out of every 100 American children of school age, we are told:

    36 are not attending school at all
    54 are attending public elementary school
     7 are attending public high school
     3 attend public night school, vocational school, etc.
     2 only enter college or university
     1 only remains in college to graduate

This means, first, that only 64 per cent of the youth of America, coming customers, are at school at all. Even this 64 per cent does not receive a complete public-school education. Their schooling averages only seven and one-half years. College and university education reaches but two Americans in every hundred; and of those two, only one completely.

Or, taking the method of Dr. Brigham, and follow-

ing the education of one thousand typical American
boys, all of whom together enter the first grade:

> 1,000 boys enter 1st grade
> 970 of them enter 2nd grade
> 940 "   "   "   3rd grade
> 905 "   "   "   4th grade
> 830 "   "   "   5th grade
> 735 "   "   "   6th grade
> 630 "   "   "   7th grade
> 490 "   "   "   8th grade

Of our original one thousand boys:

> 230 boys enter 1st-year high school
> 170 of them finish 2nd-year high school
> 120 of them finish 3rd-year high school
> 95 of them graduate from high school

Of the original one thousand boys:

> 50 boys enter 1st-year college
> 40 of them finish 2nd-year college
> 20 of them finish 3rd-year college
> 10 of them remain in college to be graduated

Although the various "Alpha" intelligence tests
rate the college freshman above the average man on
the street, we don't find even the college graduate—
the select one-out-of-every-hundred schoolboys—any
great highbrow. A recent graduating class at Prince-
ton voted "If" their favorite poem; *Tom Jones* their
favorite novel; Maxfield Parrish their favorite artist;
Douglas Fairbanks their favorite movie actor; *Saturday Evening Post* their favorite magazine, and tied
Sabatini with Booth Tarkington as their favorite

author. Up at Yale the seniors were even more conservative. Tennyson is the favorite poet; Tarkington gives way to Dickens, Stevenson, and Dumas. *The Tale of Two Cities* is the favorite novel, and D'Artagnan the favorite character in fiction.

In a canvass of our American schools to discover the most popular "recitations," the National Educational Association found that Longfellow led five out of eight grades; Stevenson, one; Scott, one; Wordsworth, one. Thirty-six thousand children in seventeen states voted *Tom Sawyer, Little Women,* and *Black Beauty* their favorite books. Long afterward through the same law of averages, young readers of *The Youth's Companion* voted with complete unanimity for *Tom Sawyer, Little Women,* and *Treasure Island.* Each branch of the New York Public Library has always out fifteen to twenty-five copies of *David Copperfield, Vanity Fair,* and *The Scarlet Letter.* Year in and year out one great New York department store reports *David Copperfield* its one best-selling book!

The president of a great university says that not one voter in twenty has any intelligent idea of why or what he voted for in any national election. A few years ago 700,000 of the Epworth League voted the greatest ten men in history as follows:

> 1—Thomas Edison
> 2—Theodore Roosevelt
> 3—William Shakespeare

4—Henry W. Longfellow
5—Alfred Tennyson
6—Herbert Hoover
7—Charles Dickens
8—General Pershing
9—Lloyd George
10—Andrew J. Volstead

Because the "intelligence" [1] of the average American—which is exactly our 90,000,000 sales resisters —is generally reckoned in terms of boys and girls slightly under high-school age and education, a list like that may be worth the attention of any advertiser. For the same reason he will be interested in an examination in current events at the Knoxville High School.

Not 500 in 1,047 of these Knoxville students were able to locate the District of Columbia. Asked "What is an Electoral College?" one said, "It's a college where you take what you want." Ninety-five per cent of the senior class failed to answer this question at all. Asked "What member of royalty died recently?" four said "Queen Elizabeth," and nine said "Bryan." Mrs. Miriam Ferguson, then Governor of Texas, caused considerable disagreement. She was called "A singer recently admitted to grand opera"; "Football player"; "Baseball player"; "Writer"; "Movie star"; and finally, "Husband of the Governor of Texas." Nine said Mary Roberts

[1] Meaning, of course, *literate* intelligence, that, is ability to cope with *words*.

Rinehart was a famous actress, while one declared Sir Walter Scott wrote the "Star-spangled Banner." Speaking of "Ma" Ferguson reminds us of another test conducted by a certain well-known pictorial periodical among another 1,650 high-school students, this time scattered all over the country. Mrs. Ferguson was mistaken by some for Babe Ruth and by others for the President of Mexico. One hundred and eighty—more than 10 per cent—failed to recognize a portrait of President Coolidge. Incidentally, only about 15 out of 1,047 of the Tennessee students knew the name of the Mayor of Knoxville—their own home city.

If Knoxville seems too extreme, turn to a similar examination in a Wisconsin Normal School where one of the prospective teachers called Steinmetz "a kind of piano"; Frances E. Willard "an American pugilist"; Mussolini "a region in southern Eurasia" and Fiume "a mountain in Japan." "Teapot Dome," to one of these young women was "an old tomb discovered in Egypt," while another affronted all Massachusetts by describing Henry Cabot Lodge as "a place where societies meet."

Or, drop down into North Carolina, where the state university instructors find that "many students who get into college cannot understand ordinary written English." One freshman there preferred "David Copperfield's novels to those written by Dickens." An upper-classman reported that "Diabetes was Milton's Italian friend." Another upper-classman, that "Lincoln's mind growed as his country kneaded it."

Or, skip eastward to the metropolis, where, speaking of 800 applicants for admission to the New York Bar, Mr. Allan Fox reported George Washington as the only figure in American history that most of them could identify. The majority of the candidates knew nothing of English literature or history. Asked whether they had ever read any biography, some of them last fall were answering, "Yes, the Private Life of Helen of Troy."

Not so long ago, reading was the nation's only means of culture. Advertising then had practically a monopoly on the news of new goods. Powerful as the printed word still is, the news supremacy of our publications is seriously threatened by at least two new ways of scattering ideas over the nation. Six million radio sets, no doubt, average an hour or two apiece every day. And for every publication in America, there is already a motion-picture theater. Probably 10,000,000 people a day see a picture. In the course of a fortnight, therefore, every person in the United States either in person or by proxy, sees at least one film. So, quite aside from additional competition for attention and in distributing fresh news, the effect of radio and movies on popular habits of thought and expression must be considered by any advertiser. Their short, staccato, picture-and-title, flippant, flash technique, infinitely reinforced by its debasement in the daily millions of tabloids, threatens within ten years to disturb even our serious literature. The mental standard for the moving-picture producer is the intelligence of the fourteen-year-old child. Professor Francis B. Tyson, of the University of Pittsburgh, holds the actual appeal more nearly adapted to a child about twelve years.

The public taste in melody is as simple as its taste in motion pictures. Advertisers who lean toward the Wagnerian form of expression might profit by a glance at what may be the most representative "request" program ever put on the radio. The New York Edison Company selected it from many hundreds of suggestions. But the vote on popular solos is illuminating. Strangely enough it was led by Balfe's supposedly forgotten "Then You'll Remember Me." Then Tosti's "Good-bye"; Bartlett's "A Dream"; Herbert's "Falling in Love."

Skipping from music to perfumes, out of several thousand people tested by Macy's, under direction of Professor Poffenberger, choices ran in this order:

Women	*Men*
Lilac	Lilac
Oriental bouquet	French bouquet
Jasmine	Jasmine
French bouquet	Oriental bouquet
Violet	Rose
Rose	Violet

And from perfumes to colors. Preferences, in general, are supposed to run:

Women	Men
Violet	Blue
Blue	Violet
Green	Red
Red	Green
Orange	Orange
Yellow	Yellow

Pure colors are preferred to tints and shades. Yellow stands always near the bottom, red at or near the top. Women generally prefer red, and men blue. Taking greater refinements, E. J. G. Bradford found, by testing a large number of people, that they liked in order: dark blue, gray-green, chocolate brown, light gray-blue, slate gray, with bluish tinge. They cared least for yellowish green, pink, bluish green. In combinations, men seem to prefer green-and-blue, red-and-blue, blue-and-purple, and even yellow-and-blue; women are more conventional with red-and-blue, red-and-green, yellow-and-blue.

After forcing himself to recognize the extreme mental simplicity of the vast majority of his audience, and their pathetic lack of adult mental nourishment, the advertiser must next realize that any workable relation between wealth and education went with the war. Our present installment selling, whereby anybody can buy anything, wipes out the last of the old buying "power" distinctions. This, of course, applies only to actual *ability* to purchase. Taste, culture, knowledge, and appreciation of fine achievements still foregather in favorable environment. Certain advertisers will find these smaller "class" groups, based today on true congeniality of interest, far more valuable than those formerly based on a supposition of superior wealth.

But, you may say, through natural selective machinery, any worth-while publication will have readers notably above average. Anybody who pays several dollars a year for magazines must be of more than ordinary wealth and intelligence. True of all publications twenty years ago, it is still true of many. Don't, however, overlook the law of large numbers. As soon as any business starts dealing with human beings in hundreds-of-thousand lots, it surrenders then and there to the law of averages. Just as there is no difference between the water of the Atlantic and Pacific, so there is no difference between circulation as it gets into millions. All the same sea of humanity; its atoms are the average man. Some humorist asks, "Who is this 'average man' we hear so much about?" The question is justified. But the answer is easy: *he* is! Except for a very few eccentricities, each of us is average. Therefore, on any given point other than the single common resemblance that first classified them—and even that may prove negligible —any given 100,000 American citizens are far more likely to act exactly like any other 100,000 American citizens than to be in the slightest degree different.

Suppose we admit, for example, that magazine readers generally are about the same sort of people who would buy the 7 per cent preferred stock of a first-class public utility corporation. Here are the occupations of those who bought a recent issue of these securities *in lots of 50 shares or more:*

Accountants	166	Messengers	91
Bakers	153	Metal workers	157
Barbers	155	Nurses	274
Butchers	115	Painters	182
Carpenters	483	Plasterers	60
Chauffeurs	601	Plumbers	257
Clerks	2,987	Policemen	347
Domestics	623	Printers	335
Draftsmen	149	Railroad men	312
Dressmakers	372	Seamen	51
Electricians	582	Secretaries	314
Factory workers	1,058	Bankers and brokers	65
Foremen	518	Dentists	63
Housekeepers	4,029	Doctors	146
Laborers	499	Lawyers	77
Machinists	499	Managers	496
Mail carriers	115	Manufacturers	153
Mechanics	530	Merchants	926
Engineers	558		

Just about the average crowd you might meet in your favorite store. Or reading your pet newspaper. Again, you might say that people who buy magazines are the sort who will buy high-grade automobiles. The Paige Detroit Company found that 13.2 per cent of their cars were sold to workmen. And, unless you are content to disconsider one family in every four, you too will have to do business with workmen. Wage earners in the United States today own $70,-000,000 worth of stocks in the industries employing them. Americans are a working people; even among the very wealthiest class, personal business activity brings in nearly half the income. On the other hand, Americans are thrifty. Of the people who paid taxes in 1924 on less than $5,000 income 6,300,000 had, over and above their earnings, an average "outside" income of $500.

In New York City, roughly speaking, one family in seventeen has an income of $150 a week. Seven families out of every eleven have less than $150 a week, but more than $60. One family in three lives on less than $60 a week. The average current income for the whole United States in 1926, divided evenly among, men, women, and babes in arms, would have given each $770. No advertiser can go far wrong calculating his per-family average at $75 a week—with two people working to produce it. To reach much above that eleven dollars-a-day-per-family income, he will have to set his selective advertising machinery wastefully enough to throw out twelve out of every thirteen families!

Hardly less interesting than the shift of purchasing power from the few very wealthy to the many wealthy enough is the relation of women to buying. One authority has drawn up a domestic life table of one thousand average American girls.

Age

15–18	110 in 1,000 marry
18–24	300 " " work; 500 marry
24–35	190 " " work; 790 marry
35–45	150 " " work; 830 keep house
45–55	140 " " work; 860 keep house or are independent
55–65	130 " " work; 210 are widows
65	420 " " dead; 500 widows; 140 work (60 widows)

But a woman doesn't necessarily have to marry to be a buyer. Even by the 1920 census there were more than 4,000,000 women earning their own living in other than household duties. The first dozen classifications of that date may still be of interest— they include nine out of every ten working women:

Teachers	639,241
Stenographers	564,744
Saleswomen, clerks, floorwalkers, and overseers	535,609
Clerical workers	472,163
Bookkeepers and cashiers	345,746
Dressmakers (not in factory) and tailoresses	267,347
Women farmers and stock-raisers	253,836
Telephone operators	178,379
Trained nurses	143,664
Retail dealers	78,980
Music teachers	72,678
Milliners and millinery dealers	69,598

Whether married or getting pay for their work, women are the nation's purchasing agents. Woman is generally admitted to be directly responsible for four out of every five sales—and probably has something to say even in the fifth. For beautifying themselves, they spend nearly $2,000,000,000 a year. All in all they are supposed to pour each year at least $32,000,000,000 into retail stores.

A recent survey conducted in various types of retail stores in New York City, shows how completely the woman buys for the whole family.

	Per cent of purchases by	
	Men	Women
Department store	18	82
Drug store	22	78
Grocery store	19	81
Silks	2	98
Pianos	22	78
Leather goods	33	67
Automobiles	59	41
Hardware	51	49
Electrical supplies	20	80
Men's socks	25	75
Jewelry	10	90
Men's neckwear	37	63

In the matter of their own clothes, an investigation made for R. H. Macy & Co., Inc., by a number of savings banks, shows, in the face of the funny papers, the average American woman spends only about 6 per cent of her husband's pay on her own clothes. The whole matter of clothes expense in families of five, with incomes varying from $2,000, is shown by this table:

Size of family income	Dollars spent on clothes for family	Dollars spent on clothes for wife
$ 2,000	$ 384.00	$ 109.36
3,000	591.00	195.00
5,000	700.00	238.00
7,000	889.00	311.15
10,000	1,190.00	452.20
15,000	1,180.00	720.00
20,000	2,400.00	1,080.00
25,000	3,000.00	1,500.00

Turning to the other side of the family, the *American Legion Weekly* asked 1,000 supposedly representative men about their clothes.

294	out of 1,000 men buy			1 suit	a year	
509	"	"	"	"	"	2 suits	" "
171	"	"	"	"	"	3	" " "
44	"	"	"	"	"	4	" " "
7	"	"	"	"	"	5	" " "
4	"	"	"	"	"	6	" " "

As to prices paid for suits:

12	out of 1,000 pay			less	than $25	
91	"	"	"	"	from $25–$35	
296	"	"	"	"	"	$35–$45
471	"	"	"	"	"	$45–$60
95	"	"	"	"	"	$60–$75
49	"	"	"	"	over $75	

Having started with schoolboys and spared a moment to grown men and women, we return to youth again. Surveys show that in buying, as well as in all other things, youth must be served. Buyers between the ages of twenty and forty are found to be responsible for sales approximating:

56 per cent in ready-to-wear goods
58 per cent in dress goods
62 per cent in underwear
64 per cent in hosiery
64 per cent in furniture
64 per cent in musical instruments
67 per cent in rugs

These figures, it must be admitted, sound reasonable. In the first place, the ages between twenty and forty mark practically two-thirds of all our activities in every direction; in the second place, most of those over forty who are ever going to have luxuries are already comfortably fixed, compared with the younger generation.

All these 1,304,300 Smiths, 1,024,200 Johnsons, 730,000 Browns, young or old, married or single, live in 29,000,000,000 homes.

220 out of 1,000 of these homes have radio receivers
450 "   "   "   "   "   "   " phonographs
550 "   "   "   "   "   "   " automobiles
600 "   "   "   "   "   "   " telephones

The average normal American, broadly speaking, celebrates his twenty-fifth birthday by shutting shop mentally and refusing to accept any new ideas. He has then the literate capacity of a twelve- or fourteen-year old child. Many an advertiser may be discouraged to realize that copy aimed anywhere above the comprehension of an eighth-grade schoolboy cuts his audience in half, while any argument over the head of a college freshman misses nine out of ten of his possible prospects. A crowd that can rank Edison above Shakespeare, and Herbert Hoover over Charles Dickens, isn't likely to be much swayed by subtle nuances. Once again the advertiser must seek his simple, sure-fire appeal. To find that appeal he must keep his eye on his audience, the way it buys, reads, talks, as it swings back and forth in tidal waves of action.   Consider the words of "Chick" Sale, master student of American vaudeville audiences.

My object is to touch the something that is in all of us—the laugh we have at others for their simple-minded folly because we know that we are simple-minded ourselves in many things. We are all hicks at heart. That explains my success. I give people pictures of what they would be but for the grace of God and the rapid transit companies.

Your average audience—which means *any* American audience as soon as you reach into the hundred thousands—is like that: $8-, $10-, $12-a-day workers; thirteen- or fourteen-year-old minds scarcely equal to second-year high school. Each gets a book every four months where public libraries reach them; four out of five haven't even this service. And one out of three families have no books in their home. They like Tosti's "Good-bye," *David Copperfield*, "The Big Parade," "Abie's Irish Rose." They all go to the movies every other week; and about one in four listens to the radio perhaps an hour a day. They like dark blue as a color and lilac as a scent. Writing themselves, they use a vocabulary generally fewer than a thousand words although each can understand, in reading, maybe six times that many. In their aggregate action the element of intellect is practically negligible. How, and why, then, do they act? What effect does advertising have on them? What do the 1,304,303 Smiths and the 730,500 Browns really know about advertising?

CHAPTER XI

What People Really Know About Advertising

Standing one Sunday morning on Main Street, Middletown, Connecticut, we counted on eleven buildings across the highway more than a hundred signs. Rough calculations indicate at least 2,000 such signs for the town—one for every ten inhabitants. So, if Middletown happens fairly to represent the rest of the country, we must, in addition to printed advertising, car cards, electric lights, and billboards, have at least ten million signs more or less permanently affixed to business buildings. There are some 1,800,000 street car cards. And thousands of miles of window displays. Some one claims to have counted 5,000 billboards on the east side, alone, of the Pennsylvania Railroad tracks between Washington and New York. This figures a sign-and-a-half a minute for the whole five-hour trip.

But all this, so to speak, is only the standing army of advertising. The transient output is staggering. Some statistical genius has figured that to read every copy of every advertisement as fast as printed would keep every man, woman, and child over eight in the United States reading 25,000 words a day. That would be equal to three fat novels every week for all grown-ups and half the children in America.

Most of this stupendous supply of advertising is

clever, attractive, and interesting. Millions of
people might pleasantly and profitably spend most of
their time reading it. More people do read more
advertising than they think they do. But discourag-
ingly fewer people than advertisers figure.

The students of the University of Colorado made a
canvass of the inhabitants of Boulder. Among the
questions asked was: "Do you read the advertising
in newspaper and publications you receive?"

> 64 said "Yes"
> 49 said "Some"
> 10 said "No"

And, to "Do you believe the statements in this
advertising?"

> 52 said "Yes"
> 19 said "No"
> 48 said "Some"

In Des Moines, Iowa, the Advertising Club conducted a more elaborate test. Among the questions:
"Do you read advertising you receive by mail in form
of circulars or letters?"

> 66 said "Yes"
> 33 said "No"

The president of the Toledo Women's Advertising Club reported a similar investigation among
women: [1]

[1] *Postage*, May, 1927.

34 per cent read all circular mail
 8   "   glance at all
 6   "   read most
32   "   read only that from their own store
20   "   read little or none.

Professor Scott browsed around the Chicago Public Library until he had observed what 600 men were reading in their magazines. He found

11 out of every 100 reading advertisements
89 "   "   "   "   "   other pages

Dr. Starch made a census of 6,000 customers in a big Boston dry-goods store. Among the upstairs customers who were asked whether they read advertising before going shopping

39 out of every 100 said always
37 "   "   "   "   "   generally
16 "   "   "   "   "   rarely
 7 "   "   "   "   "   never

Taken together, for what they may be worth, a number of these fragmentary tests, dissected and weighed, seem to indicate that no advertiser could go far wrong broadly dividing any possible audience into three parts as to their general interest in advertising.

Active: 15 out of every 100
Passive: 35 "   "   "   "
Apathetic 50 "   "   "   "

Before any enthusiast attacks this judgment, let him check some other figures at hand. Five hundred and forty-six New York business executives and professional men, asked by an investigator to list in order the things that interested them in newspapers,[1] rated advertising thirteenth in a list—just below "Book Reviews" and just above "Moral Tone." This included 127 national advertisers who ranked advertising ninth on their list, next to "Special Articles." Seventy-eight doctors placed it eighteenth, just below "Death Notices." Fifty-eight lawyers gave advertising no mention whatever, thereby ranking it, so far as they were concerned, with "Shipping News" and "Art."

Professor Walter Dill Scott also took a poll of 2,000 prominent business men, asking them what features interested them most in newspapers.[2] Advertising, this time, came seventeenth in a list of twenty, just below "Art." It considerably outranked "Storiettes," "Weather," and "Humor," but fell well below "Music" and "Book Reviews."

Dr. Starch supervised a set of personal interviews with 603 people around Boston, including 195 business men, 174 housewives, and 234 men students. All were asked whether, on receiving a new publication, they purposely looked through the advertisements. The answers were about as follows:

	Magazine		*Newspaper*	
Always	35	per cent	12.5 per cent	
Usually	22.4	"	13.3	"
Occasionally	22.5	"	23.4	"
Incidentally	20.6	"	46	"

[1] Professor G. B. Hotchkiss and R. B. Franken, "Newspaper Reading Habits of Business Executives and Professional Men." Quoted in *Æsthetic Value of Newspaper Advertising*, by Richard B. Franken.

[2] Walter Dill Scott, *Psychology of Advertising*, p. 383.

A fine showing, particularly for magazines. His further questioning, however, failed to reveal equal enthusiasm for *reading* the advertisements. About 28 people in every 100 of those who said they "look over" advertising in magazines don't by their own statement read entirely through a single advertisement. About 35 in every 100 claim they never finish a single newspaper advertisement. On the other hand, about 13 in each 100 said that in every magazine they read entirely through ten or more advertisements. And about 10 in every 100 said they read at least that many newspaper advertisements. The average person—according to this survey—reads completely three advertisements in a magazine containing about a hundred. And two advertisements in each newspaper of corresponding proportions.

Combining into one judgment the results of the several experiments made by Scott and Hotchkiss and Franken on a grand total of 3,907 people—2,410 business men, 136 professional men, and 1,361 students—we find an interest in news thirty times as great as in advertising. That is to say, if these 4,000 people accurately judged their interest—and literally followed it—each would read nearly four pages of news to every single column of advertising. Or, for every person who reads a full-page advertisement, thirty would read completely a page of news.

Considerable corroboration for these figures is found in Professor Franken's independent discovery that only 5 in every 100 readers can be counted on to notice particularly any ordinary newspaper page.

About 10 in every 100 are reckoned sure to see pages 2 and 3. The sporting, women's, and editorial pages seem to range between average and the best. Each of these pages, of course, selects its own special class of readers, 6 or 7 out of every 100 who buy the paper.

Two out of three business men are shown by tests to spend fifteen minutes a day or less reading their newspapers. Some statisticians grant the average reader thirty seconds to the average advertisement. Others suggest ten minutes or less as the total time given by an average reader to all the advertising in a whole newspaper or magazine. And we find no serious suggestion that this increases proportionately with any increase in the amount of advertising. Roughly speaking, a reader seems to devote about as much time to his daily newspaper as he would need to read really carefully a single page. In browsing through a ten-page newspaper, therefore, the average reader skips presumably nine-tenths of everything in sight, and in a fifty-page paper he skips about forty-nine fiftieths.

And unfortunately to read is not always to remember. Out of the mass of material in the radio, movies, in books, newspapers, posters, circulars, programs, and magazines, how much is retained? Dr. Strong handed one of his classes a popular magazine, telling them to read a certain article it contained. A week later he handed the same class an envelope containing all the full-page advertisements from that magazine, mixed with a fair number of others. Of the 137 women thus tested:

48 out of 100 could not recognize a single advertisement
16 " " " recognize from 1 to 5 advertisements
23 " " " " " 5 to 20 "
15 " " " " more than 20 "

In another series of five tests, including 217 men and women of every type, only 6 people in any 100 remembered the one advertisement that stood out most strongly. Only 4 out of every 100 remembered the advertisement that made the average showing.

This all sounds rather discouraging. But since it would take fifteen hours a day to read everything in a big city newspaper—instead of the fifteen minutes it usually gets—and since everybody regularly forgets far more than anybody can remember, this showing—like Chinese opera—may not really be so bad as it sounds. Check it up for yourself: Make your own test of attention qualities, *disconnected from your own selfish personal interest!* Count on your fingers the number of front covers on *Liberty,* and the *Saturday Evening Post* you remember during the year just past. Here were 104 pieces of the most expensive commercial art, designed by the ablest artists to attract attention, selected by the ablest art editors to attract attention, color-printed on the greatest magazines in a "position" no advertiser could buy, and displayed by millions with maximum human ingenuity and unremitting enterprise. Of those 104 masterpieces of display, how many do you recall?

Or, if your taste runs not to pictures, what of editorial stories and articles? Consider the vast number of topics splendidly written up in issue after issue of your whole list of magazines. Among the thousands of news columns that didn't personally concern you printed in your daily newspaper this year, how many dozen stories do you remember? Lindbergh's flight. Sacco-Vanzetti. What else?

In such circumstances certainly, it is no reflection on the art of advertising to discover that instead of being universally familiar with advertised names, the general public may be less familiar with a good many favorites than we would willingly admit.

Starting at the bottom, we notice that of the 1,000 Philadelphia high school children questioned by Mr. Donovan [1] as to their knowledge of advertised brands:

1 out of 1,000			spoke of Owl cigars
2	"	"	mentioned Ward's bread
2	"	"	mentioned Domino sugar
5	"	"	knew Ipana toothpaste
6	"	"	suggested Corona typewriter
6	"	"	heard of Huyler's
7	"	"	knew Wurlitzer
8	"	"	suggested Royal typewriters
9	"	"	knew Maxwell House coffee
9	"	"	knew Chickering
10	"	"	had heard of Kuppenheimer
10	"	"	knew Autostrop
11	"	"	heard of Oh Henry
11	"	"	mentioned Robert Burns cigars
12	"	"	had heard of Tootsie Rolls
13	"	"	had heard of Nabisco
25	"	"	knew Forhan's
45	"	"	knew Lipton's tea

[1] H. M. Donovan, *Advertising Response*, p. 26.

76 out of 1,000 had heard of Hart Schaffner & Marx
99   "   "   knew Steinway
101   "   "   suggested Pepsodent
499   "   "   mentioned Uneeda biscuit
557   "   "   knew Colgate's toothpaste
599   "   "   knew Gillette razor

Like the Knoxville High School examination in current events, this Philadelphia High School quiz might pass without notice, except that the mental age and education of this group represent so exactly those of the great American public with whom most national advertisers regularly deal.

Going a step higher, take the famous examination of 1,000 college students—men and women—made by Hotchkiss and Franken in 1921 [1] and again in 1925.[2] In the 1921 test they found that in a blank containing 100 simple headings such as "Bacon," "Baked Beans," "Breakfast Food," "Butter," etc.

800 out of 1,000 mentioned "Eastman" for Camera
771   "   "   "   "Singer" for Sewing Machine
757   "   "   "   "Campbell" for Soup
748   "   "   "   "Arrow" for Collars
746   "   "   "   "Waterman" for Fountain Pens
436   "   "   "   "Life Savers" for 5-cent mints
430   "   "   "   "Sunkist" for Fruit
419   "   "   "   "Diamond" for Dyes
396   "   "   "   "Gillette" for Razors
389   "   "   "   "Ivory" for Soap
384   "   "   "   "Colt" for Revolvers

[1] George Burton Hotchkiss and Richard B. Franken, in *Leadership of Advertised Brands*.
[2] George Burton Hotchkiss and Richard B. Franken in *The Measurement of Advertising Effects*.

353 out of 1,000 mentioned "Coco Cola" for Soft Drinks
349　"　　"　　"　　　"BVD" for Underwear
242　"　　"　　"　　　"Steiner" for Piano
236　"　　"　　"　　　"Beech Nut" for Bacon
205　"　　"　　"　　　"Pompeian" for Face Cream
191　"　　"　　"　　　"Djer Kiss" for Face Powder
182　"　　"　　"　　　"Sherwin Williams" for Paint
146　"　　"　　"　　　"Douglas" for Shoes
144　"　　"　　"　　　"Huyler's" for Candy
　97　"　　"　　"　　　"Crane" for Paper

Four years later, in the 1925 test, with only ten commodities to choose among, and the opportunity to mention as many brands of each as they remembered, the "*first* mentions" among 1,000 college students—men and women—were as follows:

563 out of 1,000 mentioned "Waterman" for Fountain Pens
523　"　　"　　"　　　"Remington" for Typewriters
456　"　　"　　"　　　"Colgate" for Toothpaste
404　"　　"　　"　　　"Elgin" for Watches
385　"　　"　　"　　　"Camels" for Cigarettes
383　"　　"　　"　　　"Ivory" for Soap
287　"　　"　　"　　　"Stetson" for Hats
254　"　　"　　"　　　"Kellogg's" for Breakfast
236　"　　"　　"　　　"Holeproof" for Hosiery
162　"　　"　　"　　　"Lucky Strikes" for Cigarettes
153　"　　"　　"　　　"Knox" for Hats
142　"　　"　　"　　　"Maxwell House" for Coffee
142　"　　"　　"　　　"Palmolive" for Soap
131　"　　"　　"　　　"Waltham" for Watches
　85　"　　"　　"　　　"McCallum" for Hosiery
　85　"　　"　　"　　　"Shredded Wheat" for Breakfast
　47　"　　"　　"　　　"Royal" for Typewriters
　36　"　　"　　"　　　"Forhan's" for Toothpaste
　31　"　　"　　"　　　"Astor House" for Coffee

24 out of 1,000 mentioned "Dunn" for Fountain Pens
8   "   "   "   "Everwear" for Hosiery
4   "   "   "   "Pears" for Soap

In 1924, Professor Cover made a somewhat similar series of experiments with 52 students of advertising to determine relative recollection values of trade names.[1] His findings emphasize, more perhaps than is generally recognized, the effect intense competition among advertisers of similar goods has in neutralizing the efforts of all. For example, when a "coffee substitute" was asked for, Postum was recalled by 88 per cent; as a "dessert," Jell-O by 88 per cent; as a "syrup," Karo by 62 per cent. But as soon as a common article like "soap" was reached, Ivory, the leader, was recalled by only 25 per cent; Pebeco, as a toothpaste, 23 per cent; Grape Nuts, 19 per cent; Post Toasties, 19 per cent; Palmolive, 17 per cent; Colgate's 17 per cent; Pepsodent, 17 per cent; Cream of Wheat, 15 per cent; Kolynos, 15 per cent; Forhan's, 15 per cent.

In another case, 42 people, interested professionally in advertising, were asked suddenly to define "Dioxygen."[2] The name was unknown to 22; 9 said it was a disinfectant; 11 described it as a dentifrice. "Calox" was identified variously by these same people as a dentifrice, soap, film, finger-nail polish, hair tonic, cough medicine, and surgical bandage. Seven of the 42 considered "Lysol" a medicine.

Back before the World War, Cheney, the silk

[1] John H. Cover, *Advertising, Its Problems and Methods*, p. 28.
[2] John H. Cover, *Advertising, Its Problems and Methods*, p. 42.

manufacturer, asked 117 of his employees certain questions about advertised products. In their recollection of slogans, the famous "It Floats" led. Seven in every 10 ascribed it to Ivory Soap. Two out of every 3 people were able to place "It Chases Dirt," and "One of the 57 Varieties." But only 3 out of every 10 credited Packard with "Ask the Man Who Owns One." And only 4 out of 10 gave Ivory Soap its universally quoted "99 44/100ths pure." Compare this with a similar test made ten years later. "It Floats" got 10 recognitions out of 10. "Ask the Man Who Owns One" again got 3 out of 10. "Covers the Earth" and "Four Out of Five" each got nothing out of 10. Five out of 10 ascribed "Eventually—Why Not Now?" to Postum.

Sixteen experienced advertising men were asked by the editor of *Printers' Ink* to identify a list of 50 famous slogans. The highest got 38 of them correctly; the lowest only 20. The average correctness was 59 per cent—or 29½ out of possible 50. Here is that list. How many do *you* recognize?

1. Ask Dad—He Knows.
2. Ask the Man Who Owns One.
3. Best in the Long Run.
4. Built for Sleep.
5. Candy Mint with the Hole.
6. Chases Dirt.
7. A Clean Tooth Never Decays.
8. Cleans As It Polishes.
9. Cocoa with That Chocolaty Taste.
10. Covers the Earth.
11. Eventually—Why Not Now?

12. The Flavor Lasts.
13. From Contented Cows.
14. Hammer the Hammer.
15. Hasn't Scratched Yet.
16. It's Toasted.
17. Like Old Friends, They Wear Well.
18. The More You Eat, the More You Want.
19. No Metal Can Touch You.
20. The Skin You Love to Touch.
21. There's a Reason.
22. Time to Re-tire.
23. The Watch with the Purple Ribbon.
24. When It Rains—It Pours.
25. Built Like a Skyscraper.
26. Makes Every Meal an Event.
27. Regular as Clockwork.
28. America's Most Famous Dessert.
29. For Economical Transportation.
30. Let the Kitchen Maid Be Your Kitchen Aid.
31. His Master's Voice.
32. No Springs—Honest Weight.
33. It Beats As It Sweeps—As It Cleans.
34. Delicious and Refreshing.
35. Soft as Old Linen.
36. The Watch of Railroad Accuracy.
37. Mild as May.
38. You Just Know She Wears Them.
39. Works While You Sleep.
40. The Coffee That Lets You Sleep.
41. Now You'll Like Bran.
42. The Quality Is Remembered Long After the Price Is Forgotten.
43. Concrete for Permanence.
44. Good to the Last Drop.
45. The Instrument of the Immortals.
46. Keep That Schoolgirl Complexion.

47. It Floats.
48. A Pillow for the Body.
49. Everywhere on Everything.
50. For the Gums.

That the traceable results of advertising don't always follow with convincing closeness the amount of money spent is suggested by the table below. Column "A" gives the gain or loss in "*first* mention" by 1,000 college students during the four years between the first Hotchkiss-Franken examination in 1921 and the second in 1925. Column "B" gives in round figures the total advertising expenditures in some thirty leading magazines during the years 1921-1924.

"A"		"B"
Gain or Loss *1925 over 1921*		*Comparative* *Expenditures* *1921–1922–1923–1924*
+ 265	Remington typewriter	$ 400,000
+ 126	Maxwell House coffee	545,000
+ 92	Elgin watch	690,000
+ 56	Pepsodent	2,300,000
+ 38	Gruen watch	520,000
+ 31	Kolynos	(Nothing)
+ 29	Ingersoll watch	370,000
+ 27	Pebeco	978,000
+ 24	Forhan's	700,000
+ 20	Shredded Wheat	36,200
+ 14	L. C. Smith typewriters	52,000
+ 8	Grape Nuts	1,100,000
− 12	Hamilton watch	245,000
− 33	Cream of Wheat	1,600,000
− 65	Kellogg's Corn Flakes	209,000

— 83	Colgate toothpaste	1,300,000
— 103	Waltham watch	120,000
— 150	Underwood typewriters	440,000

As to the direct-mail returns from advertising: Dr. Starch's analysis of 3,000,000 inquiries from 2,339 different magazine advertisements received by 98 different firms, establishes pretty definitely that an average black-and-white page will bring 225 answers from every 100,000 circulation. Or putting it another way: if you make an offer to 100,000 people as attractive as the *average* offer made by the 98 selected advertisers, you may expect a mail response from 225 people. Assume that you are enough better than the average to get these 225 with a plain page, without any coupon or free offer. Then, if you add a coupon with a "send-the-bill" offer, each 100,000 circulation may bring you 250 answers. And, if you make it a free offer with coupon, you may get back 550 coupons. If, on this last offer, you can arrange to have the coupon cashed at a store, you might boost your response to 720 out of every 100,-000 circulation. If, by any conceivable arrangement of this same free offer, you could allow your prospects, instead of visiting or writing, simply to telephone the store, you might possibly get 1,250 answers. But 12½ per cent is phenomenally high for any sort of voluntary action among a mass of people. The average advertiser, no matter what he offers will be safer if he doesn't count on direct response in any form whatever from more than 250 people out of every 100,000 who *have a chance* to read his black-and-white page.

As to direct returns through "ask-your-dealer" in stores, we quote the experience of an officer of one of our greatest trade paper groups. Five years ago, he said in a speech:

And in two years' subsequent analysis covering thousands of department and dry-goods stores we found also that of the remaining 10 per cent, less than one-third was sold by public request for it under its advertised name, and that at least 7 out of 10 per cent is sold for the same reason that the other 90 per cent was sold—because it represented the merchants' selection and his offering to his customers.

Two years later, in response to an inquiry as to whether he still stood by his original figures, this authority wrote:

As a matter of fact, we believe that in dry-goods and department stores not more than one-tenth of one per cent is asked for by its advertised name. . . . Because we wanted to be fully fair, we credited demand with three times what we really believed its just credit to be.

The *Hardware Age* investigation of about the same period found, as might be expected, a better condition in hardware stores. Here 3 per cent of all customers asked for advertised goods by name. In a Chicago drug store, out of 69 sales checked, 32 asked for goods by name; the 27 others took what they saw or were given. But of the 32 who asked for brands, 11 were cigarette buyers.

About the earliest of the indirect tests for advertising returns through stores was made way back in

1913 by the *Chicago Tribune*. It showed that purchasers of food, those days, were influenced about as follows:

> 6 out of every 100 by friends
> 36   "   "   "   " advertising
> 55   "   "   "   " retailers

The owner of several jewelry stores in California questioned his customers and found that

> 30 out of every 100 became customers through friends;
> 70   "   "   "   "   "   " location
> of stores, window display, advertising.

Eighty-two out of every 100 customers said they had read the advertising, and 53 of every 100 admitted it had influenced them.

Another interesting small-scale example of comparative motives is found in the reasons given for attending a play, as shown in blanks collected between acts for several weeks in one of John Golden's theaters. Of 13,433 who visited the show,

> 35 went because of a display card or poster
> 127   "   " of a paid newspaper advertisement
> 139   "   " it was recommended by a ticket broker
> 305   "   " of radio exploitation
> 538   "   " of favorable newspaper review
> 862   "   " it was staged by Frank Craven
> 1,408   "   " of Dr. Cadman's recommendation
> 2,196   "   " of John Golden's reputation
> 3,380   "   " they believed it to be clean and funny
> 4,443   "   " it was recommended by a friend

One manufacturer selling a several-hundred-dollar

article wrote to 450 customers, asking each for a frank statement of just what first interested him. And what closed the sale.[1] A hundred and forty-two answered as follows:

What Aroused the Interest

Manufacturer's direct-mail advertising	33
Jobber's salesmen's calls	27
Manufacturer's salesmen's calls	24
National advertising	11
Jobber's salesmen working with manufacturer's salesmen	10
Convention exhibits	7
Jobber's display-room exhibits	4
Demonstration by friends using machines	3
Jobber's direct-mail advertising	1
Combination of the above factors	22
	142

What Closed the Sales

Jobber's salesmen	52
Manufacturer's salesmen	38
Direct-mail follow-up	15
Jobber's salesmen working with manufacturer's salesmen	13
Jobber's display-room exhibit	5
Convention exhibit	4
Combination of follow-up letters and salesmen's calls	5
Demonstration by friends using machines	1
Not checked	4
	142

[1] R. S. Rimanoczy, "Factors That Influence the Sale Are too Often Mysterious," *The Mailbag*, January, 1927.

Another company selling cranes made the same inquiry of 150 recent customers. As might be expected, its percentage of replies was the same as the similar inquiry just mentioned. They analyzed as follows:

Sales Involving Only One Factor

Company salesman	22
Dealers	8
National advertising	5
Recommendation of users	3
Repeat orders	3
Price	1
Reputation of company	1
	43

Sales Involving Two Factors

Salesman plus advertising	2
Salesman at machinery exhibits	2
Observation of our equipment plus advertising	1
Salesman plus analysis of competitive bids	1
Salesman plus past experience with our cranes	1
Salesman plus reputation of company	1
Salesman plus observation of local equipment	1
	9

Studying the effects of advertising from still another angle, Mr. Malcolm Muir, vice-president of McGraw-Hill Publishing Company, in discussing industrial marketing, reported that a two-year analysis covering a thousand products showed that even those manufacturers who lead their fields in recognition have not scored with more than 60 per cent of the buyers; the next most successful class has recognition from a little over 40 per cent; the third class less than 30 per cent; the fourth, around 20 per cent; and the fifth, with a bit more than 10 per cent—which may indicate that the average seller in the industrial field is practically unknown to two out of three buyers.

A national retailers' association reports a test by representative grocers. Two similar articles, one advertised, the other not, were placed on sale in the same store. At the same price, 87.6 customers bought the advertised article, 3.6 the unadvertised, and 8.8 didn't care which. With the advertised article at a higher price, 60.5 customers took it, 24.2 the lower-priced unadvertised article, and 15.2 had no choice. Perhaps the most significant thing here is the relation between price and reputation. At the same price, nearly nine out of ten chose the better-known article. At a higher price, only six out of ten. To vary the respective prices until the demand reached a balance would have been a most interesting experiment.

Finally take the "Aunt Jemina" test. It comes as near 100 per cent perfection as any advertisement is ever likely to. An interesting personality, a real negro woman of the old-fashioned "mammy" type, who started as a demonstrator in Chicago—where the test was made—at the World's Fair in 1893, and for twenty years traveled the United States as a living trade-mark, with her "I'se in town, honey." Her smiling personality marks every package. It has been most intelligently advertised for a full thirty years. All printed matter carries her portrait. Courts have restrained competitors from using any colored woman's face on their packages. As far back as 1914 the popularity of this famous figure was so firmly established the company changed its corporate name to "The Aunt Jemima Mills Company." That Aunt Jemima pancake flours in a nine months' test sold 735 cases against competitors' 275 cases, comes as a shock rather than otherwise. To find "slightly advertised" competitors could sell even 27½ per cent in competition with Aunt Jemima seems simply to indicate the fallibility of the human mind.

These last three chapters have sketched in the fewest strokes a nation deluged with money, deluged with goods, deluged with printed matter. Newspapers for which brilliant reporters ceaselessly sweep earth and sea and sky are tossed aside at a casual glance. Magazines, after months of careful preparation, fare hardly better. For half a dollar, the younger generation drops casually into a theater that costs a million, to become mildly excited over films that cost as much as the theater. With the slightest turn on the radio knob, any hour day or night, your sons and daughters choose among entertainments for which their grandfathers would have arranged an enthusiastic trip to the city. In this newer age, when cathedrals of moving pictures gross $157,000 for the opening week, and the entire nation can hook up for a free act of Chicago Opera's

"Faust," no advertising can hope ever again to dominate through merely spending money.

On the contrary, opportunity for waste grows beyond calculation. In these circumstances, to make the showing reported in this chapter, advertising is no doubt, doing exceedingly well. Yet advertising must sooner or later conform to the new conditions. Necessity for shrewdly timed coups with immediate returns is increasing. Turnover of advertising investment is still an almost untouched field. Turnover means immediate action. To get people to act, an advertiser must know how they act. And why. Chapter XIII treats of the law of averages, touching a few high spots in a subject that could fill an encyclopedia. But before getting into the fascinating subject of how people will act, take half a dozen pages on the even more important question of why people won't act.

CHAPTER XII

The Twin Targets

When Ralph Waldo Emerson was supposed to have written it, Elbert Hubbard's famous quotation about the world wearing a path to the door of the better mouse-trap builder may have been true. Certainly it holds no longer. Today, the man who desires popular support, either in praise or in price, must blaze his own path. More, he must blazon it. He must go out and grab people from other paths into his. Or hire somebody to do it for him. "Triumph we must; our cause it is just!" was good for the Star-Spangled Banner in 1812. Today justice and merit claim all our respect, but not much of anybody's attention.

Two millionaire friends of ours celebrated the ripe conclusion of a commercial career by an adventure into the arts: one in a beautiful book on banking, the other in marvelous million dollar apartments after an ancient Piedmont palace. Though deluged with sincere compliments by connoisseurs, each in his secret heart is grieved because people—multitudes from the street—haven't rushed, money in hand, to join the demonstration. Both, in their own businesses, have successfully sold huge projects. But as artist and amateur, neither can believe that a beautiful book or marvelous apartment needs the same

141

coldly calculated, commercial exploitation as a real-estate auction.   Or a Coney Island sideshow. Church, state, banking house, and shoe store compete on even terms for the public ear.   There is no royal road to pubilicity.   The man with something finds he has nothing, unless he has a ballyhoo to "sell" it for him.

By "selling" we don't mean, necessarily, a cash transaction.   Nor even a commercial one.   We mean bringing the minds of as many people as possible into an actively favorable attitude.   A good deal of advertising has no goods to deliver; its duty on that account may be only the more difficult.

Modern advertising is not nearly so admonitory, or even abrasive, as it is explosive.   Or, better, two-explosive.   For, like a trench mortar, advertising requires a double detonation.   Circulation, the first explosion, scatters the message over a carefully calculated area.   Copy, the second explosion, upsets the equilibrium of minds.   But before turning to gun fire, glance a moment at the nature of the target. Or targets: for you shall find the great American army of sales resisters, 90,000,000 strong, dug into *two* sets of intrenchments.

The first of these intrenchments is more formidable than any of the Belgian concrete forts; in fact, a very Verdun.   It is our old friend public apathy, smartly rechristened for advertising purposes, "Consumer Resistance."

That is advertising's high sounding way of saying that people do what *they* want to do.   Man drifts into church during the second hymn. But seldom misses the opening whistle at a football game. Duty letters to deserving cousins languish for days, while a newly discovered sweetheart gets a special delivery at breakfast. Reason may be resisted, but not sentiment. Things we want to do slip easily into gear. Things we should do dissipate in a cloud of good intentions. One of the things people don't want to do is to read advertisements for profit and pleasure. The first shock in any survey of sales "resistance" is to find dozens—hundreds—thousands—millions—of people not only *not* reading your cherished advertisement, but actually struggling to avoid it.

Before selling became a science, Deacon Doe used profanely to lament, "Bill Jones won't buy that old gray mare of mine." In those horse-trading days Deacon Doe was stupid enough to blame only himself. He never thought of blaming Bill Jones. So long as advertising was content merely to spread information, it remained an abrasive process. It now assumes a dynamic responsibility. When it doesn't work, somebody is wrong. It can't be the advertising. Therefore it must be the customer. So people are blamed by the million for resisting something they never heard of.

Mr. Stanley Resor, who, of all men, certainly ought not to be prejudiced against advertising, said in the course of a speech: [1]

The average consumer has had this interest extended to such a variety of articles that of necessity he has built up

[1] From an address before the New York Club of the Graduates of the Harvard School of Business Administration.

within himself a subconscious defense mechanism. If he were to examine conscientiously the statements of all the manufacturers of products of possible value to him, he would face a doubly unpleasant prospect. In the first place, he would have to devote his entire waking hours to a study of the relative advantages of these innumerable products. And as a result of this exhaustive study he would very soon find himself a victim of nervous prostration.

How many people are aware that there are 250,000 trade-marks registered down in Washington, with hundreds of new applications crowding in each week? Or that *Printers' Ink* alone has unofficially *registered* 5,000 different "slogans" for simultaneous recognition by the long-suffering public? Or that *Printers' Ink* has also in its files more than 2,000 house organs—private publications to spur whole organizations into more savage selling?

Continues Mr. Resor:

Of the great mass of advertising, the average reader is only dimly conscious. His consciousness of advertisements may be divided into three main classes.

—*first,* his very slight notice of articles which are not and never would be of use to him;

—*next,* his larger awareness of those articles which he would like to possess but cannot afford to buy at the time he sees the advertisement; and

—*finally,* his active interest in those articles for which he is an immediate prospect; and this interest emanates, of course, not from any inherent interest in the product, but from his interest in himself and his own needs or desires.

Completely backing up Mr. Resor, yet attacking the problem from quite a different angle, Mr. Verneur Edward Pratt gives [1] a vivid picture of this same consumer "resistance" actively at work.

Out here at 2161 Lafayette Avenue, Des Moines, Iowa, is a family by the name of Jones. Every member of the family has seen and read our National Advertising. They have received, over the signature of our local dealer in Des Moines, a series of direct-mail pieces designed to create a desire for our piano—at least to persuade them to step into our dealer's store for a demonstration.

There they sit—absolutely unmoved by our efforts!

They do not buy!

What are the possible reasons?

Let us put them down:

1. Afraid they might not get large enough allowance for their old piano in trade.
2. Haven't enough cash at present.
3. Old piano being a gift from grandmother now gone, has a "memory association."
4. Have decided not to buy any new piano until John gets out of college, or until they move or until some certain future occasion.
5. Fully satisfied with present piano.
6. Have no piano, and never felt need for one.
7. No one in family can play, anyway.
8. Even if they bought a new piano, are not sure that it should be our make.
9. They know some one who had one of our pianos and had difficulty in keeping it in tune.
10. Some one told them that our make was toned for the concert stage, not for the home.
11. They remember, 'way back, a family who had an old upright of our make and it was an atrocious-looking piano.

And so on. These are not all the thoughts that fly through

[1] "Answering Prospects' Objections," *Direct Mail Selling*, February, 1927, p. 17.

the minds of Mr. and Mrs. Jones. But they are some of them; and any one is enough to prevent a sale, in spite of our elaborate advertising and selling campaign.

This, as ably stated by Mr. Resor and Mr. Pratt, is the advertising's first target—"Consumer Resistance." It is bad enough. But public apathy is only the beginning. Unless an advertiser happens to sell direct, he pounds out his vim, vigor, and vitality on a distribution system—with three hundred scintillating exceptions—as alertly responsive to advertising as a cast-off feather bed to a cold winter rain.

That is "Distribution Resistance," advertising's second target. Mr. Benson has ably described it in few words.[1]

It is not nearly so easy as it used to be to interest retailers in a product because it is being advertised. It is almost impossible to do so with any mere promise of advertising. There have been too many failures and there have been too many broken promises. The retailer has begun to suspect that previous successes were due as much to his own cooperative effort as to the advertising appeal.

What the retailer wants is more turnover for himself and less sales effort. He wants the producer actually to create demand and keep the public sold. That passes the buck back to consumer advertising, to starting a buying initiative there.

This resistance isn't wholly a matter of indifference on the part of the retailer. Like any average American, he believes in advertising. 420 out of 700 retailers, interviewed by the U. S. Department of Agriculture, thought advertising might help the sale of prunes. Out of the 106,000 questions asked by

---

[1] Address at Bok Award Dinner, Cambridge, Mass., February, 1927.

merchants of the National Cash Register Company one year, "How to Advertise" stood sixth on the list with 5,100 queries—about one out of twenty. Nor does this "resistance" result altogether from too little enterprise and too little efficiency. The American distribution system simply cannot handle everything thrust at it. There are too many stores! Too many lines!! Too many goods!!!

Next to automobile makers, the toilet-goods advertisers spend most money. Since this is mostly to force distribution through local druggists, suppose we take a look at drug stores. We find about 52,000 of them, 3 per cent, doing $33\frac{1}{3}$ per cent of all the business. Each of these 2,000 chain stores equals about seventeen of the little independents. Our 52,000 drug stores are supplied by about 980 wholesale druggists, of which only 292 remain independent of chain or syndicate buying. By these wholesalers are employed more than 3,000 salesmen. This gives one traveler to every 16 drug stores. Even with this selling pressure, when one realizes that half these little stores are in towns of less than 10,000 people, one is surprised that the Squibbs 1923 survey found the average drug store carrying an average of 43 brands of dentifrice. The average drug wholesaler is supposed to carry 50,000 items. The average corner druggist carries a stock of about 8,000 different items.

Turning to a larger establishment, most people are familiar with this often quoted list of articles on sale in the R. H. Macy & Co., Inc., toilet goods section:

1,200 different kinds of perfumes
1,300　　"　　"　　" face powders
　600　　"　　"　　" cold cream
　347　　"　　"　　" rouge
　231　　"　　"　　" lip pencil
　110　　"　　"　　" eyelash preparation
　204　　"　　"　　" sachets
　452　　"　　"　　" soaps
　742　　"　　"　　" toilet waters
　396　　"　　"　　" hair tonics and dyes
　 68　　"　　"　　" smelling salts
　 54　　"　　"　　" foot remedies
　120　　"　　"　　" cough preparations
　100　　"　　"　　" tooth preparations
　 27　　"　　"　　" hot-water bottles
　 76　　"　　"　　" sponges
　526　　"　　"　　" combs

Macy's is, of course, a great establishment, in a great city. But only one store in one city. There are, in the United States, some 1,300,000 stores, of one kind and another. These stores are located in 15,000 towns and villages scattered over some 3,000,-000 square miles. And serve more or less directly 118,000,000 people.

Now, instead of thinking of Marshall Field's, Wanamaker's, or Hudson's, or Bullock's, or Gilchrist's, or LaSalle & Koch, please visualize the *average* American store in a town of 800, serving 2,000 people in a territory a bit over two square miles. If this seems an exaggeration, remember there is a retail store of some sort for every 22 families.

To get a better picture of these struggling little

stores compare the number there are with the number scientific investigation has shown there really ought to be: According to the calculation of Mr. Hugh E. Agnew,[1] it requires a fixed number of families in a trading community.

Kind of store or business	Number of families necessary properly to support store	Actual number of families to stores in U. S.
Confectioners	450	420
Dry goods	450	341
Cigars and tobacco	650	136
Clothing and men's furnishings	500	420
Grocery	100	83
Furniture	850	620

Now, picture at the desks and behind the counters of these 1,300,000 retail stores 4,000,000 of your average little American cousins as we found them back in Chapter X. Take, for example, the city of Baltimore. Every person in town does each year about $450 worth of shopping. This keeps nearly 12,000 retail establishments, which, counting the proprietors, support nearly 50,000 employees. Each of the 38,000 clerks gets $22.60 a week for selling about $150 worth of goods. Visualize this condition all over the United States. See one out of every ten of America's workers serving as store clerks. For every three farmers to grow the groceries, one clerk to sell them; for every four factorymen to make goods, one clerk to sell them; for every railroad man to transport them, one clerk to sell them. Then you

[1] Hugh E. Agnew, *Cooperative Advertising by Competitors,* p. 126.

will be prepared for two things: first, to appreciate how distressingly unfitted are these myriads of little merchants to keep up with present unmeasured production of goods—all, as one retailer complained, "reeking with style." And then to understand the retailer's brief ride to bankruptcy!

For years fickle women have been blamed for the large number of goods returned to stores. The Comptroller's Congress of the National Drygoods Association made a report that fully half of the returns in a normal store cannot be blamed on customers. On the contrary, the first 50 per cent returns is caused directly by mistakes in size and color and defective merchandise. The next 25 per cent of the returns come from injudicious selling on part of clerks forcing merchandise on undecided customers. This puts only 25 per cent on the *femina semper mutabile!* And leaves 75 per cent of all blunders blamable on the store and its clerks. The National Cash Register asked 200 people why they stopped trading with a certain merchant. Out of 200 who answered:

Quit because of poor goods................	1
"	"	"	bad store arrangement......	9
"	"	"	slow deliveries.............	17
"	"	"	service delays..............	13
"	"	"	errors.....................	18
"	"	"	tactless business policies....	11
"	"	"	refusal to exchange goods...	4

Total on account of store faults or policies   73

Ignorant	sales people	....	6
Tricky	" "	....	18
Insolent	" "	....	16
Overinsistent	" "	....	16
Indifferent	" "	....	47

Total on account of sales people....... 103
Attempts at substitution.................. 24

200

From these two instances one may easily infer that the ordinary retail clerk isn't all an advertiser might ask. There is the further investigation by Mr. Standish Reamer who,[1] in order to test the salesmanship of clerks, visited personally Milwaukee, Chicago, Detroit, Toledo, and several smaller towns. In no drug store in any town was he asked by any clerk if anything in any other line might make up for a lacking article. In hardware stores he found clerks equally indifferent. In a few department stores only, did a clerk ask if any other service were possible. To corroborate his experience, Mr. Reamer cites the investigation for the Fleishmann Company, whose investigators visited 42 retail bakeries, instructed to buy in each store, up to $5 limit, everything suggested to them by the clerks. The total goods thrust upon their willing hands in all 42 stores was $10.60 —or about 25 cents a store.

Now take the other side of the picture. A certain popular pill manufacturer called anonymously

[1] Standish Reamer, "Direct Salesmen Rated 20 to 1, Compared to Clerks," in *Mail Order Advertising*, September, 1926.

on more than 500 New York druggists. He found 470 didn't carry his article. But 423 of them offered him something just as good. Whether the 4,000,000 American retail clerks are indifferent or overzealous, the waste falls largely on the ambitious advertiser. This fast-and-loose clerking may help explain, too, why the average clothing store lasts only 6.4 years. A hardware store, Methuselah among retailers, lasts only 7.6 years. On the other hand, it must never be forgotten that hardware stores' profits average less than one-half of one per cent. And grocers less than half that. Picture your grocer with a thirty-cent profit on forty-eight cans of soup. And five cents' profit on forty-eight cans of condensed milk. With this all in mind you will, we believe, join our judgment that no advertiser has a moral right to waste a single dollar. The fight at the firing line demands every intelligent penny he can put behind his goods.

Because the people who make—and advertise— and ship—and show—and sell—the things you use are no more efficient than the rest of us, distribution, counting waste and necessary expenses, eats up more than one-third of what you pay for any article. Roughly speaking of each dollar you spend for things on the list below, about this number of cents goes into getting them to you:

Clothing	$.33
Dairy products	.27
Drugs	.45
Electric supplies	.37
Fruits, vegetables	.50

Furniture........................... .44
Groceries........................... .27
Hardware........................... .42
Jewelry............................ .40
Meats.............................. .29
Shoes.............................. .45

These figures are probably not precise. Even before this they may have dropped. But so long as distribution costs run higher than 30 per cent none doubts they will go lower. Advertising is a distribution cost. How it will prosper in the process of squeezing out waste will depend entirely on itself. Advertising that adds expense can hardly hope to continue. Advertising powerful enough to help lower all other distributing costs will prosper infinitely. That power, however, as we shall try to show in the next three chapters, depends only partly on the advertisement, just as a transatlantic trip depends only partly on the boat. Wind and wave make or mar the voyage. Human averages make or mar the advertisement.

CHAPTER XIII

OUR WORLD'S GREATEST LAW

"You never can tell about a woman;
   Perhaps that's why we think they're all so nice.
She never does one thing any two times,
   She never does the same thing twice."

So ran the light opera tune. True, perhaps, of any one woman. Add half a dozen other women, the verse loses point. Make it a million women instead of one, and somebody can tell you precisely what they will do in any given situation.

Or, when the facts aren't handy for your particular need, you may be able without any great trouble to discover them for yourself. As Mr. G. Lynn Sumner puts it in his fascinating analysis:[1]

If you should constitute yourself a sort of census taker on your own account, and should go out and call from house to house until you had met and seen and talked to 5,000 women, you would find out of that 5,000 a certain per cent would like Norma Talmadge better than Gloria Swanson, a certain per cent would wear a 5A shoe, a certain per cent would have little daughters by the name of Mabel, and a certain per cent *would buy what you have to sell*.

This law of large numbers, or, as we more often call it, the "law of averages," is a most interesting study. Women, weather, baseball, railroad accidents,

[1] "Good Old Law of Averages," *Advertising and Selling*, July 15, 1925.

154

elections, twin babies, and bridge whist—it works impartially.

It shows, for example, that the average American's expectation of being murdered next year is about one in 10,000. This, incidentally, is almost exactly the suicide rate for the city of Brooklyn—and just one-half of that for Manhattan and the Bronx. Strangely enough, San Diego, with all its sunshine, will in 1928 have three times as many suicides in proportion to its population as Boston. Of every four who take their own lives in 1929, three will be men. Half of these men will use firearms and only one in nine poison, while one woman in three will prefer poison and only one in six, firearms.

A happier example, perhaps, is found in marriages. In 1916 every thousand of America's population furnished 10.3 weddings, and 10.2 in 1922—a decrease in six years of only 22 to every 100,000 population. Roughly speaking, one person dies for every pair that marries. In Texas 1 couple in 20 gets a divorce; in New York, 1 in 22.6, and in Georgia 1 in 19.4. Boy babies born in Kansas will live exactly seven years longer than boy babies born in New York State. And so on indefinitely. The law of averages registers every conceivable human activity. A frivolous example is the report of the English psychologist who tabulated with formal precision the elements that make people fall in love. One thousand lovers were analyzed. No surprise comes from his discovery that more men fall in love with women's eyes than any other feature. Hair comes next,

teeth third, and so on down to finger nails and feet.
Eight per cent of the men admired slender fingers.
Ten per cent of the girls called for regular white
teeth, while only 7 per cent specified broad shoulders.
Beautiful pink finger nails tie with arched eyebrows,
at 4 per cent among youths.   But alas for the song
writers, the average young man's fancy turns by 5
per cent against 2 per cent in favor of long eyelashes
as compared with curls.

Worked out from 7,000,000 cases, the law of averages tells the surety companies that only one man in
every hundred of those they bond in 1940 will go
wrong, and, of each seventy that do get into trouble, only one will do so through deliberate criminal
intent. More important, it tells them that the ideal
risk is an Englishman or Dutchman well over thirty
years of age, married and fat, quietly at work, interested in a hobby, and, if possible, quick-tempered
and profane.   Averages also tell the casualty companies that for every man or woman hurt next year
by falling off a stepladder, one man and a half will
be hurt getting into bed and three hurt climbing in
and out the bathtub.   The average age of the New
York police force or of the employes of General
Motors Corporation, or of the Long Island Railroad,
will, in 1935 or in 1950, be the same as it is today.
This simple fact enables 2,500,000 Americans to be
blanketed by group insurance.

Because the United Cigar Stores, at the very start,
took the trouble to discover that for every 120 men
passing a cigar store, one will come in to buy, it has

run a string of little corner stores into vastly wealthy real estate. The same common sense is rapidly making high-class merchandising an exact science. A certain little five-foot square of floor space, one-fifth down the right-hand side of the middle of the average store, is known to be worth one-tenth the entire rent. The same space directly behind is worth only half as much. When any solicitor tells you things like that about your advertising, listen to him carefully indeed.

Maybe you won't need an advertising man to remind you how precisely the law of averages does its work. The Chicago Cubs, with 4,183 chances, led the National League fielding last year. At the tail of the list, seven teams lower, came the Brooklyn Dodgers, with 4,085 chances and a fielding average lower by 1.1 per cent. One ball missed in every ninety chances marked the difference between the best and the worst of eight baseball clubs. In the same way, if 10,000,000 people all over the United States go to a picture show this Thursday night, you may count on the same number going next Thursday night—and next Thursday after that—and every Thursday thereafter. Until some blizzard or panic suddenly intervenes, 10,000,000 people will be at the movies every Thursday night.

To know which people depart from any such action as this Thursday night movie show—or when—or why—is as unimportant as it is impossible. All peculiarities average out so smoothly in the mass that we need pay no attention to individuals. The mail clerk in one business house regularly weighs its morning mail. He multiplies this weight by a given coefficient. Then he hands the Treasurer a slip telling in dollars and cents the morning's sales. A whole truck load of mixed inquiries, complaints, circulars! But long experience has shown that every pound of this mail will, day in and day out, contain a given number of orders with checks. And although these checks may average only $2 from one state and $6 from another, they will, as a whole, regularly average around $5 apiece.

What will you pay for a red poppy next Armistice Day? Your fellow citizens will average about 12 cents apiece. The American Legion of New York City can today safely base its 1930 plans on that assumption. Four posts this year, selling 68,000 poppies in widely varying conditions and territories, showed averages of 9.9 cents, 10.4 cents, 11.1 cents and 12.1 cents, respectively. The working of people's minds is plainly mirrored. A dime, obviously, seems about right; enough quarters come to more than offset the pennies and nickels of the generous poor.

The law of large numbers works with such astonishing regularity that popular superstitions evaporate before it. Take "June" brides. June averages only about 20 per cent more marriages—5 couples instead of 4—than May or October. Business, contrary to the popular tradition, is generally unusually good in election years. During the great summer slump only about 2 people in every 100 are out of town. Seven dollars spent by the average man instead of his regular eight marks the main difference between prosperity and panic.

Somewhere we have read of an Italian organ grinder who knew his monkey would average just a nickel a block, and so could scientifically plan his day's work. That this is not quite such monkey business as it sounds is borne out by Mr. Sumner's insurance solicitor:[1]

. . . He told me exactly how he had worked out a law of averages that enables him to use the plan with a certainty of result. He sent each month to his home office a certain number of names of substantial business men. The home office mailed out the letter I had received. A certain percentage of replies—3 per cent in this case—came back. . . . After an experience of several months he found that when he divided the total amount of insurance sold to these prospects, he had sold an *average* of $1,500 for every inquiry he had received. As he received three inquiries from each one hundred names circularized, he was, therefore, selling an average of $4,500 for each 100 names sent in. In other words, every time he sent a name to his company to circularize for him he set in motion a sales effort that *on the average* and with the usual aggressive and intelligent follow-through, was certain to result in the sale of $45 worth of insurance. . . .

Turning to still more commercial uses of our law, more soda water and candy is sold around three o'clock than at any other time of the day. The wise department-store manager, however, knows that, although more shoppers are then on the street than at any other time of the day, they are all on the

[1] G. Lynn Sumner, "Good Old Law of Averages," *Advertising and Selling*, July 15, 1925.

frivolous outgoing edge of the trip. Their high point of serious buying, he knows, won't come until at least an hour later, when all suddenly and simultaneously settle down to business on their way home.

Thousands of these rules of one sort or another are known to somebody in every line of effort. All successful business is run by more or less scientific adjustment to known preference of customers. When five people come into a restaurant the head waiter knows that one of them—on the average—will order salad, while it takes four such groups to make sure of his selling a portion of fish. And so on. As the wise department-store manager arranges to do his selling when women want, so the skillful restaurateur arranges to give people what they want. These gentlemen feel no obligation to change their customers' fixed habits; their success—on the contrary —depends rather largely on the skill with which they can turn their establishment completely to gratifying those habits.

Advertising alone seems to feel superior to these charted currents of human action. This is probably because advertising still pictures itself as controlling them. At times, no doubt, advertising has had much influence. Nevertheless, while it claims to change human habits, advertising, above all other industries, is the most completely and pathetically dependent upon the human tides. The variations in advertising returns noticed in Chapter II don't happen by chance. The law of averages, working deep below surface, makes them mathematical certainties. Once your advertising man realizes he deals with a force complicated as the permutation of planets—yet certain as the law of gravitation—his whole work takes on a new dignity. Insurance is child's play compared with advertising. Yet because the great insurance companies have grasped a few simple mathematical principles and hooked them up commercially, insurance contrives to make advertising seem a game of blind man's buff.

No one has been able, so far, to make real use of the greatest powers in all nature—the ebb and flow of ocean tides. Yet nobody doubts the presence of the force. Advertising is much the same. Small operators play tricks on the edges of human action, just as peasants at the foot of a glowering volcano turn a few pennies by letting tourists cook eggs in the hot springs. If all the effort that has gone into attempting to control human action had been spent in scientific study of its workings, Secretary Davis could not complain of "under consumption." Advertising today would be the admitted master of Mr. Borsodi's distribution age. The new advertising may yet become an economic force of prime importance. Instead of claiming an independent omnipotence it has only to follow politics, diplomacy and business practice generally in hitching up to human nature.

Stripped of all complications of its own mechanism, advertising would, as Mr. Jordan suggested, be a simple thing indeed. An advertising man would have only to sit down with an old-fashioned circus

man and a newfangled behavior psychologist to find
out how human nature works.   Then to study successful   editors,   successful   preachers,   successful
theatrical producers, successful politicians to discover how they set this human nature to work for
them.

Nor is it really so difficult to get the basic facts.
To hook on to human nature is not nearly so hard
as it sounds.   Men at business luncheons, for example, run as true to the law of averages as women
shopping.   A gentleman named Jay Lee Cross, of
the Cleveland Advertising Club, made them his special study.   He found Wednesday by far the best
day to get business men to attend meetings, Friday
next best, and Monday worst of all.   Also that two
speakers attract more than one, while three don't
pull so many as two.   Nor four as many as three.
Also that speakers draw directly in proportion to
the size of the city they hail from.   Also that the
announcement of "music" adds to attendance from
20 per cent to 50 per cent.

Now take Johnstown and Jamestown—two neighboring cities of the same size.   Their rival Rotary
Clubs run annual dinners the same week.   Both want
business men from the whole state.   Jamestown, de-
pending on advertising alone, carelessly selects Monday night and announces four speakers from small
towns.   Johnstown, on the contrary, following Mr.
Cross's facts, selects Wednesday night, has only two
speakers, one from New York and one from Chicago,

and emphasizes the "music" feature, which Jamestown merely mentions.

Suppose now, by some strange coincidence, both towns happened to use precisely the same advertisement, identical in every particular except the facts. Johnstown would have the game won, hands down, before the advertising even started. By the law of averages—applied through identical advertising— Johnstown's dinner features would attract at least three men to every one at Jamestown.

Now carry a step further! Suppose, besides knowing the law of averages in business men's dinners, the Johnstown manager knows the averages in newspaper advertising. Suppose Jamestown runs an odd-size advertisement with a long headline and without a picture. Carrying ill luck still further, suppose the Jamestown manager, taking a chance on run of paper, gets a lower inside corner of a left-hand page, away from reading matter. Now suppose Johnstown, on the contrary, has worked out a properly shaped advertisement with a picture of the leading speaker and a neat little band of white space. Suppose, further, Johnstown insists on the upper outside corner on page 3, top of column next to reading matter. That skillfully jockeyed Johnstown advertisement will, without the slightest question, be seen, read, and remembered by at least 80 people to every one who notices the Jamestown advertisement.

So, with his dinner attractiveness on a 3-to-1 basis, and his advertising effectiveness on an 80-to-1 basis, the Johnstown manager, through a practical working knowledge of human averages, will count at least 10 guests at his tables to every one secured by his equally earnest Jamestown rival.

Two psychologists of Ohio State University once decided to discover what people really talked about. Incidentally, also, whether people of Columbus Circle were any different from those of Columbus, Ohio. So wherever they could safely eavesdrop and take notes they listened to people talk—in restaurants, barber shops, and street corners. With five hundred conversations tabulated they found that:

1. People everywhere talk about the same things.
2. Men talk to other men about
    a. Business—49 per cent Columbus; 48 per cent New York.
    b. Amusement or sport—15 per cent Columbus; 14 per cent New York.
    c. Other men—13 per cent Columbus; 12 per cent New York.
3. Women talk to other women about
    a. Men—42 per cent Columbus; 44 per cent New York.
    b. Clothes—19 per cent Columbus; 23 per cent New York.
    c. Other women—15 per cent Columbus; 12 per cent New York.

Miss Gertrude Lane, able editor of the Woman's Home Companion, asked her readers what women talked about. Her answers worked out not far from these rough figures:

Children...................................... 80%
Gossip.. 76%
Hubbies and hobbies.......................... 60%
Foods and cookery............................ 30%
Personal careers............................. 28%
Church and religion.......................... 23%
Books, art and music......................... 20%
Weather...................................... 18%
Movies....................................... 11%
High cost of living.......................... 10%
Styles....................................... 6%
Topics of day................................ 6%
Travels...................................... 4%

Two things worth noticing: the overwhelming preponderance of people over things and the editorial observation "there is little variation between the interests of Maine and those of Texas; in the great metropolis and the smallest village the same topics are being discussed."

All these people all over the United States may, of course, be induced to talk about other things: a good novel, say, or a new kind of catsup. Advertising, done well with untold wealth, can *force* them to talk about anything—for a moment! But backing Niagara Falls upstream is easy compared to turning people away from their natural normal habits. And footprints in a rainstorm are more lasting. If one feels that he must compel millions of people to talk about his new novel or brand of catsup, his best chance, by far, is to hook up that book with something people are already talking about. And tie his catsup to some picturesque personality people already know. You can get people to talk about the most commonplace things: baking powder, face powder, or gunpowder, if you can honestly tie these products up with something they are going to talk about anyway. As Seymour Eaton once remarked, any advertiser who succeeds in hitching up to the weather will make a decided and everlasting hit.

Nobody can repeat too often that in advertising, as in politics, the only way to lead is to follow! And before following, one must know. Every board of directors in the United States might profitably hang in the office of its advertising man a handsome chromo of old King Canute. The king became history's biggest boob merely because he missed a tide. Had he been smart or lucky enough to stage his act only a few hours earlier—or later—he would have been famous as a first-class miracle worker. Lots of splendid advertising has failed for causes equally beyond control. The next chapter—"Human Tides" —may console some who have blamed themselves needlessly.

CHAPTER XIV

HUMAN TIDES

Makers of hairpins, combs, hair nets, corsets, knit under-wear, cotton stockings, hose supporters, lingerie and petticoats have come down to work in the morning only to find that the business they have built up by years of hard work has vanished into thin air overnight.—EARNEST ELMO CALKINS in the *Atlantic Monthly*.

NOT quite so fast as that, Mr. Calkins. Not overnight. Nor overmonth. Hardly overyear. We agree "what women have done to many long-established industries is a tale to make bankers weep and economists tear their hair." But we profess our belief that, even where women are concerned, coming events cast long shadows. Even in fashion, every great change has its harbinger; an omen, a portent so clear the dullest can see. The extent and exact direction is never so evident. Fashion experts miss a large majority of their guesses. But changes without notice are as rare as storms without clouds.

Women are certainly not buying hair nets as they used. Theoretically, anyway, the hair-net manufacturer is sleeping on a park bench, gnashing his teeth, as he glimpses barber-shop windows full of women. But women did not stampede to the barbers. Irene Castle was wearing the "Castle bob" before the World War. Irene Rooney of Seventh

167

Avenue admitted that Mrs. Castle looked cute and comfortable long before following her example. Irene Higgins of Dubuque hesitated even longer. Far beyond the centers of fashion, along with more American Indians, more bicycles, and an astonishing number of horses, you will find a good many miles of long hair still confined in hair nets.[1]

As against these few startling changes Mr. Calkins bewails we find human nature generally a conservative force besides which solid granite seems mere jelly. "No one in this world," remarks the benevolent Mr. H. L. Mencken, "has ever lost money by underestimating the intelligence of the great masses of the plain people." Certainly, none can lose much by overestimating their ordinary lethargy. At flood, the human tide sweeps all before it. At slack, human action is slow and stagnant as any shallow pool.

Consider a moment how sluggishly people act, even when their best interests are at stake.

If you drive a car in New York City on January 1 without a new license plate you will be arrested. To renew takes three minutes and a few dollars. Yet on December 19, 1926, with only eleven days left, fewer than 10 in 100 had applied for their licenses. On December 31, the last day, 60,000 jammed the offices. Even toward things that pay well and cost nothing, people show the same slackness. Stockholders of the American Telephone & Telegraph Company threw away $750,000 by failure either to

[1] At the National Beauty Contest held at Atlantic City, September, 1927, *two-thirds* of all contestants, including the winner, wore long hair!

use or sell subscription rights offered them in May, 1926. The courts have just decided for Mr. Wrigley that not over 45 out of 100 people will ever take the trouble to redeem their premium coupons.

In asking for money due, people are equally casual. On October 8, 1924, the United States War Department reported that only 1,300,000 out of the 4,500,-000 men entitled to apply for the bonus had done so. At the same time, only about 160,000 eligibles of the 500,000 in New York State had applied for their state bonus. When the privilege finally expired, on January 1, 1927, 100,000 were still to be heard from. It may have been high patriotism that held them back; but it is not high patriotism that has caused depositors in New York City banks to leave more than $5,000,000 in deposits unclaimed. Waiting only for its owners to come for it, in the United States Treasury, is about $1,000,000 interest due on Victory Bonds and War Savings Stamps. And, awaiting redemption, about $30,000,000 of bonds not drawing interest. Individuals collect money due them about as sharply as anything they do. But people in the mass are slow even in that. This is the inertia that ruins advertisers' calculations and breaks their hearts! Night after night in person, and Sunday after Sunday in rotogravure, Irene Castle proved herself irresistible before her feminine admirers dared bob their own hair. Not until women died of self-starvation in jail, and one woman died in the act of tripping up King George's horse in the English Derby, did all women begin to think they wanted very badly to vote.

If anybody wants hard work, let him try to start a fashion. For an easy time and plenty of profit, ride a fashion. Fashions seldom spring into activity with the ease of a powerful roadster getting under way. They rumble heavily and unevenly forward, like a ten-ton truck upgrade. Certainly none need get run over by the ten-ton truck! Frances E. Willard was the red flag that forboded the prohibition wave. In her own strange way, Carrie Nation was another. Maine went dry in 1858. By the turn of the century, dry towns were well nigh as common as wet ones. When national prohibition finally came, 90 per cent of United States territory and 75 per cent of its population were already dry by local law. All may object to Wayne B. Wheeler's $13,000,000 fund, but nobody can claim national prohibition came suddenly. And one weeps to remember that, instead of cleaning up their saloons and thereby turning the edge of prohibition, the brewers tried to fight it with a ridiculously inadequate advertising campaign. One of advertising's weaknesses, in fact, may be this tendency to blind men to changes they should be anticipating. Nobody blames any established business for not seeking possible discomfort and loss. If advertising could only protect old-established industries, it would need no other justification. But the thought that it gives power to stem the on-coming tide may often aid a false sense of security.

It is by watching for the always coming changes, and skillfully shifting his business in their direction, man makes his millions. Or at least retains his shirt. A New Jersey textile manufacturer complains that women have cut down their clothes from 18 to $4\frac{1}{4}$ yards apiece, and have thus caused 13 out of 20 woolen mills to fail. A Wisconsin hosiery man laments that in six years the number of types of women's stockings his mill must keep in stock has jumped from 480 to 6,006 styles. Yet the sheath skirt, with its slitted side, was in evidence everywhere in 1913. And as early as 1909 Annette Kellerman had made public appearances in the skirtless bathing suit which bears her name. Confronted with such portents, any manufacturer, if he were willing, could realize how likely were the present changes in women's apparel. That makers of corsets, cotton stockings, and petticoats should resent these innovations—and therefore ignore them—is not to be wondered at. Here, one might say, was a chance for aggressive advertising really to justify the faith of its friends. If advertising is "a tremendous force in the social world," or "the life of trade," or even "an Archimedean lever," why shouldn't it act as a magnificent conservative force in defense of invested capital? Why should it allow 200,000 ostriches to be sacrificed to a change of fashion? Why should one woman bobbing her hair, or another bobbing her skirts, lightly overcome a great deal of determined advertising backed with the prestige of well-established old firms? Advertising men themselves concede their inability to fight a "fashion." Can it be that advertising has less control of other human activities than most people think?

To raise such a question is, of course, rank heresy. But one can go only by the facts. While the Florida 1925 boom was on, California advertising inquiries were cut in half. When Florida began to wane, California advertising results returned to normal. When the bicycle boom was on, every advertisement was an apparent bonanza. When the boom began to fail, all the pages of all the mediums in America could not keep a man or woman on a wheel one day after he or she grew bored with it. Apparently Mrs. Partington and her broom have better chance of sweeping the rising tide back into the ocean than advertising has of turning about an adverse influence.

You cannot look back over the twenty-five kaleidoscopic years just past and fail to realize how such human tides have flooded and ebbed—without too much consideration for advertising. In 1900, every prominent banker and statesman in the East wore a silk hat. The phonograph was beginning to compete in a modest way with the melodeon, the piano, and the music box. The automobile was spoken of largely as a French novelty, and its American pioneers were without honor in their own country. The liquor business still had the strength of Gibraltar. Dentifrices did not come in tubes. Ferryboat operation in New York was most profitable. Baggage transfer was still a livelihood. It was cheaper to make soup than to buy it in cans. Labor supply seemed practically inexhaustible. How all this has changed! If you are thirty you have seen the automobile grow from its get-a-horse days into the key to America's prosperity. And create the wholly new profession of traffic cop. You are hearing the shoe manufactures ascribe to that growth a 25-per-cent drop in the demand for men's shoes. In 1923, the phonograph business—prodigiously advertised—was $57,000,000. In 1925 it was $22,000,-000. That was a steady drop of $50,000 a day, seven days a week, for two years running. Now you are seeing the phonograph leaders save the ship with a marvelously better machine, and with records that play an hour a setting. You are now seeing a brand-new kind of paint challenge the age-old supremacy of ordinary paint and varnish. If you are twenty-five years old, you have watched Mr. King C. Gillette sell 70,000,000 razors and 3,500,000,000 blades. You have reached the day when college athletics have an annual box office around $300,000,000 and the combined sales of sporting goods total not less than $25,000,000 a year.

Saturday afternoon, a generation ago, was a time for earning money. Now it is a time for spending. Old-fashioned folks, leading lonely lives, liked the gregariousness of the weekly church service on Sunday. Now people like Sunday as a chance to go off by themselves—to play a game as anti-social as golf, or to closet themselves into the public privacy of a sedan car.

So, after all, Mr. Calkins, these changes have not

come suddenly. Nor only in those businesses governed by the social, sartorial, and political emancipation of women.

Looking forward, instead of back, an alert advertising man can see even now the portents of some new inventions that will revolutionize the human demand. Take a small thing first: The principle of the automatic gear shift for automobile is known. What driver will stay satisfied with a hand lever and foot clutch after he is fully convinced that the epicyclic gear will work? Television is here. Hollywood is teaching its shrill-voiced motion-picture actors to speak acceptably, because the pallophotophone will soon bring their voices on the screen. And motion pictures will not be flat much longer. They will be round, as were the quaint "views" you saw through the stereoscope, sitting on the parlor sofa in the years long ago.

Dr. Steinmetz must have been looking ahead a good many years when he predicted *free* delivery of electric light and power. It was a vision fully as fantastic, when he expressed it, as was radio broadcasting ten years ago. What the universal use of electricity, whether free or paid, will do for manufacturers of lamps, domestic machinery, and farm tools, is a speculation that may interest you. Meanwhile, other scientists are lessening the production costs of methanol, a fuel made from steam and coal. Others are growing familiar with the nitrogen-fixing bacteria on plant roots, the culture of which will revolutionize farming at some date yet unseen. Still others have worked such miracles in that peculiar process, the hydrogenation of oils that you have already eaten fresh laid eggs fried in a sweet fat made from the stinking corpses of codfish. One extra atom of hydrogen in the complicated oil molecule not only deodorizes the mass, but transforms petroleum into an edible fat.

Such are a few of the new miracles. Their practical virtue may seem still far away. But small clouds on the horizon traditionally expand into hurricanes. If we agree with Macaulay that the greatest inventions are those which conquer distance, we can lend a careful eye to the air mail. Lindbergh's 1,800 hours' flying experience—more than the ordinary aviator gets in a lifetime—made possible his conquest of Europe. The skip to Paris was his 7,191st trip. Some modern marine engineers openly predict that our children will prefer to reach Europe in a couple of days by fast boat or plane, rather than to spend six or seven days in the most luxurious of the slow-moving modern ships. Rackety little racing boats already run at the rate of seventy miles per hour. A British officer down in Florida has startled the world by hitting 207 miles per hour in his automobile. The motor tourist at 30 to 40 miles per hour has produced roads just about fitted to that speed. The automobile that runs five or six times faster will, in turn, produce the kind of roads it requires. A few people are now grandiosely paying $75 for a telephone call to London. Their children will be quite matter-of-fact about calling up Melbourne or Peking for as few dimes.

In the great innovations of science the pendulum movement is invisible. The sweep of these cycles is too vast for our perception. Not willingly will people ever return to pre-telephone days, to pre-radio days, to pre-automobile days. Because, on the other hand, the decoration of women makes the most magnificently manipulated market in all commerce, Mr. Calkins can there point alarmingly at the shortest swing of the pendulum. Some cynic observes that man has for centuries sat up nights trying to think of something a woman wouldn't wear. So far without success! Skirts will change soon, if only for the reason that they are now short. And designers, as well as ladies, must live. The advertiser who can correctly gauge the day that woman will decide her knee has lost its novelty, is rich already. The advertiser who, on that day, is still trying to cut skirts shorter, goes broke. One of the classic tragedies of advertising was the man who started to buck the bobbed hair movement with double page advertisements of a new hair net. When every woman is bobbed, a new and appealing Lady Godiva will appear in long hair. Slowly, but steadily, all women will adopt that new fashion.

Even in fashion, however, the pendulum swings back and forth so slowly that it seems hardly a pendulum. Between the simple cylinder that slips over the heads of our own fair flappers, and the low-necked, tight-skirted, diaphanous dresses of Napoleon's formal court lie eras of crinoline, of black silk, of bustles, of long trains. Back all will drift some day.

Whether the stream moves toward you or away, slowly or quickly, your observation will show things going out. And coming back. Just as advertising must in the long run follow the cycle trend, so it reflects accurately, day by day, the fancy of the moment. Back when the *Ladies' Home Journal* had dress patterns, one little black-and-white Paris fashion sketch no bigger than Mr. Bok's thumb brought in more orders than an entire color page filled with special "American Fashions for American Women." Yet a color page in Montgomery Ward's catalogue one season sold $238,000 worth of coats. A good case for color you say. But another color page in the same catalogue sold as low as $43,000—scarcely more than half the selling by good black-and-white pages showing better styles. The man who measures this rhythm, whether by accident or design, gathers riches. And a reputation for great wisdom. Henry Ford is a classic example. "Society moves like a man pulling up a rope," some philosopher has observed. "He can't jump ahead. When an idea comes along that is too far ahead, it always has to wait until people get to the place where they can appreciate it." At that point, hardly sooner, the advertising we now know, can do its best work.

There is, nevertheless, vital work to be done long before this point is reached. The psychological engineer, advertising man of the future, will find that the information he brings in *from* the public is at least as important as the admonitions he puts out. Even today, the advertising manager about to receive his chromo of King Canute may reward the donating directors with the positive assurance that popular interest—not alone in women's "fashions"—ebbs and flows in human tides. And that these tides, whether ripples or waves, move in cycles. He may add that advertising, as such, has yet to demonstrate ability to control or even combat these tides. Also that any advertiser who hits the right rhythm, either by acumen or by accident, grows rich praising advertising beyond its just deserts. And, finally, that the advertiser who misses the rhythm, whether by misfortune, stupidity, or stubbornness, is undertowed into bankruptcy to become advertising's worst friend and severest critic.

Voltaire may have brought on the French Revolution, Harriet Beecher Stowe the Civil War. But forces bigger than either the wars or their prophets brought on both. And these are the forces the advertiser must watch.

CHAPTER XV

From Eve to Edison

THE manager of a famous heavyweight prize fighter, hearing his protégé dubbed a dumb-bell, defended him hotly.

"You're dead wrong," he said. "Slug knows a lot. But he can't *think* it!"

The same answer might be made to those who attack advertising. There is no vital principle, no single fact, hardly a tiny detail necessary to advertising's overwhelming success not already known and successfully practiced by somebody in the business. There is no failure in advertising, large or small, that one man, maybe ten, maybe a thousand, couldn't warn against in advance.

This knowledge is still unorganized. Advertising facts, as such, are neither popular nor necessary. Like the colored rookie who declined the cavalry because when the time came to retreat he "didn't aim to be bothered with no horse," the advertising salesman has had greater needs than science in matching the merits of his particular medium with the prejudices of each particular prospect.

If the billowy elastic cushion—the colossal shock absorber—injected into advertising by thousands of daily personal contacts between men with every

179

reason to like and respect one another were withdrawn, advertising would be dull indeed. But it would become a business. If advertising had to sell all its advertising through advertising, instead of through direct and indirect sales to and by pleasant personalities, it would lose picturesqueness. But it would peel off tons of technical impedimenta. And teach itself the astonishing strength of its own simple basic principles.

The leading advertising manual today has 21 pages on Human Impulses and 50 pages on Trade-Marks; 24 pages on Results from Advertising and 65 pages on Layout and Typography.

Important subjects: circulations, markets, solicitations, trade-marks and typography. And necessary. Yet—are they advertising's real essentials? How vital a part of its strategy? Several chapters back we sighted advertising's first target; some 90,000,000 people, a bit fed up on all selling, busy finding money for things they already want. And advertising's second target: 1,300,000 stores, trying to supply all these things, and still stave off bankruptcy the normal seven years. Against these twin targets, advertising arrays all its artillery. Fifty years ago the whole battery was a single Civil War smooth-bore howitzer. Today's arsenal is more complicated than a set of dentist's instruments; it ranges from Big Berthas to gas pistols and tear bombs. Set down in dollars, the annual roster is said to run about as follows:

Motion pictures	$	5,000,000
Programs		5,000,000
Street cars		11,000,000
Bill posters		12,000,000
Window and store display		20,000,000
Demonstrating and sampling		25,000,000
Farm papers		27,000,000
Electric and painted signs		30,000,000
Novelties		30,000,000
Business papers		70,000,000
Magazines		180,000,000
Direct mail		440,000,000
Newspapers		700,000,000
		$1,555,000,000

On one side of the battlefield, then, we find perhaps 50,000 major advertisers employing 600,000 people and spending $1,500,000,000 a year to break down sales resistance. Opposing them, we find America's 90,000,000 responsible [1] sales resisters.

This army of sales resisters, for our purposes, may be considered as made up of 90,000,000 *average* men and women. According to Dr. Hollingsworth,

The average man is 5 feet 7 inches tall and weighs about 150 pounds. He will live to be fifty-three and will have married in the twenties and have three to five children.

He believes that a couple of quinine pills and a stiff drink of whisky will cure a cold, that the Masonic order goes back to the days of King Solomon, that it is practically fatal to eat lobster and follow it with ice cream, that all Swedes have thick skulls and are stupid, that red-headed people always have quick tempers, that dew falls, that morals were purer

[1] Surely none will want to drag into this struggle the other 28,000,000 illiterate, ill, and infants under fourteen.

twenty years ago, and that the winters were longer, the snow heavier and more frequent when he was a boy.

The average woman is, of course, this gentleman's wife. These 90,000,000 don't realize any battle is on. Far from suspecting they are sales resisters, these good people consider themselves liberal buyers. And, in truth, an advertiser's money isn't spent so much fighting them—in any real sense—as it is enlisting them to fight the 200,000 other manufacturers who don't advertise. And the competitor who does.

With only a single great advertiser in each line— or confined to only a few industries, advertising as a novel monopoly could, beyond any shadow of doubt, accomplish everything claimed for it. But exactly as six Paderewskis simultaneously playing solos in the same hall would spoil all six, so six silk-stocking manufacturers advertising with equal brilliance in the same magazine would leave a woman just where she started. Except for one thing—

Each woman has some predisposition, prejudice, or weakness that one advertiser, above all others, has—deliberately or accidentally—utilized in his appeal.

Where these predispositions, prejudices, or weaknesses of one woman exist among all women in any quantity large enough to concern an advertiser, they are *averages!* Averages are steadfast as gravity— and always changing. Fads and fashions ruffle the surface. In the depths below, human nature swings, as we have seen, slowly, irresistibly, in fixed cycles of progress. Advertising can hasten these cycles;

even slightly retard them. But advertising can no more oppose, eliminate, or replace these cycles than a pair of bellows can manipulate the spring equinox.

As soon as advertising accepts itself as a magnificent hookup with human nature, it casts off complications. All is surprisingly simple. Circulations, trademarks and typography become mere tools. Bath mats or beehives—whether sold by mail or over drugstore counters—are seen to be moved by the same power. The principles of invoking this power are found astonishingly alike. Working within these principles, tests point out one *best* way to present an idea. And no genius, no brilliancy of copy, no marvel of artistry, can make any other handling so profitable.

That fact is not only the most important fact in advertising; it comes surprisingly near being the only vital fact.

The too-scientific approach to advertising defeats itself. Simplicity—easy to see, easy to say, easy to remember—is our one most needed virtue. A screw driver, within its own field, is the most scientific of instruments. With that in mind, imagine an earnest young doctor whose whole medical education came from working in a drug store. Imagine how he would talk about a doctor's business:

> Fine round pills
> Splendid big bottles
> Lovely pink liquids, etc.

Would he differ so much from advertising men when they debate

Forced Circulation [1]
Local Market Conditions
High Pressure Solicitations.

In advertising, as in pharmacy, the paraphernalia is so interesting one easily forgets that neither prescription nor advertisement has much value except as a means toward a known end. And that end, in both cases, is to start a hoped-for physical reaction inside another man.

The prescription acts *from* within the stomach.

The advertisement acts *from* within the brain.

A raw oyster, a bottle of champagne, and an ear of corn are dissimilar enough for any practical purpose. Yet the human stomach accepts them democratically, digests them into a lowest common denominator, and *takes for its own use* certain elements that chemists find commonly in a variety of foods.

The mind feeds much the same way. Mail-order advertising and general publicity, a radio talk and a billboard, a sales letter and an interview, are all more alike than they are different. All must be translated into rather similar stimuli to get into the mind at all. Once inside, all must compete on practically equal terms, as anonymously as so many calories or proteids. The man who reads advertising is appall-

---

[1] "Three specific tendencies that should be studied especially were enumerated in the speech of the retiring president of the Association of National Advertisers: First, the tendency of advertisers to go after a market with advertising before obtaining knowledge of local conditions in that market. Second, forcing of circulation by certain publications. Third, high-pressure selling on the part of the advertising medium salesmen."—*Printers' Ink,* November 11, 1926.

ingly—astoundingly—uninterested in how these sales
suggestions got into his brain. Beyond absorbing
those that appeal to him, and ignoring all that don't,
he doesn't bother.

A keen writer on physics has defined electricity
as the "behavior" of atoms in certain circumstances.
A sale, likewise, is nothing more or less than a
"behavior" of the mind. This behavior, everything
considered, is surprisingly simple and uniform. In
the main it results from an appeal to almost ludi-
crously primitive emotions. That appeal may enter
through the ear, as in personal selling. Or through
the eye, as in advertising. In either case, the effect
—or, rather, the effect sought—is always the same.
Advertising's only possible object is to upset the
equilibrium existing at a given moment in each individual mind. And to substitute a new set of relative values in which the advertiser's own article
stands nearer the top. Wherever this upsetting is
done strongly enough, the article is immediately
brought to the top. If done skillfully enough, motion
is generated toward the article. If that motion is
carefully directed into definite action, a sale is closed.
If not, that chance is gone. The advertiser has
simply scratched his mark in the sands of an incoming tide. The new equilibrium he has set up is soon
swashed over by a pressing flood of new appeals. It
may be wiped out completely. Or, some of it may
remain permanently. The circumstances vary completely in every individual case.

Advertising, however, need worry about these

missed sales no more than a mother shad about race suicide.   Both shad roe and circulation operate on a scale that allows for ample waste.   Without too much concern, therefore, for what happens afterward, the advertiser has only one main job: to get inside another man's mind, and there plant reasons plausible enough to induce that man to persuade himself to act.   For there can be no sale without voluntary action.   That can come only through the will.   And the will acts only in response to emotion.   Tomorrow's advertising man, therefore, is going to be first of all an expert in emotions.   As a practical psychologist, he will know all the various human impulses, and which will best serve him to feed the fire of desire for each bit of merchandise.   When all these causes of human behavior are accurately estimated —as they some day bid fair to be—and the real Niagaras of buying power thus brought under control, advertising will begin to do what it really ought.

Three hundred years ago good old John Sirmond wrote:

> "If on my theme I rightly think,
>   There are five reasons why men drink:
>   Good wine, a friend, because they're dry,
>   Or lest they should be, by and by,
>   Or any other reason why."

This, no doubt, is one of the first, and like as not the best, of the analyses of human motives now so popular.   Since then a dozen skilled psychologists have listed instincts and emotions for you.   Eleven

years ago Professor H. L. Hollingworth [1] handed
20 men and 20 women a series of cards upon which
were typed paragraphs taken from current advertisements, various bits of copy, reading, say,

Health—as a general tonic, 103 is unequalled. It nourishes
the system, enriches the blood, builds up firm, healthy tissue
and gives tone and color to the whole body. Prevents grippe
and pneumonia.

He then asked each of his subjects to arrange these
cards according to the degree in which they made
him desire the article or convinced him of its merits.
Of the order fixed by that pioneer jury, we take
room for only the leading ten.

Appeal	*Strength* Highest possible value 100, Lowest, 0
Healthfulness.....................	92
Cleanliness......................	92
Scientific construction............	88
Time saved.....................	84
Appetizing.....................	82
Efficiency......................	82
Safety.........................	80
Durability......................	78
Quality........................	72
Modernity.....................	72

A little later exactly the same experiment was
made at the University of Michigan on 60 students,
40 men and 20 women. The results were much the
same. Adams [2] combines the results of the Eastern-

[1] H. L. Hollingworth, *Advertising: Its Principles and Practices*, p. 85.
[2] Henry Foster Adams, *Advertising and Its Mental Laws*, p. 142.

ers and mid-Westerners, 60 men and 40 women, to show the comparative ranking of appeals when readers are *"in the advertising frame of mind."*

Here are the three appeals that this combined jury of one hundred voted first, second, and third:

> Durability
> Sanitary
> Efficiency.

The next seven were:

> Appetizing
> Time saved
> Value
> Scientific
> Ambition
> Family affection
> Safety.

The vote as a whole is chiefly valuable as indicating clearly even a decade ago the distinct preference for straightforward descriptions of *how* the article is good. And *what* it can do for the buyer. In each case the least interest was shown in institutional facts, such as who makes the article, how large the factory, how many years old, and other things that concern the advertiser more than the reader.

Poffenberger [1] varied the Hollingworth experiment a little by testing 117 women and 89 men with 15 different appeals in this form:

I want something in a toilet soap that will remove wrinkles caused by exposure or neglect.

[1] Albert T. Poffenberger, *Psychology in Advertising*, p. 85.

"Health" came first; "Pleasure" second; "Purity" third.   Below the middle of the list we find such curative qualities as "Overcome Redness" and "Remove Wrinkles."   E. K. Strong tried a similar test with 50 men and women.   His crowd put "Purity" at the head, with "Pleasure" second and "Health" third. "Economy" came in the sixth group, evidently not much more valuable, as an appeal, than the fact that the soap was made in a large factory, or that a souvenir was given with each cake.

Professor Strong again utilized much the same method in a toothpaste test, using actual copy.   Here once more "Cleanliness" leads, with "Health" second and "Appetite" third, "Economy" again in the fourth group.   "Reputation of manufacturers" and "Magnificent factory" are again at the bottom. "Cleanliness" led still another toothpaste appeal, this time in a study made by Professor Franken. "Health" was third, "Safety" fourth, and "Economy" last.

Trying a somewhat different experiment on 74 men and women, Dr. Starch found that they themselves considered "Hunger," "Maternal Love," "Health," and "Sex attraction," in the order named, the main motives for their daily actions.   "Ambition" came seventh, "Pleasure" eighth, "Approval by others" eleventh, "Personal appearance" fifteenth, "Safety" sixteenth, "Cleanliness" seventeenth, and "Economy" twentieth, nearly halfway down the list.[1]   Hollingworth gives us a list of 17

[1] Daniel A. Starch, *Principles of Advertising*, p. 275.

major motives. Poffenberger gives 16. Starch carries his out to 45. Any of these books is worth buying for lists alone. Mr. Stevenson cites [1] a Chicago bond salesman who increased his sales 20 per cent by listing the motives which made his clients buy. Any business man can recognize the money value of knowing the fundamental desires. It is ready-made demand, waiting for him to fill. But, like most of the apparatus prepared in psychological laboratories and graduate schools of business, the expert's handling of human motives is still much too cumbrous for the daily hurly-burly of professional advertising life. Turn to simpler formulæ. Mr. Alexander Black, whose years of success as able editor of newspaper features of almost unlimited circulation give him high authority says: [2] "There are only five things in which everyone is interested. They are:

Sex in its widest terms; the whole problem of man and woman, motherhood as well as romance, the baby as well as the ball dress.

Money, foremost of all blessings, root of all evil; worth more than something else, or less; never to be ignored.

Body, stomach, something to eat, to drink. Always a mystery of first importance.

Crisis of One. Any single individual struggling against superior forces whether police, pirates, natural, economic, or moral laws. Every man takes active sympathy with or against the individual, unconsciously placing himself in the other's position.

The Great Outside. In every man an elemental awe awaits

[1] John A. Stevenson, *Constructive Salesmanship*, p. 323.

[2] Alexander Black, *The Latest Thing*, p. 260.

the supreme suggestion—what comes after this life. Sentiment is as elemental as hunger.

You can easily double check to your own satisfaction this admirable estimate of Mr. Black's, or, in fact, any list of human desires. Figure for yourself, first, which of all desires applies to the most people: Hunger (or Thirst), Self-protection and Sex you will find head and shoulders above all others; all three are universal among men and animals. Secondly, check for yourself which desires hit people hardest. Hunger, Self-protection and Sex will, no doubt, again head your list.

When the U. S. army ration was increased from 36 cents to 50 cents a day, army enlistments broke all records. "Bigger and Better Beans," explained the New York recruiting office, beat the old "See the World" appeal. In equally trivial fashion, every act of every life reflects somehow the influence of one of these three main motives. A safe rule for any advertiser, therefore, is to tie up as closely as his proposition permits, with Sex, Hunger, or Self-protection. They are primitive, universal, unfailing. If anybody thinks us flippant or pornographic in advocating tying one's wagon to the sex appeal, let him turn back and reread Mr. Black's noble definition. Let him consider the "pretty girl" magazine cover, threadbare but eternal. The pleasant face of a young girl is absolutely the only design with universal appeal. Or turn abruptly to sea stories. Certainly Joseph Conrad is far from Balzac or Boccaccio. Yet in selling a $35 set of his works, the publishers discovered a tinge of exotic romance in the advertising copy made more than 100 per cent difference in sales. The same amount of money spent in two different advertisements carefully keyed and checked:

> Dignified Testimonials copy sold $3,500.
> Seductive Malay Princess copy sold $8,075.

This same new-style advertising is said to have sold more books of another world-famous—and eminently respectable—author in two days than formerly sold in a month. In eighteen months it moved 150,000 copies—a whole generation's sales by the old merit-of-the-goods method.

Modern civilization has made men's lives mighty complicated. The three simple animal instincts —Hunger (Thirst), Sex, Self-protection—all alike in the beginning, have branched and intertwisted like an old grapevine in sunny soil. And among their woven branches habits have affixed themselves like tropical parasites. These fixed habits must enter all calculations. Though showing its teeth only when interfered with, an affronted habit can bring a rash advertiser anything from sales resistance to bankruptcy. Before running athwart even a little habit, let the advertiser reread a paragraph by the late Professor William James:

Habit is thus the enormous fly-wheel of society, its most precious conservative agent. It alone prevents the hardest and most repulsive walks of life from being deserted by those brought up to tread therein. It keeps the fisherman and the deck hand at sea throughout the winter; it holds the miner in his darkness and nails the countryman to his log cabin and his lonely farm through all the months of snow.

Far more important than identifying exactly the particular motives for your appeal is to keep in mind the universal truth that your prospect is driven by an inside power. Whether that power might turn out instinct, habit, or even reason, the customer himself acts merely as its purchasing agent. All who sell a man anything at all sell him, therefore, one and the same commodity: *satisfaction* of an internal demand. Whatever your article may be, however interesting or important it may seem to you, to each and every customer it is like each and every other article—only a means toward his self-satisfaction.

With this in mind, and regardless of the more complicated lists of motives, any advertiser can get along if he will remember that humanity is thrown together and pulled apart by three parts of strangely conflicting emotions.

1. The desire to be with people.
   And the desire to be left alone.
2. The desire to be like everybody else.
   And the desire for a distinctly individual personality.
3. The desire not to be conspicuous.
   And the desire to be as conspicuous as possible.

We like to be like our superiors and different from our inferiors. So we dress and act like the rich and exclusive. They, in turn, finding us threatening their exclusiveness, hasten to adopt a new mode. So fashions are made and markets manipulated.

Just as the Gulf Stream creeps out from an obscure little sea to change the climate of continents, so in sheer boredom and petty jealousy are generated the great human cycles that control commerce.

In modern society, then, one can see more clearly why the desire for Distinction comes so close behind the urges of Hunger, Sex, and Self-protection. The moment man finds himself beyond danger and need, his first thought is to shine among his fellows. From the East Side gamin's precocious toughness to the college president's chain of degrees; from the multimillionaire who always walks to work, to the colored chambermaid who always takes a taxi; from the actress who never bathes, to the man who boasts about his daily cold tub; from the matron who has her face lifted in the beauty parlor, to the youth who risks his on the football field—all are working, in their own way, to set themselves apart from the dull, drab uniformity of the crowd about them.

The motives of the man who walks to San Francisco, the boy who dives off Brooklyn Bridge, the woman who swims the Channel, the lackadaisical dramatic critic, and, not infrequently, the great advertiser, are all off one piece in the great human drive for distinction. And all of us imitate them, all trying to show off, each in his own fashion. Any advertiser who can teach a person how to stand out—how to be strong, wise, healthy, fashionable, witty, debonair, handsome, well read, socially correct, and wealthy, especially—for great wealth is not only a distinction of itself, but opens many other opportunities—any advertiser, we say, who can show people how to do any of these things without too much work, can himself become a millionaire with even less.

Advertising practically never creates new desires. The best it can do is to arouse old desires in new ways. Man's only primitive desires were food, shelter, comfort, pleasure. Civilized man has jazzed them all but added nothing worth mentioning. An advertiser's only real problem, therefore, is how to rid himself of whatever complications come between his product and the direct satisfaction of some fundamental human desire. As coming chapters will show, one way is to simplify his sales story down to single sure-fire appeal and tell it over and over again in simple words—plain and friendly—that everybody will like to read.

CHAPTER XVI

A Pivotal Chapter

THE regular periodicals—magazines, trade journals, newspapers—are the main reliance of the great body of advertisers. And no doubt always will be. For half a century these publications have molded practically all advertising thought. Their $950,-000,000 worth of advertising is distributed among a list about as follows:[1]

General magazines, monthly and weekly	212
Women's magazines	38
Juvenile publications	27
Mail-order journals	24
Religious publications	882
Agricultural publications	560
Trade, technical, and class journals	5,460
Secret-society publications	222
Foreign-language papers	1,208
Newspapers	14,557

The monthly magazine was the cradle of advertising. He who dared spend $150 for a page in *Harper's* in 1864 stood out as sunrise on a mountain peak. Like the man who carried the first umbrella, he needed nothing else. No "merchandising" was required for that advertising. It walked on its own hind legs. Today an initial advertisement may be

[1] John H. Cover, *Advertising, Its Problems and Methods.*

196

like the bright new rug that leads the housekeeping couple first to replace the furniture, rebuild the house, and then move into a more fashionable neighborhood.   Unless a new advertiser has the sales resistance of a St. Anthony and the tenacity of an Oliver Cromwell, he is likely to sympathize with the Irishman who needed help to let go of the bear's tail.

In Eden's early days an advertiser had only to choose among a small list of excellent publications and await results.   He had to reckon with only two forces.   Most advertising, today, has a third dimension.   This third dimension, generally overlooked in theory, is becoming in practice the most important of all.   The three "dimensions," or result-bringing factors, of a modern advertisement are:

1. Copy
2. Circulation
3. Extension

"Copy," we shall notice, is an independent force. "Circulation" is the normal use of copy in any recognized medium.   "Extension," the third dimension, is its extra-normal use.   We shall give this new-fangled extension an extra chapter of its own.   And sticking to good old-fashioned advertising, look first at copy, and then at circulation.

A few chapters back we suggested that of all the death-dealing projectiles popular in the late World War, an advertisement most closely resembles a bomb shot from a trench mortar.   Both require two distinct explosions.   Both, therefore, alike require two sets of calculations.   To figure how many men a projectile can kill is one thing. To put it where it can kill them is another. Conversely, as Big Bertha taught the Germans, knowing your gun has range enough to reach the entire enemy is, unfortunately, not equivalent to ending the war.

In advertising, likewise, a true strategist has to figure for every separate advertisement.

1. How far the copy will *go*
2. How much the copy will *do*

There is a projective force, dynamic or static, to carry the advertisement. That is circulation. And an explosive force that the advertisement carries. That is copy.

"Circulation" is the number of people who may legitimately be claimed by the seller to have a reasonable opportunity to observe the copy of any advertiser who buys it. This circulation is a projective mechanism only. Circulation creates nothing. Circulation adds nothing. Circulation merely multiplies. That a broadcasting station is powerful enough to be heard by all the Persians, half the Esquimaux, and every third family in Terra del Fuego, isn't the slightest guaranty its message is worth broadcasting across the street. Ten million listeners won't make its bedtime stories a bit more snappy. Nor its saxophone solos mellifluous. Nor its political speeches any less monotonous.

On the contrary, the "kick" to awaken interest and induce action comes only from the copy. Extraordinary copy will shake a slight response out of almost any circulation, no matter how small or mediocre. By the same token, even a feeble advertisement carried to a big enough list will bring some returns. The law of averages guarantees that any drag net, no matter how slight, through any million human units must always haul out some fraction of a per cent. In practically all cases, there will be found people who have already decided on the article offered, and are either

(a) waiting to be reminded of that decision, *or,*
(b) waiting to learn how it can easily be carried out.

Furthermore, in any big list—or in a well-chosen small list—are always added a very considerable number of people who, unconsciously or consciously, want a *sort* of article. They have never happened to realize the particular article advertised could so nearly—so easily—satisfy that want. Or they may have known and forgotten. Some, according to temperament or urgent need, will act at once. Others will file the buying information for future use. The advertisement itself may be torn out and kept. We have seen orders for Christmas held six months. Or the facts may be intrusted to memory and, possibly, forgotten until another advertisement revives the desire.

In all these cases, circulation offers only the *opportunity*. If the consumer doesn't want to buy, or the advertisement isn't able to sell—all is blank. Circulation, in that case, is as void as time in which nothing happens. The residuum of good-will from an ineffective advertisement—no matter how big or how widely circulated—may easily prove valueless and impermanent as the noise of a great explosion. A giant cannon is effective only because it shoots a giant projectile. Unless the load measures up to the gun, the artillery practice is weak and wasteful. Unless your message is at least as important as the circulation behind it, you are overspending. On the other hand, until your circulation is as big as your copy is important, you are underspending.

Zero multiplied by the biggest number you can think of is still zero. No matter how many copies you circulate of a blank page, you never make it say anything. The last of the last million of a feeble advertisement is exactly as ineffective as the first copy off the press. The dumbest little mail-order advertiser knows this. Unless his advertisement can get a certain planned-in-advance response from a known number of people in each thousand reached, every extra copy paid for merely increases his loss. And within the next few years advertisers will, we think, come to realize that this appeals even more strongly to general publicity. When we use the word "response" we don't mean necessarily—nor even generally—an order by mail. Nor a clipped coupon. We mean some definite response tangible enough for a business man to buy, like any other commodity, in thousand or hundred thousand lots.

If this sounds strained, consider insurance. Insurance is as intangible as anything a sane man could buy today. Yet the nation puts $6,000,000,000 a year—four times its advertising expenditure—behind its faith that insurance actuaries have harnessed up the law of averages to everybody's benefit. The same law of averages that makes modern insurance an exact science will some day be utilized to guide advertising response. And to guarantee it! The fundamental laws are at work with mathematical accuracy. The fact we don't know how to use them is our fault, not theirs.

For those who don't appreciate the astonishing regularity of the law of averages in advertising, let us cite a single typical example. A manufacturer of power equipment with sales averaging about $300, is a large user of trade-paper advertising. During the past five years he used more than 200 different advertisements in one paper, always with the same space in the same position and advertising the same article. "With all these factors remaining constant," reports Mr. C. R. Long,[1] "the physical appearance of the advertising (*i. e.,* copy and layouts) was almost the only element controllable by the advertiser which varied. Copy and layouts did vary widely; numerous series, based on perhaps a dozen different themes, were used, as well as a large number of 'single' advertisements featuring noteworthy installations, sales records, etc." With this complete variation in copy and constant change in outside industrial conditions the replies by years were as follows:

[1] C. R. Long, "Seasonal Trend of Inquiries Is Shown by Five-year Tabulation," in *Class and Industrial Marketing* for June, 1927, p. 30.

Year	Yearly totals
1922	256
1923	274
1924	292
1925	288
1926	296
Average	281.2

The greatest variation between any two consecutive years is less than 8 per cent. The last three years were practically constant.

Many advertisers are not interested in fundamental laws. And, in fact, are altogether unconcerned about advertising response. An immense circulation seems to satisfy. Merely to look at the millions of copies totaled up on their advertising schedule thrills with a sense of achievement—a feeling *they* have done something. Yet these men wouldn't waste time firing blanks merely because a trench mortar was big. Nor would they pay for a transatlantic trip on the *Leviathan* tied up at dock. Even if her engines turned out 400,000 horse power right under their deck chairs they would still insist on getting somewhere for their passage money.

No disrespect is intended those who still pin their faith to sheer force of circulation in saying that they belong, like the whale, to an earlier and easier civilization. There was a day when the original Leviathan had more than a sporting chance against any craft man could send against him. Also, there was a day when every magazine reader might reasonably be counted a reader of every advertisement it carried.

Our grandfathers, consequently, could be satisfied with a plain advertisement well displayed to any good round number of people. Our sons will find circulation not nearly so simple. They will have to recognize—as their fathers almost do—that the more modern conception views circulation from three angles:

1. NORMAL CIRCULATION: The entire number of people to whom any advertising copy is exposed.
2. SIZE: The unit of space-effort made by any advertising copy, in any medium, actually to reach normal circulation.
3. POSITION: The advantage—or disadvantage—through good location—or bad—any advertisement in that medium has in reaching normal circulation.

Closely intertwined with these mechanical factors of size and position, which shall have a chapter of their own, is "duplicate" circulation. Also that quality called "cumulative effect." Circulation will have our whole attention as soon as copy has its say. But so many advertisers are absorbed in the mathematics of advertising—statistics of markets and populations—that copy cannot get the attention it deserves once these other factors are allowed to take the floor.

On the other hand, neither is copy alone the whole story. Some critic once remarked that a great work of art is never finished; that each new observer brings it something all his own. This is even more true of an advertisement. Strictly speaking, copy can create nothing. Carried by circulation to a vast variety of individuals, copy simply selects those who happen to *bring to it* exactly the right mental or emotional ingredients. With them it coalesces into a sort of dynamic affinity.

In the past few chapters, therefore, we have tried to chart the sea of humanity, to sketch 90,000,000 American people, how they act, and what they on their part, are likely to *bring* to any advertisement. Now we turn to the advertiser. We examine his means of approaching these people. But before tackling copy consider just a point or two, which while not copy in themselves, will do more to make or break a copy writer than a thousand books of rhetoric.

Captain Matthew Webb swam the English Channel in 1875. To get the next man across took 36 years. People now believe there are only five days each year in which any one can hope for success. So certain kinds of advertising find sharp restriction. Three weeks before Christmas the toy department of a New York store is the biggest and busiest of all. Thousands of feet of extra space are jammed and crowded to the point of suffocation with a fearsome mob of parents and children. Within a week it shrinks to a tiny corner where only an isolated aunt prowls at long intervals in search of a birthday toy. Full-page advertisements in every newspaper in New York would not breathe life into that moribund department the day *after* Christmas. During the Mah Jongg craze we happened to see written, printed, and mailed, all within a week, a twenty-four page catalogue of sets and accessories.

This cost $4,000 delivered to 20,000 selected stores. Answers came by telegraph and mail. Before they stopped, the advertiser had received keyed orders for more than $25,000 of sample sets. The catalogue was good, but not so good as that! It simply swept on the full tide. Little, Brown & Company published a biography of Walter Camp. Of such books only a few hundred copies are ever sold. In the autumn of 1926, however, a series of Walter Camp Memorial football games was played. Sharp interest was aroused. By circularizing a list of Yale graduates, returns of more than 6 per cent were secured. As soon as the brief season of football was over the Camp biography became merely a biography. No further circularizing could be made to pay.

Timeliness, then, is all-important. But even before timeliness comes the question whether your article is the *kind* of article that will repay advertising even at flood tide. Musical doormats, pocket parsnip peelers, tobacco pipes with involved plumbing arrangements, non-refillable bottles, perpetual-motion machines—some one is fully convinced that each has only to be advertised to be sold. Tragedies cluster around this kind of reasoning. Take, for instance, a patent parachute to save hotel guests from fire. The inventor calculates that, once advertising begins to work, a traveler will demand, before registering, whether his room has the parachute, and, if not, will seek another hotel. Or, for a more practical example, take the author who came to a publisher with an excellent manuscript about railroad trains.

He argued, correctly, that of the millions who ride on trains, many would like to read a book about them. The publisher was able, fortunately, to show him how these people were so widely scattered that the cost of selling them the book would be prohibitive. Untold quantities of gold, silver, copper lie untouched, although their location is accurately known. The metal is as fine as any. It simply does not run high enough in proportion to its surroundings to offset the cost of extracting pay metal. Similarly, many products and services which pay handsome little profits when skillfully handled in nicely limited operations, can by their very nature never sell enough to justify extensive advertising.

Every advertising agent is called upon to resist such propositions. And not by any means all from crank inventors. Presidents and sales managers of successful companies are always likely to catch the fatal fever for advertising something merely because it has merit.

Finally, even when your article is practical, and the time propitious, your prices must be right. The public's attitude toward prices is already an interesting study. Within the next five years it will be the most important of all studies. Our opening chapter suggests that the psychology of advertising is a buying psychology. The question of price furnishes a good example. To the seller, a few cents off the price is merely a change in figures, a smaller percentage on certain costs. To many a customer it may mean a chance to own something until now entirely out of reach. Or, better still, a chance to buy that *and* something else. Only the woman who contrives her week's shopping to squeeze a new pair of gloves out of pennies saved has any idea of the real meaning of lower prices. And only the man who has watched that woman buy can adequately visualize the nation's constantly lowering commodity prices as the road to a magnificent prosperity.

Economy of itself is not a popular appeal. Yet a low price, like a pretty-girl magazine cover, is one of the few appeals everybody understands. An unusually low price becomes *news*. On the other hand, while a low price for known value is the most important single element in selling, minor price changes *as such* often make surprisingly little difference. So as long as you avoid the unreasonable, you need never cut prices simply to get business. Twenty years ago Lorin F. Deland enumerated one of the most important principles of advertising: "The *reason* for a price is as important as the price itself." Many a man, with a good sale at a dollar, has been disconcerted to find that he did not double, or even appreciably increase, his sales by slashing to fifty cents. And many another, shrewd enough to test before he leaps, has found that he could add five cents, ten cents, fifty cents, or even a dollar to his price without proportionately cutting his sales volume. In fact, advertising, when justified at all, will often pay an independent profit if one takes Mr. Percy S. Straus at his word and adds its cost into a higher price for the article.

There, then, is your paradox. Low prices are the
only assurance of a great business. And the only insurance of any business. Yet in many cases the price
may be moved sharply upward before sales fall off
enough to matter. Between these two antitheses,
however, operates with implacable force of the guillotine one eternal principle: *The price must seem
reasonable.* You are about as badly off to have your
price seem too low as to have it seem too high. It
must feel right, sound right, read right. It must fit
very closely the average person's conception of about
what he or she should pay for the given article.
In the long run, people won't—and don't—pay more
for one article than for another that seems about
the same. The right price, fortunately, can generally
be foretold to the penny by proper testing. For
example, three test advertisements identical except
as to price, showed for a certain book:

    At $3.00— 48 sales
    At $2.00—118   "
    At $1.00—290   "

With test figures like these and his manufacturing
costs before him, an advertiser can easily determine
his proper price.

After a low price for known value the next most
important factor is familiarity. That the public is
avid for something new is a wide-spread delusion.
Nothing is less true. The public constantly gropes
for the old, clings to the conventional, joyfully recog-
nizes the familiar. Take the young people in Ring

Lardner's story who jumped at a chance to go to New York City from their Chicago home because it would give them the chance to compare the New York production of "Abie's Irish Rose." Or the elderly couple in his *The Golden Honeymoon,* who enjoyed Florida, the new land of opportunity, where they went for a change, because they found some of their old friends there.

People like "Hamlet" *because* it is so full of quotations. Operas live by one well-remembered aria. Musical hits of today are Strauss and Schubert, *réchauffés.* The most successful early automobiles were those that most resembled the well-remembered buggies and buckboards. The leader among mail-order books is a single-volume edition of Shakespeare. Radio stations hold their audiences with urgently requested old favorites. Tourists overlook the fresh and fine, seeking hackneyed memorials. Ask a newcomer to Cape Cod whether she would rather see the new ship canal or Plymouth Rock. Notice at the Boston Navy Yard whether the latest submarine or *Old Ironsides* is more interesting to visitors. Ask yourself why the film production of "Ben Hur" outpulled, in every city and town, the most flaming novelties Hollywood ever produced. Ringling Brothers could find no possible substitute for red-and-white clowns and dusty elephants; without them the circus would close in a week. When George White's expensive "Scandals" was about to fail, he took four old joke books and rewrote it into a success.

Novelty is no asset in advertising. It is a danger, a liability. To freshen up an old truth is far easier for the advertising writer than to plant a new one; to satisfy an old need is infinitely more profitable than to create a new. The writer of advertising, above all, must use the utmost care in weaning his prospects away from old favorites. His first and foremost thought must be to see that his new ideas are firmly hooked up with other people's established beliefs.

As Mr. Stevenson so attractively explains: [1]

The human mind, possibly on account of the heritage it has received from animal ancestors, tends to put unfamiliar ideas into an unfavorable class, unless curiosity interferes, and to give a "no" response. The child runs away from the stranger not because of any unpleasant experience with strangers, but because the idea of speaking to that stranger presents a situation with which he is unfamiliar, and consequently he avoids the situation.

In the same way, a woman who has always swept her house with a broom unconsciously puts the idea of a vacuum cleaner in an unfavorable class because the idea of cleaning her house that way has never presented itself to her. . . .

The human mind, too, has a tendency to reject plans which will necessitate a rearrangement of ideas. Students have known for a long time that the original author of the familiar Cinderella fairy tale didn't intend to add to her difficulties by making her dance in glass slippers. The first translator made the error of confusing the old French word meaning a certain kind of leather with a word spelled in much the same way meaning glass. But so accustomed have we become to the idea of Cinderella's glass slippers, absurd though the idea may

[1] John A. Stevenson, *Constructive Salesmanship*, p. 271.

be, that, in all probability, no publisher would even make the attempt to correct the story.

Above all things, every advertiser should keep in mind the dictum of Hesketh Pearson's in *The Whispering Gallery,* which says:

. . . the majority of self-made famous men achieved their eminence by virtue of their excessive ordinariness, by the extremity and intensity of their reactions to the commonest impulses; and that the rest of them, those who were born eminent, attained whatever popularity they possessed by their defects rather than their finer qualities.

By admitting on the witness stand he thought Benedict Arnold a "writer," Henry Ford probably made more real friends than by any other single small act. People love to find in others their own weaknesses. Conversely, they distrust any who affect airs of superiority. We know an advertiser with a sensitive eye for type and layout, who nevertheless won't allow a plate to go to a country newspaper. The home-town interpretation of a finished proof leaves him still a trace of distinction, yet fits into the crude little newspaper with the tact of a perfect guest. So, in turn, we suggest to the thoughtful advertiser a study of the homely tongue, the eye, the mind, and, most of all, the heart of his fellow men.

CHAPTER XVII

Vox Populi

AMONG the aborigines of Australia one still glimpses man's mind in making. In a land of giant fern, kangaroo, and boomerang, abstract thinking is hardly expected. Yet it is shocking to find even bushmen without a word for "tree." "Gum tree" and "nut tree" have their separate words. But "trees" as a class don't bother them. They have nouns for the "white cow" and "red cow," but no collective noun to call the cows.

These primitives prove why Americans sell one another faster by word-of-mouth methods than by expert advertising. Our nation has 25,000,000 boys and girls in lower grades. And 4,000,000 in high schools. But only 500,000 in colleges and universities. There are many excellent magazines and newspapers. Even so, Americans are far from a literary people. More money is spent each year for advertising than for the entire educational system from little red school house right up to university. Of 118,000,000 Americans 50,000,000 are still out of reach of a public library. In such cities as have libraries, only three books a year go out for each citizen. And, worse yet, a recent public-school survey showed that 34 per cent of the children's homes contained no books whatever.

The educated can be reached in small groups. But generalities are a cultivated taste even among the educated. Readers of popular American publications know no more about the spectrum, say, than Australian bushmen about abstract trees. Say "blueness" or "greenness" and leave your readers cold. Try "sky" or "grass." To the lads drafted in the late war "Imperialism" meant less than nothing. Only when they were invited to "kill the Kaiser" did the hostilities take on an active personal flavor. Professor Poffenberger asked 37 people, all of whom had stopped short of finishing high school, and were, therefore, of about average American literate intelligence, the meaning of a number of words. Twenty-seven out of 37 failed on "zest," and 22 on "slush."

"Quality," "supremacy," "service," "distinction," like "imperialism," are deceitful words. To the advertiser who dressparades them into his copy they swank with style. Worn thin as a Scotchman's nickel, they slide over and off the mind of the average reader like a slick eel off a smooth rock.

Take the one word "epicure." Certainly it has the much-sought smart sound. Certainly everybody would instinctively prefer "epicure" to a low cannibal from the Philippines. As many may recall, the word was once blazoned on our crowded city streets on a widely distributed poster:

"An Epicure's Way of Baking Ham."

A skeptical scientist made two small reproductions of this poster. The first was an exact duplicate. The second was the same in every respect, except that the savage "Igorot" was substituted for the elegant "epicure," making the alternative read *"An Igorot's Way of Baking Ham."* The two proofs were placed together before 53 housewives with the request that each choose between the two. Twenty-nine chose the "epicure," while only 24 took the "Igorot." But, questioned, 12 of the 29 admitted they were guessing and had no idea what epicure really meant! Yet "epicure" is a meaningful word compared with many. A long list of these elegantly empty sarcophagi is popular among our best advertisers. Sam Slick suggests that if divine fate removed about ten words from the vocabulary, automobiles could no longer be advertised. His ten words are:

outstanding	supreme
achievement	thrilling
acclaim	advanced
stamina	luxurious
grueling	finer

Apparently it is thought vulgar to use simple words in expensive space. If people in the Social Register, the Bankers' Club, and Bradley's Beach do have any one common characteristic, it is, most likely, a laconic directness of speech and a humorous abhorrence of all high-sounding banalities. If those who pay for distinctive three-syllable abstractions had any suspicion how little "kick" such words had for anybody other than themselves, the copy in much of our handsomest advertising might immediately take on a new and honest interest.

Every copy writer ought to be compelled as part of his job to read one week a year the New York tabloid newspapers. In their coldly calculated, commercialized editorial stooping to the average American mentality, he will find a perfect laboratory of the picturesque concrete. Everything is labeled so plainly that no eight-year-old child can hope to escape. Arrows, diagrams, cross-marks-the-spots, frankly avoid any need for the most rudimentary elements of thought. Circulation charts prove overwhelmingly the success of this method.

To return, however, to the use of "sky" and "grass" instead of "supremacy" and "distinction." In the matter of finding its words, the advertising profession is just beginning to awaken to the value of a vocabulary study made by Professor E. L. Thorndike, of Teachers College, Columbia University—years ago. To get a true cross-section of everyday language he had counted and sorted a total of 4,500,000 words. His sources ranged from daily newspapers to children's classics; from business men's letters to elementary schoolbooks. Out of those 4,200,000 words he undertook the colossal task of choosing the 10,000 most commonly used words and arranging them in order of their everyday popularity. Here are the twenty words used most frequently by the average American writer:

and	on
that	it
with	but
be	have
of	he
as	his
all	there
at	they
not	out
for	when

Dr. Thorndike's work was intended primarily for teachers and writers. Professor Cover, of the University of Denver, went one step further in applying it for advertisers. To get a fair example of the words used by a man with an active vocabulary of 2,500 words he takes the second words from the top of every column in Thorndike's list covering that range. Here they are—the sort of words used by a rather better-educated-than-average man.

about	dust	lovely	score
but	government	plenty	Tom
family	listen	seventy	accident
high	perhaps	they	column

As Professor Cover points out, this is not an impressive list. Yet it fairly represents the typical vocabulary. Here follow a few words he claims to have selected more or less haphazardly from a variety of current advertisements in popular publications.

cremis	obstetrical	vellumesque	condiments
beiges	prenatal	kalsomine	inimitable
brochure	exhilarating	volatile	nutriment
sloshing	skimpiness	fitment	uniformity

Compare these monstrosities not only with Thorndike but with a similar sample of the 4,000 words required to pass New York State's literary test for new voters. Three out of every four of these first voters' 4,000 words are found also in the Thorndike first 4,000. The few not found there—the longer Latin derivatives—had to go into the New York quiz to test the voter on his proposed civic duties.

able	ball	cane	considerable
dime	exclaim	fury	honest
lace	milliner	ours	preside
restore	show	strict	top

Whenever dictionary publishers put out a new edition, the newspapers are filled with discussions on "How large is the average man's vocabulary?" Ten thousand—twenty thousand—thirty thousand words are in the interest of publicity, generously bestowed on men who in actual conversation never by any chance use half the words included in those two-column newspaper discussions. Professor L. M. Terman, of Leland Stanford University, suggests a quick method of settling such disputes by letting every man measure his own vocabulary. All one has to do is to select a hundred representative words out of the dictionary and count how many he can define. Professor Terman's estimate of the probable average result indicates:

Number of Words Understood
(or Passive Vocabulary)

8-year-old child	3,600
10 " "	5,400
12 " "	7,200
14 " "	9,000
Average adult	11,700
Superior "	13,500

Tests such as these are like looking in the mirror to tell how tall you are. Moreover, they relate to *passive* vocabularies—words that may, perhaps, be understood when dragged into highbrow conversation, or when some writer elaborates in a book. When it comes to *active* vocabularies—old-shoe words a man himself uses comfortably and understands without a pause—these big vocabularies shrink with astonishing rapidity. From the 11,700-word "passive" vocabulary, generally credited to the average adult, it is interesting to work down toward the average American's active everyday language. Colonel Leonard P. Ayres, one of America's foremost statisticians, decided one day to abandon banking and count words for a change. He got hold of thousands of actual written communications, in twelve different groups, ranging from love letters to collection letters. When the repetitions were subtracted, Colonel Ayres found his 240,000 words total boiled down to a list of 2,000 different words, which, he concludes, is the true size of the letter writer's active vocabulary.

Now for the next step. Combining his analysis

with three other similar studies previously published, Colonel Ayres found:[1]

"The" and "and"—two words—account for nearly 10 per cent of the words we write.

"The," "and," "of," "I," "a," "in," "that," "to," "you"— nine words—account for 25 per cent of all the words we write.

Fifty words—including the nine already mentioned—account for 50 per cent of all we write. Only one of these fifty words has more than one syllable.

300 words account for 75 per cent of all we write.

1,000 words account for 91 per cent of all we write.

This leaves the top 1,000 words of the average man's vocabulary—the more decorative and less useful half—to be used only 9 per cent of the time. Unless your copy writer wants to spend your selling money on educational work, he will view two syllables with suspicion. And three with alarm! For years it has been the fashion to claim that more brains go into the advertising pages than into the editorial. Be that as it may, writers and editors have, at least, the comfort of relying on the intrinsic value of what they say, while the advertiser dolls himself with trick typography and a vocabulary stiff and shiny as a bridegroom's collar. So much for the tongue. Now a glance at the eye.

[1] Fred C. Kelly, *The Fun of Knowing Folks*.

CHAPTER XVIII

WHERE ART BEGINS

THE human eye is built for moving objects. Primitive man had to catch the slightest change in his surroundings. Thousands of our ancestors perished because they happened to overlook one fatal change. The superior ability to view with alarm has bred a habit of instinctive alertness. People still retain a strong reflex to anything new.

So long as advertising was new—a change—it commanded interest. Back when motor cars and moving pictures attracted attention on their own account, a double-page advertisement did the same. When *Collier's* introduced color advertising in 1907 it had the force of an explosion. New kinds of advertising, each had its turn. Advertising, unfortunately, is no longer new. And, like the Broadway revue, its cost has become so great, few advertisers dare risk anything original even if it occurs to them. Only seven advertisements in a hundred depart from two or three rigidly fixed types.

Some advertisers try to fight this lowering visibility by still stronger attention stimuli. Among the more thoughtful, however, is coming a quiet revision of attitude. Having worn down the surprise value of big spaces, big type, and big statements, they look around for a new angle of approach. Finding that the old shock formulæ no longer *force* attention, the more progressive copy men have set out to *win* attention. This means abandoning the theory of arousing interest by slam-bang outside the reader, and skillfully appealing to things within him.

Imagine, then, the advertising in any publication as a great road race. The prize is the trade of a million people. Each advertising message is a racing car. The copy man is driver. Layout man and compositor are mechanicians *only*. By allowing the layout man to drive, advertising has done much to educate popular taste. And thrown away millions of other men's money! In a good advertisement, as in a good racing car, appearance counts little compared with power. When appearance adds to power, its value is inestimable. But the chief duty of the mechanician in advertising, as in motor racing, is to keep humming along with a smooth and powerful swing.

Advertising power comes mostly from the message itself. The best two methods of applying it, as your layout man well knows, are headlines and pictures. When we say "pictures" we make definite reservations. We don't mean "art." Any student of H. G. Wells can recall how many centuries it took men to achieve the crudest drawing found scratched in the ancient chalk pits. Until magazines, moving pictures, and radio brought about mass reproduction of popular favorites, good art was more or less synonymous with starvation. Nowadays we attain vast mechanical distribution of very good art—drawings by Franklyn Booth, paintings by Maxfield Parrish, Norman Rockwell, many others. But, unfortunately, we cannot also arrange to have their work appreciated by machinery. And as every true artist knows, the appreciation of art among our citizens is an astoundingly thin veneer.

Many a fine piece of art in an advertisement has really impressed only two people—the art director who bought it, and the artist himself, as he cynically cashes the check. For the artist is not fooled. He knows that in all America are only a few dozen people who care about his work enough to buy it for their homes; and only six or seven museums whose directors will buy it for their walls.

All this applies only to Art—to Art with a capital A. It doesn't mean pictures. As the Eastman Kodak Company proves, there can be very good pictures indeed. Soft focus "art" photographs thrill connoisseurs, but don't sell cameras. What sells cameras is the very best and clearest "shot" that can be taken of ordinary folks, doing ordinary things. What advertising art really needs—we are speaking to art directors now—is more Landseers, more Browns (the Brown who did the eternal newsboys), more Luke Fildes's (remember "The Doctor's Visit"), more Tads and Briggses and Sidney Smiths, who know the one true road to the public mind and heart. "His Master's Voice" is advertising's greatest art. The man who painted "Washington Crossing the Delaware" would have sold more Buicks and more Estey organs than all the National Academy of Art's membership combined. To quote a line of Kipling's, every picture "should 'ave the 'igh shine of a photograph."

Don't flatter people mentally by thinking they enjoy better pictures than you do. If they did, the best pictures in the Metropolitan Museum would be surrounded by crowds. Year after year, these pictures hang lonely on the walls while the visitors, with unerring taste, gather around the only two really bad paintings in the building. Don't O. K. any picture for an advertisement unless *you* honestly like it. And your secretary must like it too!

Your secretary, if she is a normal girl, likes pictures a lot better than stories. So do the rest of us. Pictures are nearly six times as easy for us to recognize as words. And half again as easy to recall. They can be made to do a lot more work in advertising than they do now; not by being bigger, but by being better and more convincing. The improbable scene where the wife in immaculate white tells the husband she just loves the Bigbunk Sanitary Swillpail, it smells so sweet, is going to vanish in favor of a photograph or literal drawing showing how *you* can put garbage into the pail without touching it with your hands.

People would rather look at pictures than read words. And they like pictures of people doing things. The picture of an object is usually less convincing than the picture of a person using it. Sometimes you can suggest a whole person just by showing one of his fingers. But show the user somehow. That's what the art director is for. You can show jellies so translucent they melt in the mouth, and fried eggs so beautiful they almost stain the whole page yellow—but you will sell more goods, say the experienced advertisers, if you get people as well as still life into your pictures. If you want to sell a bond, it pays better to show a happy party of bondholders at their wassail on a steamship than to show—no matter how beautifully—the mere bond itself.

Optimism, good humor, ease, comfort, the happy ending; these are the things which the advertising artist should mix with his paint. And above all, life! Generous, fortunate, care-free life—life as it ought to be, life in the millennium, life free of burdens and worries and cares. All of us want it. Every advertised article is supposed to contribute in some way to this kind of life. See that its contribution is made clear in the cut!

The good old A-I-D-A *motif* has been played so often one hesitates even to mention it again. *A*-ttention *I*-nterest *D*-esire *A*-ction has been drilled into every earnest advertising *motif*. Any good advertisement must first get itself looked at. Attention, at best, however, is only a preliminary reaction that pulls the rambling mind together more closely to concentrate on the problem at hand. An advertisement may be wonderfully successful in getting attention, and fail completely in getting anything else. Therefore, the quality of attention must not be strained. Somebody has suggested:

A polecat in the road will attract lots more attention than a $10 bill on the park bench, but not so much desire for ownership.

With pictures as with polecats and physics, any act of attention may be accompanied by an opposite reaction. *"$100.00* in Prizes"—we recoil in slight disappointment from the two extra nothings the advertiser has stuck on simply to catch the eye.

A plump pink Godiva with bobbed hair would certainly attract attention. Also a white Death's Head freckled with black spots, jagged teeth, chewing a squirming snake striped zigzag like a zebra. So will pretty pictures, swashbuckling headlines, circus display, and trick offers. But all this unselfish attention is likely to back-fire. Casual readers are one thing; prospective buyers quite another. *Selfish* attention is the only attention that pays at both ends of an advertisement. When attention is selfish enough, turning it into interest—the next step in the AIDA formula—is easy.

The ablest show-window designer in America once cautioned us: "The one thing to avoid is drawing a crowd! Any boob can block the pavement enough to bring out the police reserves. The hard thing is to catch the eye of every possible customer—*and keep the others walking past!*" He meant that in advertising, as in window display, the only attention worth trying for is that which rightfully belongs to the proposition itself. A pretty girl fitting her dancing slippers in the window of a select shoeshop would attract a crowd. But the regular customers

would seek seclusion across the street. When
Anthony Comstock raided "September Morn,"
Monsieur Ortiz took the little picture out of his window. Not because he feared arrest. But because
the crowd drove away his customers.

Old traditions still regard an advertisement as an
end instead of a means. The mechanical side of
attracting attention is, therefore, still hugely over-
estimated. And overworked. A man whose private
eye will pick his own name in the smallest type
instantly out of a whole newspaper page will, as an
advertiser, gravely load his space with heavy illustrations, large type, and larger logotypes.

Those advertisers who hope to force people to accept goods by sheer strength (as well as those who
fancy a strong "institutional" resemblance) will save
money by keeping in mind that skillful *variation,*
not size or repetition, is the right stimulus for attention. So long as there is a change—bigger or
smaller—louder or softer—faster or slower—the *di-*
rection of that change may make little difference.
Even a clock ticking regularly in the room will attract your attention by quietly stopping. The more
powerful a fog-horn and the louder it blows, the
more certain we are to notice its stopping. If the
operator blows continually with full force we soon
set our nerves against it. If the operator is cunning
enough to toot his fog-horn for varying periods at
constantly changing intervals, he can keep us toss-
ing awake all night.

This variation of attention stimuli requires considerable skill. Unless an advertisement be kept quite simple, the reader will get lost and give up. On the other hand, an advertisement can be too simple for its own good. Motoring continually on a straight, smooth boulevard soon loses all interest. Same with a monotonously simple advertisement. Ten years ago, Hollingworth suggested that in order to keep from boring the reader by its very simplicity, any advertisement simple enough to be easily read should combine with its orderly arrangement a carefully calculated dash of complexity.

In calculating this complexity there are two limitations that should be kept in mind. First, that five (5-5-5-5-5) of anything is about all the human eye can comprehend at one glance. This five may be five letters, five words, five dots, or five patterns; but whatever the unit, the eye refuses more than five of it at a single look. Six objects (6-6-6-6-6-6) require two separate looks; and eleven, three. This is particularly valuable in writing headlines, or setting them.

The second principle is that without motion of the eyes the mind cannot at normal reading distance attend to any object or objects that won't fit into a space one inch square or less. This is the average maximum. The average minimum is one-half inch square. The "ideal" average is, therefore, about three-quarters of an inch square. The human eye, remember, is built for motion. Since printed matter doesn't move, the eye must. It stops just long enough to grasp one part, and then skips ahead to the next field of vision. But it cannot, as we observed, read while moving. For the same reason the eye cannot sweep a whole advertisement in one long look. It skips from top to bottom in a series of hops-and-stops. Both to get itself read and to create a pleasant impression, every good advertisement must be constructed cunningly to humor these hops-and-stops.

Never forget that attention at best is brief enough. It flutters like a nervous humming bird. But don't forget, either, that complete control of the direction in which your reader's attention shall shift from first glance to last, is within your power. By logical arrangement and mechanical ingenuity in your layout, you can trap the reader's eyes like two white mice, and coax them consecutively through the successive parts of your advertisement precisely in the order you wish it read.

This trapping of attention through logical, seductive ad-architecture belongs to whomever designs the advertisement as a whole. The part of the compositor is unselfishly to turn out a smooth message, not to achieve a striking bit of typography. Just as actors play up to each speaker in turn, focusing the audience's attention where the lines demand it, the skillful compositor must subordinate his art to sense, rather than play for slanting exclamation points or splendid fancy brackets. Once attention has been caught, the compositor's only important job is to make reading easy.

From our earliest "I-see-a-cat" days in the little

red First Reader we have been taught to start at the upper left-hand corner of a page, work to the right straight across each line, dropping easily and regularly down to the lower right-hand corner. Every device that falls in with this incurable habit adds, of course, an increased probability that the whole advertisement will be read and understood.

But smooth, strong, even lines, however important, are only the beginning. Any fair compositor can handle the black space. It takes a real artist to use the white space.

No more, no less, white space should be paid for than is needed, and every em of white that is bought should be studiously utilized to make the copy easier to understand. Logically distributed white space is the surest way to a quick grasp of the message. At the first glance, spacing must indicate the natural relation of material. Letters should be closer together than words; words closer than lines, and lines than paragraphs. Extra white space should, in advertising, practically never be "justified" as in good book setting. It should be taken up between sentences where possible; if not, between clauses; where absolutely necessary, extra spacing can come between words; but in no circumstances should it disturb the regular space between letters. Far better let spaces run uneven than to "square-up" lines by unusual spacing.

As to the white-space margin: taking one thing with another, a good rule of thumb is to let your white margin on each edge be one-tenth as wide as the space occupied by the copy itself. One-eighth may do better on dull newspaper stock.

Short headings should be set in one line, where space allows. Where longer lines must be used for the heading, the words at the ends of those lines should break not arbitrarily, for appearance sake, but naturally, by the sense of the words. The lines of two-line, three-line, or four-line headings should not be separated with a band of white space. Hold them tight together as one unit. Use the white space as a frame to make that unit stand out.

As to the shape of your advertisement: when in doubt, use rectangles, preferably the classic "Golden Section." For centuries masters of art have agreed on its desirability and developed its possibilities. Famous canvases, pleasing book pages, and especially magnificent architecture, have refined its uses and accustomed our eye to its attractions. That rectangle, reflecting the proportions of approximately three to five, is the most pleasing of all forms. Turned side-wise, so to speak, with a base of five and a height of three, the oblong still achieves harmony possible to no perfect square.

As to type: familiar, well-designed, not too fancy faces assure instant recognition. They speed us forward pleasantly. So do short, tidy sentences. So do crisp paragraphs. Not more than three or four type changes of any sort—whether from size to size, or face to face—should be used throughout the whole setting. Italics in quantity will be found weak, rather than emphatic. Bold face, overdone, will rack your advertisement like a steam calliope in a business office. Instead of convincing the reader it scares her.

Except as pure decoration, capital letters can never be used in long sentences; or worse yet, in solid blocks. In reading, we slide along the upper half of words. The dull uniformity of capitals contrasts unfavorably with the curve and variety of the lower case. Besides, people are much more familiar with lower-case letters. Cover up the lower half of any fairly large line of type in lower case, you will still be able to read along with surprising ease. Try the same thing with a line of capitals. Then you will understand why a block of copy set in capitals is so annoying. The human eye is neither accustomed to reading capital letters nor interested in them. To think out a headline for the purpose of attracting attention, and set it in capital letters, is simply to write in with one hand and rub out with the other.

As the eye skips along we neglect the bottom of all familiar words. More than that, people regularly skip all but the first few letters, taking a chance that words will end according to their guess.

Occasionally this confidence is misplaced; but the saving is worth the risk, and the advertiser should protect himself. Another point to be observed, particularly by layout men who follow the ingenious Heyworth Campbell, is that the eye habitually reads words and not single letters.

Naturally, as anyone can think out for himself, our eyes are at their very best when swinging back and forth along the printed lines in perfectly regular mechanical rhythm. Lines should, therefore, be of uniform length. They should begin and end uniformly. Any changes in length, either at beginning or ending of lines, makes strain and discomfort. Think twice before you disturb, on any account whatever, the regularity of your type swing. For strain and discomfort either cause the reader to quit reading or distract so much of his attention from the message that he might as well have quit.

Along with the theory that people won't read a long advertisement comes the contention that people won't read small type. This persists in the face of every proof to the contrary. Small type is the accepted type. For at least two hundred years before advertising, books accustomed people's eyes to 8-, 9-, 10-point type. Larger advertising type dates back less than a half century. Today—newspapers and magazines, theater programs, financial reports, and every sort of business and social communication are, almost all, printed in 8, 6, and even 5 point. People read small type regularly in everything else. When they won't read small type in advertisements, it's the advertisements they won't read, not the type!

We can dismiss this matter of type size with one paragraph of Mr. Sumner's analysis:[1]

Although it is intended for the same eyes, the advertiser thinks 12 to 24 point type is necessary, while the editor is satisfied with 9 and 10 point. . . . The advertiser averages 250 words to the page, the editor five or six times as many. The editor reserves one-half to three-quarters of an inch

[1] G. Lynn Sumner, *Advertising and Selling,* March 24, 1926.

around the edge of each page as a margin or border of white space. The advertiser is not satisfied with this. Either he increases the margin or he puts a border of some sort around his message.

It is always interesting to run through a magazine and see the advertiser—who pays for space and not words—turn his allotment back into white paper, while the editor—who pays for words and not space —crams his space chuck full of words and pictures! With these pages barely scratching the surface of the subject to which more competent authorities devote volumes, we begin a suggestion or two on the subject of copy. Strictly speaking, not even a pencil sketch or layout should be made until the copy is completely finished. Then the art expert should bring his utmost technical skill to putting over that message. He is an interpreter, not a creator. Shakespeare, one might say parenthetically, *wrote* Hamlet before any of the thousand men who have tried to figure out a stage setting for it. None of these settings would fill the house a single night. "The play's the thing"—not the scenery. The personality of a great art director, like that of a master stage director, shows greatest in the skill with which it is submerged.

CHAPTER XIX

Where Copy Comes In

"I wipe my pen and cork the ink bottle," replied a famous copy man, asked about his first step. That, of course, is a copy writer's way of saying he stops to think. One thing he might think about is whether he writes to fill space already ordered. Or whether space will be bought only when he perfects an idea which will justify somebody's spending $10,000 taking it to the public.

That thinking, of course, belongs to the man who pays for the advertisement. But he, more than likely, is thinking about meeting a schedule. So again and again, expensive advertisements are run without anybody asking anew, in the light of completed copy, whether the message is worth the money.

More often than not, as advertising agency men know, copy is written more or less to fit a preconceived layout.

The layout, of course, is predetermined by the space.

The space is predetermined by the schedule.

The schedule is predetermined by the size of appropriation.

And so, in the last analysis, we find the copy in a given advertisement, if not the actual idea behind the message, dictated not by what the space might be made to pay, but by what was appropriated to pay for the space.

This may sound unimportant. It is vital. If the copy man had to write something to justify new space, if the advertiser had to decide afresh how much space to order, some clearer thinking about copy might come. One great advertising man has already suggested that size and shape of space should be determined by the importance and nature of the finished message, just as a packing box is determined by the bulk and value of the object to be shipped.

To any executive tempted to slight these really important matters to dabble in his own advertising copy, we repeat *Punch's* famous advice to a young man about to be married, "DON'T!" Get the best copy man your money can buy. This doesn't necessarily mean the most expensive. In copy writers, as in so many other things, the best is the cheapest. An extravagant price paid a copy man may, of course, reflect his ability to sell his copy as much as the ability of his copy to sell. But most really good copy men have not sold themselves nearly so skillfully as they have sold others. So there are still excellent copy writers with less pay than a really fashionable plumber. Get hold of one of them—a good one—pay him well—and tell him what you want to *do!* His business is to translate what you want to say into whatever will make people do what you have in mind.

If you are the man who pays the advertising bills, here is a short parable for you: Some years ago, when a famous ball player was cracking out a home run nearly every day, a news association sent its equally famous sport reporter to persuade the star to write a short signed story about each and every home run. The reporter sat in the press box. The slugger lugged his heavy bat to the plate. Half a minute later he was trotting around the bases.

"Well, now," said the reporter, "what do you want to say? It looked to me like a high, fast ball hit into the right-field stands. But I may be mistaken. Will you please give me full particulars?"

"Say," answered the hero, "you're a writer, aren't you? And I'm a ball player? All right, then. Let's both stick to our own stuff and we'll both get by."

This is about all we have to say to the man who pays. If the writer can't put over your message, fire him. But don't break his heart by endless little "corrections." You won't improve the copy. You merely drive the writer into trying to write for *you*. We are all ignoramuses about one another's professions. See that it's your message; but let one man fix the words. Leave writing to writers.

"Every copy of the *Saturday Evening Post* goes to press," says a cynical agent, "with the best line in each advertisement buried in the waste basket of the man who O.K.'d it." "The client," says another agent, "has an absolutely God-given ability to detect the strongest paragraph or phrase in any piece of copy—and to strike it out!"

Some day in a higher civilization advertising agents will decline to serve clients who cannot button up their blue pencils. Yet those agents themselves may run off on a pet tangent. The ideal arrangement is a compromise. The advertising buyer prescribes precisely what he wishes to accomplish. The advertising writer interprets that policy into copy. Wherever revisions are to be made the advertiser will state his reasons. The writer will put them into writing. And so, back and forth, until the advertiser is absolutely satisfied. But every word in the copy will belong to the copy writer.

That is all there is in this chapter for the man who pays. The rest is devoted to a few patriarchal personal words to the young man behind the copy desk. Any others read further only at the risk of eavesdropping. To copy men we say:

You cannot learn to write a sonnet from a schedule of its scansion and rhyme plan. Your young nephew Orville, perhaps, knows them perfectly. You won't, nevertheless, mistake his work in a high-school magazine for that of Shakespeare and Milton. If you are Miss Abigail Hecklebury you may study up motivation and characterization of the short story, and still fall far short of O. Henry's best work. Rules are well worth learning. But human experience is worth most. It is worth while to know every rule. And then to know how to be bigger than them all.

In the next chapter are the stories of three remarkably successful advertisements. All three have been reprinted over and over again—scores, maybe hundreds of times. This reprinting of successful copy is something that the "general publicity" advertiser disdains to do. Having achieved a really good advertisement, he usually runs once in his list of magazines and snatches it out as if ashamed. Actually, he thinks "everybody" has seen it. "Everybody" is a big word. If you could see "everybody" all at once, you would be stunned for a week. And if you had to teach "everybody" simply to say "Oh" when they met you—well, eternity would be too short. The more businesslike mail-order advertiser, therefore, does not change his copy just for the sake of a change. He finds his one sure-fire appeal and sticks. He keeps his best copy running until it is threadbare. He knows that, even when years old, it may still outpull his best piece of new copy. He knows he needs almost infinite repetition of a single idea to batter his way into the public consciousness. Remember the oft-quoted observation of Mr. E. M. Swazey:

Every market is constantly dropping off from the top and building up from the bottom. Each year 2,500,000 newly-born Americans begin consuming, 400,000 somewhat older Americans are graduating from high schools, 1,250,000 brides begin housekeeping and 1,250,000 young husbands begin spending their pay envelopes in a different way. Each year 2,000,000 families move into new homes or apartments. On the other hand, every year 1,400,000 Americans die, and almost an equal number, perhaps, lose their productive capacity. Thus, in a few years, a market may become entirely new.

To some advertisers this constant change may discourage altogether any hope of a real impression. Wiser heads find in it the consolation they need never worry about novelty. Mr. Mead, of the Mead

Cycle Company, used to say that not for $10,000 would he change a word of his little old advertisement. In the famous *"$2.00 may save you $200"* copy used steadily for fifteen years, *Vogue* has an eternal advertisement.

Mr. J. Howie Wright, in describing the most profitable piece of direct advertising he had ever seen, tells of a list that had been worked three times a year steadily for six years, bringing in, nevertheless, on a particularly effective mailing, 420 return cards from every 1,000 circulars.

The Barrett-Cravens Company used the same letter sixteen times in one year, some lists receiving it as many as five times. It brought in $29,352 worth of business at a cost of $4,158. Says Mr. E. J. Heimer,[1] secretary of the company:

Our test mailing of 500 was so satisfactory that we immediately sent the same letter to our entire list—with gratifying results. When it came time to send this list another letter, we were unable to write anything that suited nearly as well as this first letter. So after a little preliminary discussion we decided to send the same letter to the same list. We did, and again it pulled well. From then on we have been using this letter ten and twelve times yearly, not necessarily on the same lists, but often so. During the year 1925 we used it sixteen times, some lists receiving it as often as five times, and each time it pulled well.

One extraordinary advertisement, run a hundred times over, will do more good than 150 less convincing advertisements run once. If people like your

[1] *Printers' Ink,* May 27, 1926.

advertisement, and are influenced by it, they will be just as faithful to it—over a period of years—as they are to "Abie's Irish Rose" or to Rosa Bonheur's "Horse Fair," or to Abbey's murals in the Boston Public Library, or to Niagara Falls. People are just like that! They don't help you one bit. *You* have to help them. It takes long, continued, tireless hammering at just one idea to force that idea into their reluctant minds. When in doubt, stick to your original idea. When up against it, rewrite your best advertisement. Better still, run the best advertisement over again. When it bores the man who pays the bills, it is probably just beginning to make a dent on the public's mind. We repeat. The public is wonderfully well able to skip your advertisement, to resist your "argument," to know nothing and care less about you. When up against it in a tennis match, Lacoste doesn't try a new trick service. He serves his regular, placed delivery. Bobby Jones doesn't try a new club when an open championship hangs on a single stroke. He takes his regular iron or mashie, and plays his regular shot to the green.

Therefore, the first rule for young copy writers to unlearn is that an advertisement will attract attention only if it is "different." Whole lifetimes are wasted in advertising agencies by men trying at all costs to be original. A reader, unfortunately, is not necessarily more attracted by a different advertisement than he would be by a different breakfast. If he likes bacon and eggs, you can easily get his attention (for perhaps an unfavorable second) by offering him antelope steak and a bottle of beer. If, less original than this, you merely offer him hominy and kidneys, he may wave you away languidly so that you cannot feel you have harpooned his attention at all.

Walt Mason, Dr. Frank Crane, Mabel Urner, Eddie Guest and the other most widely read writers in America would tell you. They play just about the same tune every day. They are well paid for it —far better than if Mr. Guest suddenly tried to write a grand-opera libretto, while Dr. Crane produced a novel in the style of Sinclair Lewis. Probably they would enjoy the change, but not the results. Therefore they sit tight. And the public pays them daily, weekly, and annually for doing their own kind of work every time.

Second of the rules to unlearn is that you can so charm the reader with the *looks* of your advertisement and beauty of your writing that he will be charmed—also and simultaneously—with your product. There are advertising men who insist, above all else, their copy shall be beautifully decorated and adhere to the time-honored canons of the typographic art. It is these men who lay out an advertisement first; then summon a copy writer to supply "87 words of stuff." And that is what he obediently supplies—87 words of stuff!

One really good idea, constantly and skillfully harped on, is worth more in advertising than Caslon's most perfect masterpiece; more than the greatest picture Orpen can paint; more than a brand-new piece of copy by Rudyard Kipling himself. The "Say It with Flowers," slogan, backed by 4,500 florists all over the United States, is estimated to have increased the sale of cut flowers at least 400 per cent in seven years. Another sales idea nearly as effective is the "greeting card." Co-operative advertising started seven years ago to induce all-year use of these cheerful little messengers enabled the manufacturers not only to sell three times as many Christmas cards, but to sell, without Christmas, more cards than they previously sold in a whole year.[1] The first Twentieth Century Limited went up the New York Central tracks June 1, 1902. It carried 54 passengers. Today, the Twentieth Century Limited carries about a third of all the passengers between New York and Chicago—as many a year as all the Atlantic liners carry between New York and Europe in their first-class cabins. Incidentally, it earned in 1926 more than $10,500,000.

It is lack of ideas like the "XXth Century Limited" or "Say It with Flowers" that makes so much short advertising copy seem long. And wastes so much money for advertisers who try to make up for blankness by adding white space.

Josh Billings didn't care how much a man said so long as he said it in a few words. Brevity of words is always acceptable. Generally indispensable. But not brevity of ideas. Brevity of advertising means, rather, the telegraphic style; the quick paragraph;

[1] Hugh E. Agnew, *Cooperative Advertising by Competitors.*

the few phrases that crush into a single sentence not only one buying motive, but powerful combinations of buying motives.

The theory that a man or woman who will read a short advertisement won't read a long one has little to commend it. People read what they are interested in. If anything interests you *enough* you will read it through a magnifying glass hours at a time. A man interested *enough* will search a whole library looking for a single additional fact. The only way bigger space can be made to pay for the increase is to put in more copy. Larger advertisements using the same words seldom give larger results. Over and over again tests have proved that bigger type alone will not proportionately improve pulling power, and that a simple increase in white space helps only the poorer advertisements. Copy and headlines count.

A good advertiser uses confidently all the copy he needs. He heads it with strong display to catch the interested eye, just as a newspaper editor fits a headline. For the experienced advertiser knows that, even in large quantities, the effortless attention of any person who won't read a reasonably long advertisement has no great value. There isn't so much difference in people. A man won't listen if he is not interested. He won't read if he is not interested. He won't buy if he is not interested.

Mr. Pickens' observation on length [1] may be worth noting:

[1] James H. Pickens, *Business Correspondence Handbook.*

It can be said without hesitation that the long letter is normal and that a short letter is not normal; that the long letter is safe where the short letter is dangerous. The word "long" here means complete, rather than quantity of copy.

Experience shows that even those who order from notoriously long mail-order advertisements seldom read all the copy. Each studies enough to satisfy himself on the particular points that most interest him. Yet the mere fact all the information is there inspires confidence that brings his immediate order. So Abraham Lincoln spoke for advertising when he said a man's legs should be long enough to reach the ground. That is the quickest, surest way to measure copy. You have, naturally, to talk longer to sell a man life insurance than to induce his wife to accept a free sample of face cream to make her beautiful. Brevity is important, but not nearly so important as personality—red-hot hustling life. If your business is really active and anxious to be of service, set that spirit glowing in your every paragraph.

The young copy writer will find nearly all the rules of advertisement writing negative rules, like those against length. "Don't use long words," says one authority. He proves his point by instancing the Lord's Prayer, the Twenty-third Psalm, and the Gettysburg Address. Yet the Gettysburg Address foams out in its very first sentence into a shower of polysyllables. It is *not* written in plain Anglo-Saxon, but in most ornate Latin English. Nothing is more remote from common speech than to say "fourscore and seven" when you mean plain eighty-seven. Even so the average copy writer does well to step clear of long words. Also to go easy on negative suggestions. Like brandy or dynamite or parachutes or puns, all may prove wonderfully effective for those who know just how to use them. But they are dangerous used with less than maximum skill.

Forgetting all the things *not* to do, remember that a frank, sincere, personal tone is—the quickest method of securing confidence. And sales. An attractive, forceful *friendly* personality showing through the copy helps more than any thing else to turn noncommittal attention into a steady, trustful interest. There is a town in Illinois called Walsh. It has—or had—a population of 36. A general store run there by Mr. Henry A. Hinderer does a business of $100,000 a year. Every week he mails a mimeographed selling bulletin to each of the 500 or so homes on his list. It costs him only $18 a week; but it takes maybe $50,000 a year away from the big Chicago mail-order houses.

"Eight years ago," explains Mr. Hinderer, "an idea struck me that if I would send a letter into each home in this territory and make it read as if I was talking to them, they would look forward to receiving it the same as a letter from some relative or friend." The weekly letter is a carefully selected lot of news; auction sales, church socials, other neighborhood interests, with a suggestion or two on farming methods, and plenty of jokes.

In a town much bigger than Walsh, another man determined to test for himself the personal note in

selling. He divided 5,000 names on his mailing list
into two equal lots. Lot "A" he mailed simply as a
form letter with nothing more personal than his
signature. With lot "B," however, he took the
trouble to look up each of the 2,500 names in the files
and, through a glance at the correspondence, was
enabled to add a really personal postscript. (Imagine any ordinary advertiser taking this much
trouble!) But it paid this enterprising letter writer
well. Lot "A" in simple circular form brought only
$386 in orders. Lot "B," from the same number of
mailings to the same list, brought $2,144. In other
words, each personal postscript throughout the whole
2,500 letters added $7 worth of business.

  Seymour Eaton used to tell how he once won a
dinner by the same experiment:

A Boston manufacturer was selling a commonplace household article through a magazine advertisement asking prospective customers to write for his circular.

To each reply he was sending out an imitation typewritten
letter with the name and address filled in.

My friend had a hundred inquiries on his desk. I suggested
that he take any ten of these inquiries. Then sit down comfortably and dictate a personal letter to each. . . . Then
take these ten personal letters and have his stenographer use
them as models for duplicate form answers to the other ninety
inquiries. . . . I bet him a dinner that he would get more
orders from the ten personally dictated letters than from the
other ninety. I won the bet.

  A mail-order house, in dull season, put out 18,000
letters. The 4 per cent reply scarcely paid for the
stamps. Fifteen men were called together to dis-

cuss the situation. (An interesting comment on the importance of a single mailing among professional men of letters!) Instead of following the accepted fashion of advertisers, and all trying to improve one piece of copy, they decided each should write and mail a special series of his own. Each was to make his letters as personal as he wanted and as different as possible from ordinary, everyday stuff. Twelve out of the 15 series pulled a combined average of more than 30 per cent, as against the original 4 per cent. Even averaged among 12 different men, the personal touch was worth 26 additional answers for each 100 letters—more than three times the possible improvement suggested for all advertising by Mr. Pickens and Dr. Starch.

Even in printed catalogues the personal note—provided it be sincere, straightforward personality—pays rich profits. Henry Field of Shenandoah, Iowa, sells seeds. He is said to distribute more catalogues than any other similar business. Anyway, he is successful enough to hire 400 people in season. Here is the way he talks to his customers—in his 1926 catalogue:

Any of you who visited me last summer will recognize this picture as the way I look when I sit and visit with you from my old armchair in my office. And this is just a little more of that same visiting. We have a chance for a good visit once a year, whether you come to see me or not. . . . And tell your neighbor about us. That's the way our business grows. I have been working along with you in this seed business for a long time, now, twenty-five or thirty years, maybe more. And I hope we may be together for a long time yet to come.

Call this Old Home Week, if you like. But in a prosaic metropolitan business, far removed from an Iowa seed farm, the president set out to bring closer contact between the company and its customers by humanizing the company catalogue with photographs of executives and notes concerning their work and policies. Personal letters began to flow in from all over the country. Another equally simple change in attitude on the part of another colossal corporation brought in a single year—*without cost*—an addition of 130,000 sales leads.

"People prefer to know individuals"; wrote Seymour Eaton. They like to feel that they are being served by men, and not simply getting their goods out of the hopper of a treadmill. And, if people have any kicking to do, it is mighty unsatisfactory, for instance, to kick a Standard Trading Company, or a Midwestern Railroad.

"There is no doubt," adds a prominent banker, "that the development of the electric light and power companies has been sadly hampered, in their effort to reach the farms, by the fact that they are called by such names as the Twin Falls and Southeastern Company. If they had been named the Henry Roberts Electric Company, or the Brown, Jones & Smith Company, progress would have been much faster." Using the name "Graybar" for the "Supply Division of Western Electric Co." is one of the wisest steps in recent business christenings.

For somewhat the same reason, the most interesting form of expression, to most people, is a story.

Few people, if you will notice, can talk to one another for as long as one minute without dropping into the narrative form:

"I went ——"
"She came to me and ——"
"It seems there was an Irishman who ——"

All such phrases introduce narratives. Oddly enough, most advertising writers ignore this almost universal preference to venture the vastly more difficult trick form of "argument," or high-sounding statement. The most famous persuaders in history knew better. Whether appealing to any of a man's pocket nerves, or to his wife's social aspirations, or to his fear of death, or to anything else in people's minds and hearts, it is usually safe to plod along after Saint Paul and Abraham Lincoln, and see if the point you want to make can be gently introduced in narrative form.

But no amount of story-telling nor even of personality will ever overcome indefiniteness. Some time ago, Mr. T. J. Buttikofer and the writers were experimenting as how best to get subscriptions for a certain magazine. Our not too-good-looking letter, boiled down to less than a page, brought in 1½ per cent subscriptions from a reasonably large mailing to an only fair list. A little later a noted woman copy writer was paid $1,000 to do something really worth while. Her expensive language, appropriately dressed by the printer, brought just three-eighths of one per cent returns—not enough to pay the postage. She was selling editorial policy, abstract ideas, general glory! We were selling subscriptions. Nothing is half so important as a clear idea of exactly what you are selling. An able advertiser will, in addition, have pictured in his own mind precisely what the reader is going to think—*and do*—upon reading the copy.

For, even with all the good qualities suggested in this chapter, your advertisement will never do much until it gets them to focus sharply on bringing the reader to one definite action. The more definite the suggestion, the more definite the response. As Professor Walter Dill Scott once put it:

The possible customer cannot be depended upon to do any constructive thinking. Unless the advertiser has made the method of securing the goods so plain that the mental picture must be seen by the new customer, he will not see it. *And will be likely to leave the advertisement with no thought of securing the goods advertised.*

Said the charming Miss Ina Claire in a dressing-room talk with Karl Kitchen:

I learned one very important thing about the art of acting from Cyril Scott. It is: Never do but one thing at a time. For instance, don't make a gesture and speak at the same time. For the audience will watch your gesture and miss your speech.

Arthur Brisbane told his listeners at a Sphinx Club dinner years ago almost exactly the same thing. Said Mr. Brisbane, as closely as we can remember:

You must send your ideas through your readers' minds like freight cars through a tunnel. One idea at a time! and each one tightly coupled up with the idea just before and just behind it!

The first and last thing for a copy man to remember is that if he hasn't in his own mind a clear picture of the definite action he expects from his readers, he will fare little better than a golfer who merely swings at the ball and hopes for the best. Good advertising, really, is a lot like good golf. Not a matter of brute force. Nor luck. Your skillful advertiser knows the few basic motives that govern all human action. His trained copy writers know the average man's response to various printed words. He knows exactly what he intends to do with every sentence. So, with carefully calculated appeal, he makes large numbers of people perform some one simple act he has in mind. For, like the professional golfer, a really good advertising man tries always to hole out. He is not content just to shoot in the general direction of the green in the hope the hole will help him. When golf holes begin to meet your putts halfway, readers will begin doing, on account of your advertising, things you didn't definitely ask them to do.

CHAPTER XX

How Three Successful Advertisements Were Written

BACK in 1909 a young publisher in New York sat down to write an advertisement for an almost unknown fashion magazine he had just bought. He needed subscriptions. He had little to spend getting them. He could not afford crews of canvassers, nor expensive news-stand campaigns. He needed copy that would pull strongly whether used in other publications or in circular letter form.

Now, any ordinary copy man, grinding out three or four pieces a day, would infallibly thrust his mind into neutral gear and write something like this:

Dame Fashion is Capricious

You will know her "infinite variety" by reading this exclusive magazine. It gives you fashion sketches from Paris, and the latest news of the smart Fifth Avenue shops. Exclusive photographs of people in society, etc.

Beautifully illustrated, set in Cheltenham Mild, and signed by the publisher in large letters, that advertisement would have satisfied any man already in this fashion field. It was the accepted method. But did it satisfy this particular young publisher, with vigorous ambition? It did not. He buried himself in his private office for several days, littering the furniture with typed scraps of paper. He drove a patient secretary through a storm of rewrites. His copy technician abandoned all hope of home. He called in other assistants and picked their brains. And after a three days' battle the printer was called in to set this:

> ### "$2 Spent for *Vogue*
> ### Will Save You $200"
>
> The gown you buy and never wear is the really expensive gown. Hats, gloves, coats, shoes that just miss being what you want are the ones you cannot afford to buy.

This copy pulled from the opening day. It was particularly effective in the Social Registers which nothing else could touch. It even brought in subscriptions, at a profit, from newspaper space. Repeated, it pulled again. Word for word it is still pulling, after eighteen years. Today it sells subscriptions to débutantes just as it once sold subscriptions to their débutante mothers.

You will observe three rather interesting things about it.

Instead of a merely "clever" catch phrase, this headline jumps right down to cases and offers the reader a chance to save $200. Two hundred dollars is important money.

Instead of forcing the reader to read the whole advertisement, this writer sums up his case so that it can be taken in at a glance.

It has been said over and over again that readers have little curiosity about an advertiser and his product or problems. Tests prove this every day. People have themselves—*and themselves only*—constantly on their minds. Women face a definite clothes problem. Each one wishes she could be better dressed than she is. Mr. Condé Nast promised each woman that she could achieve this and still save money—not just a little money, but a really good lot of money. But did he start off in a bookkeeper's humdrum way and tell her that $200 was the equivalent of a hundred theater tickets, or make her realize pictorially that it equaled the first payment on a motor? No. He let the word $200 do its own work. Inclusion of obvious details is the sure sign of an incompetent writer.

After gaining attention and successfully securing attention and conviction—two very necessary elements—Mr. Nast carried on from that point as gently as the Twentieth Century Limited gathers speed. It has always been a principle of his to "keep the reader nodding in agreement." After gaining attention and successfully securing confidence, Mr. Nast's only remaining task was to flog the convinced reader into action. His "closing paragraph" came, for those days, with the crack of a whiplash.

SEND NO MONEY: Merely use this coupon, etc.

This is old stuff now. It was not old in 1909.

Three days' concentrated effort by a man of real genius produced an advertisement that has worked for him steadily for seventeen years and may work for seventeen more. Three days seem a small price to pay for it. But few men are able to concentrate so long on a single problem without swamping themselves in complications.

Three years elapse, as they say on the theater programs. We meet another man willing to work hard at a difficult job. He was a young man in those days— 1912. But he had had good experience. He had peddled things from house to house (which ought to be compulsory early training for every advertising writer). He had a subordinate position in a large publishing house. Among its books was a three-year-old set of the World's Greatest Literature, in fifty volumes. The publishers had exhausted the conventional ways of advertising. They used copy about like this:

KNOW THE WORLD'S IMMORTAL LITERATURE

In these beautifully bound volumes you have spread before you a feast of great stories and essays; these books will be an ornament to your home. . . .

Miles of such stuff were written for these books; the public yawned it into the waste basket. Sales reports were adverse. The set seemed, like so many other "novelties," gradually relinquishing its hopes of eternity.

And then this tall, quiet, thoughtful young chap sat down and wrote an advertisement. (But before quoting it, let us add that he found an old print somewhere of Queen Marie Antoinette. It was a chest-

nut of a picture.   But most people have a vast fond-
ness for chestnuts—if you doubt it, listen to the
"stories" they tell and listen to.)   Anyway, here's
the advertisement:

THIS IS MARIE ANTOINETTE RIDING TO HER DEATH

Do you know her tragic story?   How the once beautiful
queen of France, broken and humbled, her beauty gone, was
jostled through the bloody streets of Paris to the guillotine?
. . . Out of all the millions of books in the world there are a
few, and only a few, so great that they will never die.   These
are the books that every intelligent person *must* know.

This copy brought in coupons at a rate that
astonished the publisher, who had practically abandoned active sales effort for "Harvard Classics."   The
young man—his name is Bruce Barton—proceeded
to write other advertisements.   They pulled, too.   In
a year his copy had not only helped put Dr. Eliot's
Five-Foot Shelf back into the public consciousness,
but had set afoot a revolution in *all* book advertising.
An advertisement headed with an interesting picture
and a headline taken right out of the book itself is a
commonplace now.   It was radically new in 1912,
and Barton was its inventor.   Largely because this
set of books was well advertised, and vigorously sold
by salesmen who gained a new and vivid appreciation from the advertising, it has enjoyed since 1912
more than $15,000,000 in sales.   Instead of dying in
three years, as did the *Memoirs* of General Grant,
and other passing sensations, Dr. Eliot is stronger
after fourteen years than ever before.

Now for another long skip. The writers of this book have been in business together, in one way or another, for seventeen years. Sometimes in the same office and at fairly adjacent desks. Writer B was Writer A's assistant copy writer for *Vogue* and *Vanity Fair;* afterward he became for some time writer A's advertising agent for the Five-Foot Shelf, the Collier-Lakeside Single Volume Shakespeare, Wells' *Outline of History,* and various other books.

Moreover, at other intervals in the pursuit of a livelihood, both have been intrusted with mail-order advertising copy for many different commodities. There are few articles of merchandise they have not advertised and few possible services—ranging from business courses to employment agencies, theatrical performances, and many more. Also, both writers have been editors, at one time or another, of magazines of large circulation, and have thereby had an opportunity to study professionally the effects of almost every conceivable type of appeal. Let these words of autobiography suffice as an excuse for the personal details that follow.

There came about between them one day the question of selling as a popular single volume the famous *Autobiography of Benvenuto Cellini.* It is in every public library. Also in this same Dr. Eliot's Five-Foot Shelf, and many other collections. We had been observing for several years the popular trend toward history and biography. Here, sold only to a few hundred cultivated book lovers, was one of the most vivid human documents the world has ever produced.

Not even tonight's fresh tabloids excel the lusty effrontery of Benvenuto bottled up four centuries ago. Moreover, Joseph Schildkraut's success in the play "Firebrand" had been just the spark needed to touch off a popular demand for our dash into classical romance. So Writer A determined to offer a single-volume Cellini—the first on the market.

And what about the man called in to write copy about it? What were his mental processes? They can be quite easily summarized. He thought, first, that he ought to read the book all over again—his memory of it was hazy. It took him about twenty hours, which he largely spent in reading himself to sleep. But it is not, he decided, a soporific book.

(Upon your true familiarity with the product or service you are advertising depends largely the pulling power of your copy. Make a note of this. It is why, for instance, so many department store advertising managers and writers fail; they know or care so little about the merchandise they are advertising.)

Of course, while Writer B was doggedly reading Benvenuto—which took about two weeks, in the manner described—his client, the publisher, was yelling and shouting for copy. These yells, when epistolary and not verbal, went into the writer's wastepaper basket. Finally, the writer finished his reading and sat down to write the copy. And here, faithfully recorded, are his mental impressions as he sat, staring at the white paper in his machine:

This is a pretty fine old book, after all.
Wish I had lived in those times—more color and life than

you find around Manhattan nowadays. Oh, well! Better to read about these things than do 'em.

Nasty old character, Benvenuto, but quick on the draw. No—he used a sword. Rapier.

Made good silverware, too; better than Paul Revere did.

And called a spade a spade.

Frank, like Pepys. Lots of men have the same adventures and impulses now, but they don't confess them, in their autobiographies.

Wish they did.

The frank record of any man's life would be the greatest book ever written, but nobody dares do it.

Wonder how to start this copy, anyway?

Bet you a lot of men and women would like to read this book, if they really had confidence that old Benvenuto was a real character, and a highly picturesque one, and tore things up in his day. Now, let's see. . . .

So passed a morning, with a lot of sheets of paper crumpled up and thrown in the basket, where reposed the client's fourth letter beginning: "It is now three weeks since we asked you for copy on our Cellini volume. We do not wish to seem insistent, but —"

"Damn your insistency," murmured the copy writer, as he went out for lunch.

But after lunch (which is generally the worst moment in all the day for concentrated thought) he sat down again and evolved these built-up headlines:

LOVER, SWORDSMAN, DEBAUCHEE

Supreme Artist in Gold and Silver

Here is your chance to own the Complete Unexpurgated Autobiography of Benvenuto Cellini.

It was the word *"debauchee"* that took the longest

time to write—you will observe that it is the word you see first and remember longest. The writer picked it out, after long trial of all the possible synonyms, and there are at least a dozen. *"Debauchee"* seemed to be the most unusual, and yet not so unusual as to be unknown to the reader. The writer guessed—correctly as it proved—that this was a word that would attract attention. (It—the single word *"debauchee"*—caused one nice little publication to drop the advertisement and brought a procession of protests from equally dull larger publications.) It was the only word that really fitted— Cellini was not a mere prodigal, not a wastrel, not a *roué*. He was either a libertine or a *debauchee*. And, of those two words *debauchee* is less hackneyed.

After that, the copy really wrote itself:

Friend and boon companion of Michael Angelo—protégé of many Popes—duelist, carouser, perfect artist in metals, sculptor of Hercules in marble and bronze, and designer of the great "Medusa" which has thrilled generations of artists. . . .

As we came to the end of that copy, Writer A said "Good enough so far as it goes. You have made them want it. But you have left out the most important part of all. You haven't given them the *excuse* for buying it. All sales are based on emotion; but the deeper the emotion, the greater the necessity for the appearance of intellectual action also. Give me your pencil!" And Writer A added:

Are you interested in Art? Here is a priceless manual of the age of Michael Angelo. *In History?* Here are Italy and

France from 1500 to 1562 pictured by one who swung a sword with his own hand in the sack of Rome. *In Sociology?* Here is the sixteenth century violent and licentious, lived before your very eyes. *In Literature?* Here is a masterpiece of narrative, written by a braggart and a murderer, a sculptor and musician.

And the finished advertisement has run successfully for two years as this book goes to press.

Actual time spent in composition of this advertisement:

> Preparation (reading the book)...... 20 hours
> Copy writing .... 4 "
> Revision, arguing with client, etc..... 2 "

But, as 5,000 copies were sold at $3 a copy, this time was a good investment for all concerned.

These three pictures may mean nothing in particular. At least they are real. The advertisements are far from the best ever written, but they accomplished precisely what they were sent out to do.

CHAPTER XXI

The Gentle Art of Getting Results

A poor white in Texas, who won himself $1,000,-000 by being too lazy to move from a starving chicken ranch where some one discovered oil, was invited to contribute to a college.

"Why?" he asked.

"For posterity," he was urged.

"What in h —— did posterity ever do for me?"

Ignorant and profane, the old fellow's point of view is understandable. It parallels Professor Ripley on huge corporation surpluses. And B. C. Forbes, when he says:

Heads of corporations have told me, with a chuckle, that their annual report skillfully concealed such and such a number of millions of dollars of assets. They sincerely felt that they were doing the right thing by being, as they would call it, "very conservative."

So "conservative" that the average manufacturing business hands out to its stockholders only about three and one-half cents of each dollar of its earnings. If the average laboring man were equally cautious with his Saturday pay, some of these great businesses would have no surpluses to conserve. Advertising, anyway, is one industry that owes its prosperity to the optimism of the spending millions.

When their buying stops, prosperity stops, and when prosperity stops, advertising wilts.

Nevertheless, we find even advertisers building, in theory, anyway, toward a two-, five-, or ten-year objective with no apparent concern for the present. Is this magnificent breadth of vision? Or what?

"The only good Indian is a dead Indian," was an early Western aphorism as to unreliability. The only good advertising—from a cold business view-point—is the advertisement that does it now! Our boyhood recollections are filled with Columbia, Rambler, and Pope-Hartford bicycles. Later on we recollect Heatherbloom Petticoats. Where now is the cumulative effect of advertising bicycles and women's petticoats? Where is Sunny Jim? And Spotless Town? And Prudential's Gibraltar?

These ideas, no doubt, repaid long ago the millions spent establishing them, and so are no longer on the books. That merely enforces our suggestion of harvesting advertising immediately it ripens. If, on the other hand, Gibraltar and Spotless Town—not to mention bicycles and petticoats—didn't in their own day completely repay the cost of their advertising, who is to pay it now? And to what current account will he charge the still uncollected portion?

Take Phoebe Snow and the Smith Brothers! "Trade" and "Mark," at best, were never Valentinos. Since whiskers ceased, they seem even less winsome. Phoebe Snow, quite contrarily, was an altogether charming creation. But the ungainly Smith Brothers continue an asset of ever-increasing value, while lovely Phoebe languishes. What is the financial status of an advertising idea thrown overboard at the height of its popularity? Machinery and equipment are written off for wear and tear; patents and copyrights for obsolescence. How does an honest, intelligent auditor account for discontinued advertising? And, along the same line of reasoning, when advertising isn't calculated to produce immediate results, how can any accountant justify a failure to set up a reserve for its depreciation?

That advertising is "salesmanship on paper" we have been glibly told for years. But the reason for salesmanship is the signed order. Any salesman who reports only "good interviews" becomes a joke. One of the most incisive criticisms ever made of advertising was Mr. E. T. Gundlach's quiet suggestion that an advertiser should always remember to put into his copy some good reason for buying.

Any dollar brought back by any advertising today is certainly as good as it will be in 1938. And, unless there is a ghastly error in the merchant's rapid turnover or the banker's compounded interest, the quick dollar should be the valuable dollar in advertising as well. Furthermore, until America's population catches up with its production, the first need of American business is buying—liberal, universal, continuous and immediate. Then again, while advertising is often considered an investment, never forget that in these kaleidoscopic days some new invention, unexpected competition, radical political situation, may wipe out that investment just as it arrives at a golden old age.

Nevertheless, grant for sake of argument it is still an economic, patriotic thing for an advertiser to plant his advertising vineyard so its accumulated immortality will enrich his stockholder's grandchildren. Even so, it is not so easy. Contrary to accepted theory, advertising for future results is a dangerous and difficult task. Planting advertising depth bombs to explode among posterity requires nice calculation. It is like shooting a gun softly. Or jumping gently out of the window. Or trying to pull a brassie swing down to a putt. Mental reactions are hard to put into a refrigerator. They are too like your morning cup of coffee:—either hot or nothing. Sam Slick defined a progressive mortician as one who knows how to collect for his service while the tears are rolling. Quick action and large regular sales are advertising's surest and safest way to future fame. Sears Roebuck and Child's are likely to be household words when fifty of the most impressive Bokprizers of their period have been forgotten.

"Fingy" Connors of Buffalo, on being reproved for his dazzling diamonds, retorted laconically, "Those as has 'em generally wears 'em." Lots of advertisers dissemble all interest in advertising results. Beneath this apparent indifference, we suppose every advertiser wants his advertising to pay. And profitable advertising means four things in one: *reaching* (1) *as soon as possible* (2) *the greatest number who will* (3) *buy at the earliest moment.*

And doing this, so far as possible, (4) *without paying an extra penny to reach another solitary soul.* This accomplishment, needless to say, calls for abundant skill. All advertisements are subject to strong outside influences.[1] Besides the major cycles that affect a whole campaign, each separate advertisement has its own peculiar problems. Seasons, holidays, national calamities, local celebrations, make unexpected differences in results. In a rainy spell the family reads and mail-order advertisers profit. A fine-weather holiday week-end takes everybody outdoors. And advertisers in the Sunday newspapers pay for it. After the big Southern hurricane in 1926 the Bermuda traffic fell to nothing overnight. To bring bookings back to normal took ten days. An Eastern blizzard during California's winter advertising never fails to stimulate a heavy increase in inquiries.

The bigger mail houses keep a staff of observers timing their industry to weather and crop reports. But the ordinary advertiser blissfully ignores most of the intangible elements that make or break his campaign.

Monday finds both the housekeepers and business men almost too busy for advertising. Nor is Saturday a great deal better. Summer week-ends need watching. Just as Wednesdays and Thursdays are the most responsive week days, the middle of the month tends to better selling than either end. The middle of the year, however, is quite another thing.

[1] For the effect of these influences, see pages 12 and 13.

Circulars or keyed advertisements that look profitable in November or March melt away miserably in July. August is perhaps the slowest month; February, perhaps, the best; October, close behind, is nearly twice as good as July. Returns, around Labor Day, Thanksgiving, Christmas, New Year's, Fourth of July, Decoration Day, and Lincoln's or Washington's Birthday will often be cut in half. These holidays sometimes reduce results as much as 75 per cent. Besides the regular feast days that thin down attention, we have noticed, in selling high-price units, that the public gives itself a buying holiday about the time income taxes must be paid or the tax figures calculated. A slow business season, a market too well worked recently, a market not yet educated to a new sort of goods, social disturbances, wars, murders, and elections—all cut sharply into any—and *all*—advertisements. The only sure way to avoid risk is to make tests so far below average conditions that any proposition which pays in the test may be counted certain in actual advertising.

All this fluctuation is, of course, amply allowed for in the rates you pay for your circulation. People are always talking about throwing circulars into waste baskets. Three out of every four circular letters may be thrown away unopened—and still leave ample room for profits. One firm selling securities by mail makes a good profit from sales to eight-tenths of one per cent of the original list. For high-class magazines, the average rate per agate line is only $2 for 100,000 circulation. And in newspapers only eighteen cents per 100,000. Even with an article selling as low as $1 an advertiser can pay the cost of his page in the *New York Times Sunday Magazine* by selling only 240 people in every 100,000 circulation he buys. This leaves him a safety margin of 97.7 per cent. Within this magnificent margin the wise advertiser plays for immediate profits. He knows that people don't read the same magazine articles twice. Or look again at the same news photographs. And, therefore, that people are equally unlikely to read successive advertisements of the same article unless they are immediately interested in a personal way.

Able advertisers soon learn their strongest selling arguments. By comparing results from various headlines and coupons they gradually accumulate a list of things valuable enough to use in every piece of copy. Then they "shoot the whole works" in each advertisement. This, of course, deliberately spoils some chance of a second reading. They neither expect nor need it. Their returns come from new readers. And in any circulation there are always more than enough absolutely untouched prospects to make a gloriously profitable enterprise of any advertisements that can reach even one in a hundred of them.

The finest tribute to the great Chicago meat-packing houses is that they utilize every part of the pig but his squeal. Advertising can be made equally thorough. Nothing is too small to help pay. One ingenious mail expert made a discovery worth $64,-000. He found by actual test he could count on exactly $3,864 a year more *profit*—6 per cent a year on $64,400—by having the boxes on his return postal cards printed:

| A penny here will bring back dollars. | *instead of* | Place Stamp Here |

The ordinary advertiser, and indeed the inexperienced advertising man, finds difficulty in grasping the astounding power of human action in the mass. And the astonishing regularity of its expression through the law of averages.

In the long run, about so many people will do one thing and about so many will do another. In the course of a year, for example, two or three people in every thousand will write to their newspaper. (The *New York Daily News* has more than a million letters a year. Two hundred thousand women wrote the *Chicago Tribune* in six months.) But it would require incredible exertion to increase this average to four in a thousand; and ten in a thousand would probably be impossible. Fifty per cent action seems to be the mass maximum, no matter how easy the deed or profitable its accomplishment. Six to twelve out of every hundred will "inquire" about almost any reasonably attractive offer. But when it comes actually to buying by mail, two in a hundred is fair enough and six in a hundred astonishingly good. Determined follow-up of "leads," either by mail or canvasser lands about one in three, which brings us back to two or three sales in our original hundred inquiries.

This is human action at its sharpest, under the prod of professional skill. When one remembers that magazine advertising passes its peak within ninety days, and that the human memory forgets about 80 per cent within the first half hour, one realizes the waste that can come from a lazy advertisement.

There are three good reasons for urging every person who reads an advertisement to take definite immediate action:

First: because some are ready to buy at once. And their money will help pay for the advertisement.

Second: because others will register their interest with inquiries, of which not less than 25 per cent may be sold by subsequent follow-up correspondence.

Third: because even those readers who neither buy nor write will, nevertheless, recieve a sharper and more lasting impression if the advertising copy is vigorously directed toward immediate action.

In any piece of copy the emphasis on how to get the goods is far more than mere information. It is a strong stimulus to action. And to memory! To make the reader see the brand is good. To make him see the goods is splendid. To make him see himself with the goods is the climax of selling. To make him picture himself—one step at a time—going through the motions of buying will do more to clinch a sale than any other single bit of copy writing. Whether he buys or not, the impulse is still sketched upon his brain.

Furthermore, fortunately for the aggressive advertiser, seven out of ten people are more or less positively moved by suggestion. No advertisement, however long, is long enough until it assigns every reader something definite to *do*. If he is to answer a question, tell him the answer. If he is to vote, tell him how to vote. If he is to write, tell him what to write. If he is to buy goods, tell him how to get them.

The best two ways to assure direct action from any advertisement are, of course, headline and coupon. The headline is the most important factor. Some authorities rate it as half the entire advertisement. Yet a survey of more than $3,000,000 worth of recent advertising found only one really good headline in every nine advertisements.

One publishing house, testing circular letters, found that eight out of fourteen business executives had developed the habit of reading the return card *first*. In advertising, similarly, many people read nothing but the coupon. Others read the headline and jump to the coupon. Or they glance at the main copy and study the coupon for the offer. Tests have shown the coupon to have such strategic importance that most readers will accept an offer exactly as the coupon states it, even if the copy half an inch above contains the same offer in purposely more attractive terms. A coupon, therefore, regularly produces at least four inquiries where only three would come without it.

Besides the general reasons that apply to any form

of stimulating action, there are four special reasons
for using a coupon.

1. *Mail Order:* to secure a direct order by mail.
2. *Leads:* to secure inquiries by mail to be converted into
   sales by some local dealer or agent.
3. *Store Visits:* to induce calls on a local dealer or agent for
   samples, information, or service.
4. *Tests:* to ascertain and compare the relative values of a
   variety of appeals or media.

A coupon not only makes action definite; it crystal-
lizes immediate action. Even among the readers
anxious to answer an advertisement, something interesting in or out the paper will within five minutes distract a large number. If before they forget,
you get them to send in their names as prospects, you
can finish the sale at your own convenience. Preventing sales evaporation, therefore, almost any
coupon, or even an expensive sample, will pay well.

The best reason of all for coupons is copy insurance. An experienced advertising man can discard
pretty accurately any number of bad advertisements,
and approve—in general—any number of good ones.
He cannot, however, always guess the one best.
Without a positive check, most advertisers run whole
series of appeals far weaker than their best. When
not overstimulated by free offers or fevered copy, incoming inquiries will register as accurately as a
doctor's thermometer the *general* interest each advertisement creates. Since a coupon automatically
magnifies by 25 per cent or more the size of this
answer, its value as an effect detector is as distinct

as the magnifying lens of the doctor's thermometer which enables him exactly and promptly to read a patient's temperature. In Chapter XXVI we go to some pains to warn that the number of replies from an advertisement is far from the final test. Nevertheless, to run any previously untested advertisement in costly space without a coupon by which to measure its effectiveness seems to us a quite unnecessary risk of money.

One of the oldest fallacies is that the only answers to advertisements come from farms and small towns. Papers with large rural circulations and only a small share of the juicy institutional advertising have been forced into "mail-order" advertising. From this fact has naturally arisen the tradition that farmers are natural-born advertisement answerers. Close analysis of the origin of inquiries from a large group of women's publications, however, has disclosed that, compared with the corresponding circulation, a greater proportion of inquiries come from middle-sized towns, between 10,000 and 50,000, than from either the great cities or farming districts.

This is not hard to understand. Middle-sized towns are more progressive than the little ones without being as busy as the big. Human nature is notoriously uniform. The same impulse to act dwells in the top story of the tenement as in the front room of the farmhouse. In both places that impulse bears a certain definite relation to the total number of people who read. The radio managers, we are told, figure one out of every hundred listeners will,

sooner or later, write to the station. Working back-
wards, they intelligently visualize their real audience. Whether or not their answer is correct, their
method is one all advertisers might ponder. Working from known returns to real circulation may some
day prove a good deal simpler than the present
method of figuring from theoretical circulation to
probable results. At any rate, engineering training
is no doubt responsible for the willingness of the
leading radio managers to forget the imaginary millions who might be listening; and concede that, even
in the largest centers of population, a radio station
must be exceptionally good to attract a regular audience of 100,000.

But that runs ahead into our next subject. In
these last three chapters we have mentioned a few
of the simplest points about copy. Now we have
reached the other side of the problem: How can
the advertiser distribute his copy widely enough to
produce important results, yet cheaply enough to
make those results profitable? That brings us to
circulation: first, in its simple, good old-fashioned
A B C form. Then to *real* circulation, as actually
delivered through size and position. Then circulation as affected by duplication of one sort or other.
And, finally, to a new sort of circulation, infinitely
intensified.

CHAPTER XXII

Butterflies and Little Bloodhounds

If advertising had a Mussolini to decree that every man, woman, and child in the United States should read regularly his 25,000-word-a-day share, the real circulation of any given advertisement would be easier to figure. Lacking such an imperial traffic cop evenly to distribute its flow, advertising becomes its own worst competitor. It piles up like rush hour in the subway. Advertisers fight one another's advertisements in the same issues of the same mediums. And these mediums fight one another even more fiercely for the same markets. So any advertiser who follows the conventional schedule must be prepared in the busy months to find his pet copy crowded like Sunday morning on the Boston Post Road.

Because nobody has yet identified the less obvious but more mischievous effect of this congestion, it is still viewed with equanimity by advertisers who vigorously object to duplicate circulation. In any list of great publications an advertiser may find duplication (theirs, *not* his!) running from 40 to 60 per cent. Even in the most exclusive "high-hat" magazines, readers may overlap as much as 15 to 20 per cent. Any home that has a magazine at all is likely as not to have half a dozen. Two independent investigations have established that the average

275

number of magazines in the american magazine
home runs nearly three and one-half to the family.
And we need hardly add that into these same magazine homes go nearly all the best newspapers. Practically all theater programs. And a huge lion's share
of all direct mail.

On the other hand—and of the utmost importance
—few elements in advertising are so badly judged.
Or, so badly juggled.

Exactly as statistics represent a "market" without estimating its one vital factor—*desire,* so statistics measure circulation without estimating its one
vital factor—*attention!* "Coverage" is a noble term.
But it doesn't mean much. It belongs to the same
type of abstract conceptions as the "protection" we
have had when we start a new year without having
collected any insurance. Nobody can deliver a market. Each time an advertiser runs a good enough
advertisement in a good medium he will get some
of its circulation. If he runs simultaneously in several media he will naturally have a slight overlap.
But he certainly needn't lie awake nights worrying
about people who are *not* interested reading his advertisement twice.

And for those who are interested he can afford to
duplicate his advertisement just as often as they
will read it.

It's the people who don't read the ads at all that
cost money.

Not those that read them twice!

If single advertisements really dip deep into any

publication's entire circulation, the surest way to assure maximum duplication would be to keep right on advertising in that publication. Yet a whole year's schedule in a good magazine—"100 per cent duplicate circulation"—might easily pay better than any less stable program.

Right here, however, we encounter one of those crazy quilts of reasoning which makes advertising such a fascinating game. Repeating advertising to the same people in the same magazine is agreed to be beneficial. It is understood to produce "cumulative" results. Reaching those same people with that same advertising through another magazine, however, is "duplicate" circulation. Therefore, waste. So far as the "waste" goes, skillful and patient repetition of the same idea is the only certain formula for advertising success. There seems little difference whether advertisements are repeated tandem or abreast. Which is better in any given case depends entirely on what the advertiser is trying to accomplish. Anyone wishing to entertain himself with advertising's more metaphysical aspects might enjoy a rainy Sunday deciding whether, in that given case, the selling advantage gained through cumulative effect offsets the investment loss through duplication of circulation.

To prove to his own satisfaction how absolutely groundless is the average advertiser's fear of duplication, Mr. T. H. Beck tried an interesting experiment. Back in September, 1925, he had two identical advertisements inserted in the same issue of the *American*

Magazine. Twelve pages apart, in the middle of the magazine, both had precisely the same position. These two advertisements together happened by coincidence to cost almost to the dollar what six advertisements, exactly the same, cost in a list of six magazines and newspapers chosen independently by the advertising agency—in ignorance of this test—for the best possible promise of direct mail results. Carefully keyed and scrupulously checked, the two duplicate advertisements, pulling together in the same magazine, got thirty more orders than the total of all the other six advertisements pulling independently. To accomplish this, moreover, the duplicate advertisements overcame an *adverse* circulation balance of 1,600,000 copies! So long as professional mail-order men find a profit in running two, three, or even five advertisements in the *same issue* of the same magazine, less exacting advertisers need not worry about duplicate circulation at over-lapping edges.

In the early days when circulations were small and advertisements novelties, duplication may really have been a waste. But not today. Circulars, car cards, elaborate outdoor set-ups that would have made talk twenty years ago, scarcely catch our eye. The present three-and-one-half magazines per family are lucky if, all together, they get as much attention as did *Harper's* or the *Youth's Companion* alone in our boyhood days. And, as Professor Cover observes:[1]

[1] John H. Cover, *Advertising, Its Problems and Methods.*

The chance for duplications, if an advertiser is using space in several publications, is decreased. If three mediums received by one reader get only about the total amount of time that one such medium got from a typical reader in former periods, it may be necessary for the advertiser to use two of these mediums, or maybe three, to get the same amount of attention that he formerly got from one.

Back in our first chapter we spoke of the "regimental chaplain" conception of circulation by which any advertiser who bought 100,000 circulation pictured himself as addressing 90,000, 80,000, 50,000, or even 40,000 or 20,000 or 10,000 people regularly through his advertising. Not infrequently we see statements like this:

Advertising of X——— will be continued in the leading women's publications. A careful audit of the circulation of these publications shows that we are *telling 10,000,000 readers monthly* about the advantages of X———.

Only a blind faith in advertising and a complete ignorance of circulation prevents this sort of thing from being intolerably dishonest. For every circulation proposition has two distinct sides:

1. *Seller's Gross*—A. B. C. physical circulation, delivered fully and honestly. As fixed and safe a buy as any high class bond.

2. *Buyer's Net*—or the advertiser's Try-and-Get-It share of the above. Varying and unknown.

That is why advertising needs two sets of calculations. Newspapers, magazines, billboards, circulars, do their whole duty when they deliver their circulation to the public. *They can't deliver an equal num-*

ber of the public to the advertiser. Or anything remotely near it. To reverse the old proverb, they can carry water to the horse, but can't make him drink. That is up to the advertiser. Theoretically, duplicate circulation is a matter of advertisements distributed. Practically, it is a matter of advertisements *read.* Any man who hasn't seen your advertisement can never be "duplicate circulation" for you —no matter if he buys a hundred different magazines containing your advertisement.

For advertisements are like bullets in a battle. Only those that hit count. All others fly unnoticed. Mere repetition will no more polish a prospect into a purchaser than a hail of passing bullets will gradually kill a soldier. To be affected at all, each individual must some time or other definitely notice your advertisement. Unless that advertisement sells him then and there, you have lost your best chance. To continue to hammer that individual with the same advertisement, or even one which resembles it, is like trying to teach fish to bite bait they won't touch.

"I belave anything at all if ye only tell me it often enough," wrote Mr. Dooley. Taking his jest too seriously has cost advertisers a lot of money. Repetition may be reputation. Or may not. Anything worth saying to a group of people is worth repeating to them. For, in a *group,* the repeated advertisement comes as news to some and a reminder to others. But repetition to any given *individual* tends to defeat its own end. Repetition of a sensation, already familiar, breeds apathy. And more. It engenders a habit of resistance. If this were not true we would never get rid of a popular song. No man could work in a boiler factory. Nor lean against the wind on the ribs of a forty-story skyscraper.

Without ingenuity, freshness, and variety, repetition simply dulls. A pebble in my shoe or stye on my eye starts with my whole attention, but, as other new interests distract, gradually loses its hold. The panorama through a railway window, the throbbing of a steamer screw, soon reach the point where they can attract your notice only by stopping. A Swedish friend once told us of a gigantic chocolate sign in Stockholm. It stood house-high halfway across the public square. For years he walked by it unseeingly on his way to work.

One day the sign attracted his attention.

It was gone!

Yet, in spite of my Swedish friend, the flying bullets and the steamer screw, we find books about advertising filled with this sort of statement: [1] (The italics are ours.)

> While thousands of people attain the mental act of noticing advertisements, *millions pass through the physical act of seeing, unconsciously*, perhaps. The effect of the advertising on people who merely see the advertisements is very important in achieving results.

Even Mr. Dooley didn't say "say it often enough." He said *"tell* me often enough," which is quite different. A man or a community familiar with a brand doesn't always buy it. Of the 10,000 "first mentions"

---

[1] Constance E. Miller, *How to Write Advertisements*, p. 86.

in the recent Hotchkiss-Franken test, only 3,394 were by people actually using the brand mentioned.[1]

To increase sales by blindly smearing advertising into the public subconsciousness is psychologically incorrect. In these days, moreover, it is financially impossible. No less an authority than Mr. Truman A. DeWeese[2] says of his own selling!

If you put the words "Shredded Wheat" in large electric signs on the top of every building in the United States I don't think it would increase the consumption of the product by one case.

Keeping the name before the public may be good business, but it is a whole lot less than good advertising. When the right appeal reaches the right man at the right moment, it needs no repetition. One sales manager, keen to build a new sort of dealer organization, went out and lived a month in the stores he wanted. Then he wrote his copy direct to the dealers he had met. His single page in the *Saturday Evening Post* brought back 1,653 replies out of a possible 3,000 dealers in that line, or 55 per cent of all his possible prospects at a single shot. Another less informed advertiser to the drug trade got only 42 replies from the *Post* and *Liberty* put together. An editorial article in the *People's Home Journal* simply describing some new housekeeping tools— dustpans, cream separators, to be had in any grocery store—brought 3,334 cash requests to buy.

It's the mind that makes the market! Not the

---

[1] Hotchkiss and Franken, *Leadership of Advertised Brands.*
[2] *Printers' Ink.* April 21, 1927, p. 186.

circulation. Nor the locality. Nor the pocketbook. Risking a bad pun to drive the point home—it's the mind that must be mined! Divisions of wealth that work out on maps so smartly in red, blue and yellow function more slowly in greenbacks. Unlimited ability to purchase—statistically—doesn't necessarily represent quick sales. That, as we have seen, comes in human tides. Flesh and nude stockings, for example, have been worn so thin so long, we get a delightful shock from trig legs in modest black. Every woman outside the poorhouse has money enough to buy herself a pair of black stockings the minute stores open tomorrow morning. Some day the whole world of women, like a line of tumbling tin soldiers, will decide to change. And, one after another, regardless of comparative wealth, each woman in turn will see black stockings as her one great necessity. Her place in that buying parade will depend not at all on her pocketbook. Simply on her stocking sensitiveness.

The effects of any advertising campaign are much the same. Just as raindrops run together on the windowpane, so simultaneous action by people in the same neighborhood must appear related, no matter how completely disconnected it may be. Any coincidence of individual buying, whether influenced early or late, whether by one advertisement or several, whether by seeing goods others have bought on account of an advertisement, or from some impulse entirely independent of any advertising—must, naturally, seem to the advertiser to have come as a cumulative result of this series of advertisements acting in smooth succession on the same people.

Nevertheless, as you have observed, it is the *group* —not the individual—that absorbs advertising. Instead of regarding his audience as millions of sixpenny nails, each waiting patiently for his next tap on the head, an advertiser might, more profitably picture it as millions of tenpins, each falling or standing, according to the force and accuracy with which each new appeal hits him individually.

Our lawyer, for example, counts 200 names on his list of clients. According to their own needs, they turn up in irregular rotation often enough to keep him busy every day. Our dentist tactfully reminds, now and then, that a filling in time saves a gold crown. But our own ache determines our visit. No matter how able a young doctor, he must wait patiently until his "practice" averages enough ills a day to keep him busy.

The new boy in a strange school—the little barber in a new neighborhood—the salesman in an unfamiliar territory—the manufacturer of an unknown article—the advertiser with his first new insertions —are all about on a par. If all are fairly good, and work with equal energy each at his appointed job, their respective curves of success would, no doubt, all turn out pretty much the same shape. The reason seems simple. Barber, doctor, or advertiser, each makes for himself an ever growing circle of friends and possible customers. When he has acquired enough to allow the law of averages to operate successfully in his favor, he has established a real and, presumably, a profitable business.

Moreover, each of them, while becoming known himself, is, in turn, perfecting by a sort of trial-and-error system a practical working knowledge of his customers. In other words, in advertising, as in any other business, a newcomer gets acquainted with his prospects just as they get acquainted with him. This growing skill in public relations gained during earlier experience is no doubt responsible, in many instances, for the accumulated effects of advertising—whether success comes gradually or bursts suddenly forth.[1]

This tenpin hypothesis of clean-cut advertising effect—each appeal picking its own prospects at the psychological moment—hardly pretends to describe exactly what happens in every given case. Yet to a reasonable mind it may be more acceptable than the popular conception indicated, for example, in the following paragraph from an advertising magazine! (The italics again are ours.)

A man will say to me: "Oh yes! I get a lot of letters every day and most of them go into the waste basket." Of course they do; no one expects him to save them. But, whether he knows it or not, *each one of those letters has made an impression on his subconscious mind.* . . . The first name that will pop into his mind will be the one impressed there by six, eight, ten or twelve messages.

[1] "I am of the personal opinion that most belated advertising successes are due to an education secured at a most costly price. The real success might have been secured easier and better on the start, had the eventually successful plan been the one tried first, rather than last." William A. Shryer in *Analytical Advertising.*

This is the poison-ivy theory of advertising receptivity. Strangely enough, it is, in greater or less degree, almost universally believed. Few thoughtful people swallow it whole. But few dare totally dismiss it. By its naïve philosophy, none can handle a single circular or see a single advertisement without automatically establishing in his subconscious mind one-sixth, one-tenth, or one-twenty-second, or one-one hundred seventy-eighth of a complete response to whatever its message happens to be. The process is understood to be quite unconscious. But inexorable! One's mind becomes an indefatigable adding machine, carrying forward toward inevitable action thousands of constantly increasing totals—all different, and all in vulgar fractions!

So firmly has this poison-ivy theory taken hold, even those in the advertising business find a constant temptation to join the popular religion that the repeated appearance of a given piece of copy will, by physical absorption, finally affect every individual it reaches, whether or not he ever consciously reads it. Each member of the Canadian police is supposed to get "his" man. Advertising is understood to go the Royal Mounted one better; it is supposed to get every man! As soon as his subconscious mind has reached just the proper exposure—like a cake baking in the oven—the wholly unconscious prospect suddenly springs into action and—like Trilby beneath Svengali's hypnotic glare—buys some advertised article he has so often not needed. Literal acceptance of this doctrine abrogates the doctrine of free will. It puts your whole future, this moment, at the mercy of whoever happens in the past six months or six years to have been mailing you circulars you never noticed. Whether you are interested in oil stock, evergreens, or obesity cures makes no difference. If your name gets on those mailing lists, and the advertiser's postage holds out, you must, sooner or later, buy all three.

This theory is, of course, exactly the reverse of the truth. Thousands of cases happen every day where consistent advertising moves to final action an actual prospect, once remote. But in millions of other cases the supposed prospect couldn't be swayed by any possible succession of arguments continued a thousand years. And few advertisers of any unit smaller than ocean steamers can afford to spend money flirting with shy and far-flung prospects. The quick buyer, not the philanderer, makes advertising possible. A woman reads, knows her mind, shows her purchase to neighbors, and thereby sells another —she is the one who pays the advertiser to advertise.

Firm faith in advertisements as Little Bloodhounds of Business persists, nevertheless. And some ingenious ideas have been evolved to support it. Most interesting of these, perhaps, is the theory of a radical difference in state of mind between a man reading a mail-order advertisement and reading general publicity. From this assumed difference in mental attitude has arisen, in turn, a tacit tradition that mail-order advertising fades away like the spring violet, while general advertising has some indestructible quality like the century plant. Or the seventeen-year locust. And, consequently, if this indestructible publicity quality be not drained off in direct orders, but allowed quietly to accumulate, its submerged effect may almost any day suddenly burst forth to metamorphose the happily advertised article from a red-ink caterpillar into a golden butterfly.

With or without advertising, any good business will accumulate momentum so long as each year brings more customers and good will. Intelligent advertising, courageously sustained, will generously add to this momentum. But the theory of constantly mounting cumulative results from successive advertisements of a series is no longer accepted. More modern practice, based on innumerable records, realizes that in normal conditions any proposition "pulls" best in a given medium when first advertised. Also that, regardless of change of copy, the cost-per-order continues, thereafter, to advance so long as that advertising persists without sufficient intermission before the same body of readers. The certainty of ever-increasing returns from successive years of well-organized advertising will never be questioned by well-informed men. "Cumulative" is denied here only in its old special sense of the pyramided effectiveness once supposed automatically to accrue to every new piece of copy as a hang-over from every previous advertisement.

As a natural corollary comes the conclusion, equally well tested, that advertising returns tend to keep up the best from mediums with flexible circulations. It is the fresh audience that makes profitable any consistent repetition of advertisements. The more new readers there are, and the faster they change, the better the publication from an advertiser's viewpoint. In a thoroughly unorthodox fashion Mr. Shryer states the extreme position of this belief:[1]

A good many publications devote considerable effort to convincing advertisers that their readers renew in large proportions. I would rather have new readers, gained in almost any way, than old ones renewed constantly. Free subscriptions are better than the same old readers month in and month out. Every new reader is a new prospect, likely to be appealed to through the novelty of your first appeal to him. Changing copy or changing the entire style of your appeal is less effective than having new readers for old copy.

Old circulations seem to slow down like old civilizations and ancient rivers. Mining camps and mountain torrents are not always alluring, but they have the force of youth. So with fresh incoming circulations. Some day some Newton among circulation managers will discover that he can do with lots less circulation—if he keeps it well aired. He may even go so far as to rest certain portions of it, as a farmer his fallow fields.

In the meantime an alert advertiser can profit by the same principle to continue in magazines he likes best. With a few months rest now and then, publications which might show an increasing net loss, if used continuously, can be turned into first-class profit

[1] William A. Shryer in *Analytical Advertising.*

payers. By running a favorite piece of copy and skipping every subsequent issue until that insertion is found to have paid for itself, even the most exacting mail-order advertisers use publications that would bring a loss without this interval of rest. That those who keep close track of their advertising cannot afford to slam-bang on an express schedule, is no reflection on any circulation. It means merely that under stress of modern conditions the cream of actual prospects comes slowly to the surface. Therefore prospects in quantities that an advertiser can afford to work occur only once in so many months. For the advertiser who has enough money, patience, and determination to conquer a chosen market, regardless of decreasing advertising efficiency, this principle is less important. Even that advertiser, however, may profitably study its significance.

CHAPTER XXIII

When Is Circulation?

IMAGINE exactly 1,000 motorists a day driving over a one-way road. Imagine a huge billboard squarely facing that road at an advantageous corner. Busy with their own affairs, only a certain proportion of that thousand motorists are in any circumstances going to "apperceive" that billboard. But the owner of the billboard site will—and should—sell his space on a basis of a full thousand-a-day circulation.

Suppose, instead of buying the whole billboard, with this a thousand-a-day circulation, some advertiser buys only a quarter. Three competitors take the other three quarters. How will this affect the first advertiser's circulation? Will it drop to 250 a day? Probably not. But since each motorist has four signs to look at instead of one, none of the four advertisers can well continue to count the whole 1,000 a day as *his* circulation.

Now, forget these four little signs competing with each other. Assume, instead, that the original advertiser takes the whole space for one big sign. He buys therewith its full thousand-a-day circulation. But suppose, as the sign is built, it must be turned away at a sharp angle that makes many certain to miss it. (If the sign were turned completely backward the advertiser would, of course, refuse it altogether. In that case real circulation is obviously reduced to zero.) How far sideways, out of full position, however, would the buyer be justified in allowing it to slant and still count for himself the benefit of its entire circulation? The same thousand motorists are always driving by, so the gross—or *space seller's*—circulation remains exactly the same. The copy remains the same. Size and position alone vary. And, with size and position, varies the *advertiser's* circulation!

By changing the size of the sign from ten square feet to ten thousand, a relative increase can be made in *its* circulation.

By swinging it sideways from 10 degrees to 90 degrees a relative decrease can be made in *its* circulation. And just as size and position affect the circulation of this sign, so size and position will be found automatically to increase or decrease any advertiser's circulation anywhere.

Theory? Quite the contrary! We know one advertiser in a big list of popular magazines who won't use anything larger than single columns. Nevertheless, he invariably adds up the entire circulation of the whole list as *his* circulation. Extra-good position may help his quarter-page catch more readers than the average quarter-page would entitle him to. Extra-good copy may make his quarter-page sell an extraordinary percentage of those readers. But even if he thus overcomes the handicap of small size, he is like a man who hires a taxi and runs alongside to help it go faster. Even if he is smart enough to squeeze full-page results out of his single column, he is still stupid if he figures himself getting normal circulation.

What he orders is less space.

What he gets is less circulation! If he wants to be sure of full circulation he must buy full-size space and, if necessary, pay extra for full position. The advertising agent for this quarter-column optimist happens, in another account, to handle an exact antipode. Here each advertisement must pay not only its expenses, but its own profits. For this advertiser, the agent finds many magazines in which he can use *only* back covers, no matter how much more they cost! Therefore, he gladly pays the higher price for more circulation than he can possibly get in the ordinary run of the paper. When the added attraction of color—a copy element—is offset by comparing back-cover results with those from an identical color insert, the 45 per cent superiority of his back covers is found to be entirely a matter of 45 per cent more real circulation—paid for and delivered!

It is evident, again, that there are two kinds of circulation:

(a) *The circulation the space producer sells*, with delivery as honest and accurate as a high-class bond.

(b) *The circulation an advertiser gets*, which varies with a dozen different factors—chiefly size and position.

The two chief factors that determine the actual circulation any advertiser gets—as distinguished from the gross or "opportunity" circulation he buys —are size and position.

Let us look first at size: Nine hundred and ninety people out of 1,000 will joyously bet their bank books that a full-page advertisement attracts at least twice as much attention as a half-page. All feel that advertising, by its very nature, not only sets aside the law of diminishing returns, but actually reverses it! Unfortunately not. Size in advertising, when other things are equal, follows accepted general principles.

Take first, for example, the matter of store rent:[1]

When a man has a store, with, say, twenty feet of frontage on a busy street, and increases this to forty feet, he is not justified in paying double his original rent.

To be exact, the additional twenty feet is worth to him only 68 per cent more than he has been paying. If his rent has been $100 a month it should now be $168.

If he jumped from twenty to eighty feet frontage, or, in other words, if his store is three and a half times as large as formerly, his rent should be increased by only 112 per cent— from, say, $100 to $212 a month.

This, you will see later, parallels increase in advertising size: To double his $100 store space is worth $168, to double his $100 advertising space is worth $158. To light two candles instead of one or beat an extra bass drum will give about the same diminished result. Experiments in quick repetition of the same copy are still few. Adams found the same advertisement too quickly repeated worth only one and one-half times as much as a single insertion.

[1] Fred C. Kelly, *Business Profits and Human Nature*, p. 79.

This, too, seems to follow the general principles of physical stimuli. If it were possible to compare, as a whole, the effect of all advertising in 1928, as against all advertising in 1908, the results would, no doubt, be found in surprisingly close accord with the same law of diminishing returns. Which would, of course, help explain why much better advertising to-day isn't getting the response of twenty years ago.

That advertising response lags behind an increase in space is one of the few known facts of advertising. Take the results of nine tests made by seven different psychologists, over a period of twelve years. These tests include 1,023 people. They range from simple comparison to an unexpected request to recall in writing actual advertisements seen in a recent publication. Combined in one table, and grouped as closely as possible into sizes corresponding with eighths, quarters, and halves of the given unit, they work out as in the table below. For convenient comparison we set down alongside the count on actual returns as reported by Mr. Freyd and Dr. Starch.

Actual size (of space shown) Average black-and-white page—1.00	Square-root ratio	Experimental ratio (The result actually obtained)		
		Tests by seven observers	Actual returns Freyd	Starch
.13 (Eighth-page)	.36	.21	—	—
.25 (Quarter-page)	.50	.42	—	31.9
.50 (Half-page)	.71	.63	.81	53.
.67 (Two-thirds)	—	—	.95	—
1.00 (Page)	1.00	1.00	1.00	1.00
2.07 (Double page)	1.54	1.58	—	—
4.09 (Newspaper sizes)	2.02	2.01	—	—
6.50 (" ")	2.50	2.60	—	—

Your advertising response, direct or indirect, does not increase or decrease with the size of the space itself. To double its original results, other things being equal, an advertisement must be four times its original size. If you get 100 orders from a trial half-page, you naturally expect 200 orders when you double to a page. They will come nearer 160. But when you cut that trial half-page to a quarter, expecting only half as many orders, you will be delighted to get around 70, instead of the logical 50.

Mr. Max Freyd [1] in counting up for several years the keyed returns of seven different advertisers found that statistically, at least, the advertiser's most economical form of space would have been, in order,

> Half page
> Two-thirds page
> Back cover
> Full page

Incidentally, he makes the suggestion that the publisher is unjust to his overheads when he sells small space at pro-rata page rate.

Size of advertising bought, nevertheless, remains more or less accidental, except in so far as it is— quite legitimately—influenced by the sellers. Some day accurate records will show for the benefit of everybody the relative value of similar pieces of copy in various sizes, shapes, and positions. A pioneer advertising man who carried a study of this

[1] Max Freyd, "The Analysis of Keyed Returns," *Harvard Business Review*, April, 1926.

sort to astonishing perfection found 6-line classified advertisements his most profitable producer, with 56-line display next most efficient. The Dennison Manufacturing Company, also, has proved the value of small advertisements intelligently used. For a number of years they have been developing advertisements, from 28 lines to 50 lines, and skillfully and gradually decreasing their inquiry cost from $8.33 in 1908 to 38 cents in 1923.

Except, however, for that infrequent advertiser who knows what he is after, and who, by careful keying, is feeling his way toward his goal, there is much to be said in favor of large space for any who can afford it without let-up. First, size itself may carry a prosperous prestige. Secondly, a full page offers greater opportunity for more copy, striking layout, better type and pictures. This, as well as the greater cost of space, assures more care to make a larger advertisement really effective. The consequently greater attractiveness, as well as preference on account of larger size, regularly—and properly—secures more favorable positions. Whether or not these three advantages are worth the extra cost, there still remains the additional fact that a full page or a double spread makes certain no competitive advertisement, good or bad, can steal any of your thunder.

Before dismissing size and passing on to the question of position, it is only fair to warn that any large-scale comparisons of average results for contrasting groups—full page against smaller sizes, right-hand page against left, and so on—are always likely to contain a submerged joker serious enough to impair their practical value. The returns a given advertiser gets from his keyed full page may often determine not only the continuance of his account with a given publication, but to some extent the reputation of that publication as a profitable advertising medium. To a keyed full page, therefore, any make-up man outside the insane asylum will automatically give the best position anywhere obtainable after his most sacred cows are fed. Consequently, in all large-scale comparisons of average results, the strongest full-page copy will regularly be found registering in favor of the choicest right-hand positions. And, worse yet, the left-hand pages and all smaller units not strong enough to force make-up favors have not only to work from a weak position, but have to snatch their results in active competition against these selected full-page advertisements in the hand-picked right-hand positions.

Beyond reminding ourselves that the law of diminishing returns works as accurately in advertising as elsewhere, and pointing out why larger space may, nevertheless, often prevail against it, little is left to say in the matter of size, except the interesting fact that to make your advertisement look bigger you must add at least 5 per cent to its area. Conversely, you may cut 5 per cent off the size of any odd-size advertisement without making it look any smaller. In this or in any other case, it is a businesslike rule to use not a single line of space more than you need to accomplish your purpose. Money saved is not the principal reason. Always there is the possibility of salvaging enough wasted extra space to enable you to run three advertisements instead of two. Or to add still another attractive publication otherwise unable to squeeze itself on to your schedule.

So much, then, for size as a circulation factor. We have seen that an advertiser can increase *his* circulation 50 per cent by doubling the size of his space. Now for the circulation effect of position:

"I know how to write our advertising," writes the advertising manager of a famous tooth paste. "The style of each ad. is the same—following the outline of our most successful efforts. Yet one month, the inquiries will bury us; and the next, make us feel like old Mother Hubbard's pup. . . . The reason is simple. . . One month my ad. will be placed toward the front or extreme rear of the advertising section. The next month it will be buried in the middle. When it is buried, it can't work. Enough people don't see it." [1]

This fairly states the position of the man who keys his returns. As we suggested some twenty chapters back, the man who doesn't key his returns is experiencing exactly the same hardships. But since he doesn't know it, he doesn't worry.

In 1924 the *Advertising & Selling Fortnightly* published a valuable contribution [2] to knowledge of position as an important circulation factor. This article tabulated results from a leading advertiser received by 757 insertions in a list of 95 magazines

[1] *Advertising and Selling,* February 10, 1926.
[2] William T. Laing, "What Is the Value of Position in Publication Advertising?" *Advertising and Selling,* February 27, 1924.

and farm journals. Covering a period of eleven months, a list as varied as this makes the test broad enough to be entirely trustworthy. Without going into detail we may indicate that a right-hand page well to the front of the book seems to reach more than three times as many people as a left-hand page in the middle of the magazine. And to reach nine times as many as an average page in the ordinary run toward the back. Or putting the proposition in its more usual form: Mr. Laing finds a difference in position can make a consistent variation of as much as 90 per cent in results. Since his count is large enough to average down to identity both copy and publisher's gross circulation, the difference in results can, of course, be explained only in terms of real—or advertiser's net—circulation.

Every good manual of advertising contains some very interesting and fairly substantiated facts on position. A back cover, for example, is often held to have nearly three times the "attention value" of an ordinary inside black-and-white page. That means three times as much power to convert publisher's gross circulation into advertiser's net. In the same way, an advertisement on the outer margin of a page may thereby have one-eighth more circulation than it would otherwise. An advertisement at the top of a column is said to have one-tenth more real circulation than one at the bottom. The variations run up and down, in and out, sideways and reverse. We once found a variation of 31 per cent in results due to a comparatively slight difference in the editorial runover brought back alongside from the front of the magazine. Leaving these finer variations to more competent hands, we will notice here only the general relations between front and back sections of an ordinary magazine.

Mr. G. Lynn Sumner, whose personal experience on this point is at least equal to any man's, wrote,[1] reporting results of three years' research tabulation and analysis of keyed copy which had brought profitable sales:

Every month for thirty-six consecutive months, with six to eight advertisements in each issue, the *first* six advertisements in the magazine had produced far more inquiries than any other. Yes, no matter what piece of copy drew first position when the publisher spread them through the book, *that* advertisement pulled by far the largest number of replies.

The best results were invariably secured from the first advertisement. The next best results were secured from the second advertisement.

An advertisement appearing toward the end of the first advertising section produced better results than one in the middle of that section.

An advertisement at the extreme back of the issue produced better than one in the middle of the book advertising section.

Again, a year later we find Mr. Carroll Rheinstrom writing: [2]

To my office every month come dozens of advertisements from all over the country. . . . The page positions in the magazines in which they appeared are noted. . . . Of these

[1] *Advertising and Selling*, August 12, 1925.
[2] Carroll Rheinstrom, "Why One-price Space in Periodicals?" *Advertising and Selling*, February 10, 1926.

advertisements, conceded by their authors to be outstandingly successful, more than 80 per cent had appeared in positions before reading matter, in pages 1, 2, 3, 4, and 5, after reading matter, and on the last two or three pages.

Working with theory rather than actual results, Professors Hotchkiss and Franken found in a flat magazine a difference of 30 per cent between the attention value of advertisements in the first ten pages of advertising and a group that followed toward the end of the book. Moreover, they found practically the same situation with regard to positions in newspapers. Every man must decide for himself what these figures prove. But no advertiser may overlook the fact that three independent investigations as reported by Laing, Rheinstrom, and Sumner, and checked up by the collaboration of Hotchkiss and Franken, have so closely coincided.

It may, perhaps, be worth adding that the 12 per cent or 14 per cent extra attention value in the right-hand page is largely, if not wholly, artificial. The left-hand page—not the right—is the naturally strong position. One might as well expect a Chinaman to start at top of his column and drop downwards as to expect an American to start anywhere but at the left. Before magazine editors, without too much taste or judgment, began forcing the right-hand pages with heavy illustrations, cutting off like so many misplaced dams the smooth flow of text, the left-hand page had been for centuries recognized by book builders as the place for frontispieces and illustrations. Publishers have built themselves a Frankenstein in their right-hand position. Even now it may not be too late to return to the natural basis.

The size element in circulation is easily handled. An advertiser has simply to pay for as much as he wants. The position element is more complicated. To offset the loss of circulation through a bad position puts it up to the advertiser to buy larger space. Or furnish exceptional copy strength. Or both. Yet position—like kissing—goes largely by favor. "Good positions requested" is the agency order stereotype. Advertising rates are presumably based on the average position. There is no more reason why advertisers should "request" extra-good positions without extra cost than "request" a free bonus of 50,000 or 500,000 additional circulation in any other form. Advertisers who eagerly wire extra money for a lower berth, a favorite hotel suite, or front-row seats at the Follies could hardly complain if publications followed the general law of supply and demand. Newspapers are already businesslike enough to charge for all extraordinary space. Magazines might readily follow their example.[1] In the meantime,

[1] An amusing, but not too practical note is found in a letter by C. D. Maddy, published in *Advertising and Selling*, January 24, 1926. He writes:

"I have combined the various factors mentioned by Mr. Rheinstrom and Mr. Sumner, together with figures of my own, to a copy of the old stand-by, the *Saturday Evening Post*. Applied to determine the relative value to the advertiser, and then measured in cost. All pages are assumed to be in one color, and also full-page advertisements. The unit cost (that now asked by the publisher) is fixed as the worth of page 140—the *poorest page*."

every advertiser and space buyer should make himself familiar enough with the influence of position on circulation to refuse either to blame or overcredit either the magazine or copy in any case where position is the really responsible factor.

Given a reasonably large circulation to start with, the make-up man is, we find, more important to the advertiser than the circulation man. He can change real circulation for an advertiser far faster than the circulation manager can change it for the publisher. Now that publisher's circulation is so thoroughly under control that a page is as safe a buy as a good bond, the A B C might, in fact, profitably turn its experts to a study of this dominating internal factor. They can start with the knowledge that so far as "circulation" signifies anything to any given advertiser, certain positions add or subtract not merely

	Approximate Page number	*Relative value in dollars* (Compared with poorest page at $7,000)
Best page	Inside front cover	$29,400
	2	26,600
	3	16,200
Facing reading matter	35	26,600
	50	9,800
	70	9,100
	85	8,670
	105	8,120
	125	7,560
Poorest page	140	7,000
	160	7,700
	175	8,960
	195	13,300
	Back Cover	19,600

by tens of thousands, but by hundreds of thousands.

If the average advertiser were really as seriously interested in his circulation as has become our fashion to pretend, such variations could not, of course, go unnoticed. But advertising's new third dimension—extension—now assumes circulation's burden. Extension does directly, at first hand, what widespread advertising was once called on to accomplish through indirect influence. So circulation becomes less and less a dynamic force to influence consumers and more and more a gigantic statistical divinity to impress advertisers, salesmen, and retail merchants. Let us look next, then, at Extension—the active little David who shoots 'em down with his slingshot while Goliath awes them with his ponderous spear.

CHAPTER XXIV

ADVERTISING'S THIRD DIMENSION

A NUMBER of hosiery manufacturers got together to spend $100,000 in cooperative advertising. Before preliminaries were adjusted the selling season was near. So the campaign was rushed. In the excitement, nobody remembered advance proofs, or any of the conferences ordinarily used to keep everybody enthusiastic about his own advertising. And so the whole $100,000 was spent, and the last bit of copy run, before the hosiery manufacturers discovered their schedule had even started.[1] Here is one campaign, anyway, that lacked extension. "Extension," was in the beginning, as its name implies, only a by-product. In these days of intense merchandising the situation is often completely reversed. The advertisement serves simply to focus and coordinate a swarm of equally important auxiliary operations.

In spite of growing importance, extension may still be defined as any activity given an advertising idea beyond its regular exposure to the ordinary circulation of a recognized medium. This extended use may be before the advertisement is published, as in advance proofs mailed a list of retailers. Or it may come after publication, as in a trade paper repro-

[1] Hugh E. Agnew, *Cooperative Advertising by Competitors.*

duction of consumer advertisements. Or giant proofs pasted in a dealer's show window. A recent article lists "22 Ways to use an Advertisement." From preliminary display at salesman's conference to following up mail inquiries after publication, all activities beyond the actual publishing of the copy may well be classified under the head of "extension."

Extension sounds trivial. In modern advertising it has grown into a matter of life and death. Practically every campaign intended to move goods on a large scale relies primarily on something beyond simple old-fashioned advertising.

Take the coffee trade reprisal against Postum. For each dollar spent in advertising, 300 extra pounds of coffee were sold. *"For"* each dollar in advertising, is the correct statement. In this campaign, as with the paint manufacturers, the oak-floor manufacturers, the woolen-goods manufacturers, the salmon packers—and, most of all, the California fruit growers—the advertising serves as a gleaming battle flag. With it as a common meeting point, competitive leaders sell one another cooperation all along the line. And, as advertising actually swings into schedule, the organized industries coordinate a well-planned aggressive forward movement of their entire distributive machinery.

This extension of advertising until it influences or controls even production details comes generally, but not necessarily, under the head of "merchandising." Although the results from all such extra operations are, as a rule, politely credited to the advertising itself, high-pressure extension is seldom openly recognized as an essential part of an advertisement.

To get ourselves some sort of a perspective on the relation of extension to the primary old-fashioned advertising factors, let us glance at two analyses that happen to hand. The Dartnell Company made an investigation of thirty-one different lines of business, getting from several hundred advertisers confidential details as to the distribution of their advertising.

A comparison of all expenditures reported would average

	Per cent of appropriation devoted to each	Number out of 31 firms using each
Magazines.................	29.23	27
Dealer Helps................	16.46	29
Newspapers................	14.40	20
Direct mail................	8.68	11
Trade papers................	8.12	27
Outdoors..................	2.59	10
Novelties...................	1.64	10
Business Shows.............	1.38	14
Sampling..................	.39	10
Directories................	.33	7
College publications........	.16	3
Catalogues, etc.............	.10	2

Another enterprising investigator [1] made a still more detailed study of the same subject. Of 2,782 selected manufacturers, covering all New England, asked about their advertising, 631 answered. But

[1] *A Survey of Advertising Used by 631 New England Manufacturers*, Tolman Print, Inc.

only 472 of these considered themselves "advertisers." Of these advertisers—

285 of 472 reported using direct mail
252 of 472   "   trade paper advertising
160 of 472   "   "miscellaneous" advertising
147 of 472   "   dealer helps
108 of 472   "   *newspaper advertising*
80 of 427   "   *magazine advertising*

As to their preferences in what we are calling extension, of the whole list of advertisers

283 of 472 reported using sales letters
245 of 472   "   "   folders
217 of 472   "   "   follow-up letters
189 of 472   "   "   envelope inclosures
184 of 427   "   "   catalogues
160 of 472   "   "   booklets.

While of these special 285 who reported themselves as active users of direct mail

285 of the 285 use sales letters
245 " " " " folders
217 " " " " follow-up letters
188 " " " " envelope inclosures
180 " " " " catalogues
157 " " " " booklets
123 " " " " display cards
103 " " " " window cards
 91 " " " " broadsides
 80 " " " " blotters
 66 " " " " novelties
 66 " " " " package inclosures
 60 " " " " window cut-outs
 51 " " " " window strips
 46 " " " " house organs
 46 " " " " price tags

As to the comparative value of these several forms of extra circulation promotion, the combined vote of these 285 New Englanders gives the following interesting estimate:

Sales letters.................	100	per cent
Folders.....................	54	"
Catalogues..................	50	"
Follow-up letters.............	42	"
Booklets....................	42	"
Envelope inclosures..........	42	"
Broadsides..................	23	"
Window cards...............	23	"
Display cards................	23	"
Novelties...................	15	"
House organs................	12	"
Window cut-outs.............	12	"
Package inclosures...........	8	"

Representing the boiled-down selling judgment of 2,782 New England manufacturers, these figures are not without intrinsic interest. We bring them in here, however, merely as a footlight flash on the variety and importance of modern advertising's third dimension.

Turning to another very different sort of extension, take "Linoleum Week," when 1,500 merchants are intelligently induced to center their selling attention on that particular floor covering. Sherwin-Williams recently sent a large list of paint dealers ten elaborate mailings in as many weeks. California Fruit Growers distribute each month 260,000 bulletins to school-teachers. In 1915 and 1916 Wrigley put out nearly 10,000,000 copies of his children's Mother

Goose booklets. The International Harvester Company offers schools thirteen different kinds of charts, lantern slides on eighteen subjects, and motion pictures on nine.

For still another example of how the extension tail has come to wag the advertising dog, turn to books. In the good old days when books were books, not merchandise, mention among the "six best sellers" was understood to be a sign of literary merit. Hear, in the words of the man who made one, how a best-selling book is made today:

First, a special trade edition, containing a sepia portrait of the author and a few words of advertising, was mailed out to a large list of booksellers. Then advertising pages in the *Publisher's Weekly* to the book trade. Then for window display a giant replica of the book, and a three-foot easeled poster reproducing the gaudy jacket. For the smaller bookstores, five-color 7 x 11 inch posters, stickers for the dealers, letterheads and bills, and, lastly, 300,000 postal cards to be imprinted with the dealer's name.

"With this material in the dealer's hands or ready for him," says the enlightening advertising manager, *"we started to plan the direct advertising that would help move the large number of advance orders. We* bought a page in the *New York Times Book Review* and a page in the *New York Herald-Tribune."*

This ordinary form of extension by trade papers or direct mail is so general we mention it only as a reminder. It is child's play compared with the organized effort America's great newspapers—and some of the greatest magazines—put behind an advertiser's advertising.

As an example we cite, in some detail, the work of the *New York Evening Journal* for Duco. If there were one company able to buy success through straight advertising, it would be the DuPonts. If there is one newspaper able, by throwing great concentrated circulation into a single high market, to sell straight advertising results, the *New York Journal* is that paper. Yet this Duco campaign is the *Journal's* 626th of the kind, and the *New York Journal* is only one of a list of thirty or forty great newspapers from Boston to Baltimore, from Oregon to New Orleans, regularly doing this high-pressure extension work for their advertisers.

The *New York Journal* alone, in the course of its first three years:

—made over 1,200 investigations for agencies and manufacturers;

—made more than 400,000 personal calls on retailers in the interests of advertisers;

—placed on doors, in windows or on counters, 198,000 pieces of advertisers' window display;

—mailed to retailers more than 1,000,000 trade papers—of ten to twelve full newspaper pages each.

The necessity for this astounding amount of apparently gratuitous work—the sort of drudgery one would expect *in the place* of advertising, rather than in addition to it—was once explained by the sales manager in charge of that work for the *New York Journal*.

To get the full value of the consumer preference or consumer demand created by newspaper advertising, it is necessary to get William Jackson to push goods from his side of the counter as well as to get customers to ask for these goods from their side.

This can be done only through active, personal enlistment of dealer cooperation.

One time the manufacturer tried "forcing" William Jackson to carry his goods, but that finally failed. Then "bluffing" William Jackson as to advertising results was tried and given up.

Finally, the logical, common-sense solution of the problem of dealer inertia or resistance came along—late, as most common-sense solutions do—"Let us HELP William Jackson sell our goods."

And here, we are told, is how the *Journal* and the Duco Company HELPED William Jackson sell:

February 1 to March 10

(10 weeks before advertising starts)

Duco salesmen covered entire city, getting the best possible outlet in each neighboring group of four selected stores.

March 10 to April 7

(4 weeks before advertising starts)

Merchandising men of *New York Journal* called on every listed dealer, telling them about proposed advertising.

Duco salesmen—on their second trip—followed with their portfolios of sample advertising in forty-eight hours. Got orders and promises to use window displays; three-section easel-style; cut-out; window strips, and instructions how to pyramid cans.

April 7

(3 days before advertising appeared)

The *New York Journal's* merchandising men—on their

second trip—again went the rounds for the Duco advertisers, *pasting on each dealer's window* the color-page advertisement coming in the Saturday evening paper. Also reporting those dealers not using window displays as promised.

April 10

The advertising starts.

Napoleon himself might have been proud to be connected with this campaign. Naturally the Duco Company sold in the first three weeks more than they thought might be sold all summer. It is magnificent. But is it "advertising"? There is, of course, no element of deception. On the contrary, the *New York Journal* is justly proud of its achievement. And not surprisingly the Duco advertising executive writes:

Other factors being approximately equal, we would naturally choose the publication which offered the most intelligent merchandising aids.

On the other hand, sending one's own staff around with advance proofs of another man's advertising can hardly be counted as ordinary circulation.[1] Checking up a merchant's window display can hardly come under the head of copy. Therefore, advertisers must either openly ignore this third dimension, or openly recognize and classify it somewhere as an essential part of advertising. The general term "merchandising" excellently covers the

[1] Nothing takes the place of circulation. For twenty-eight consecutive years the *Evening Journal* has had the greatest evening paper circulation in New York.—*Advertisement*, Tuesday, January 16, 1927.

case with Duco. In many other instances, that term is quite inappropriate. Moreover, "merchandising" can exist—and does on a tremendous scale—quite detached from any advertising.

Using a vivid side light to conclude the shortest possible chapter on a subject that engages at least half of all advertising discussion today, let us quote the words of no less an authority than the editor of *Printers' Ink* himself:

Here—briefly summarized—are the nine reasons he suggests help kill off the dealer's cooperation that any advertiser might reasonably expect:

In the first place, copy is frequently written with a disregard of local conditions.

A second case is that, since the writer of copy is not able personally to visit each merchant and explain the value of the advertisement, the merchant is not always aware of the aims of the campaign and discards the advertising as being unsuited to his requirements.

Third is the practice of making advertisements too large in comparison with the annual sales.

Fourth reason is the tendency to leave only a quarter of an inch or so at the bottom of the advertisement for the dealer's name.

Five is the tendency to write copy that does not truly represent the dealer.

The sixth reason is the practice of throwing dealer campaigns together as one would a ready-made bungalow. The human element is overlooked.

As the seventh cause we can assign the failure of manufacturers to consult merchants before preparing copy.

Number eight lies in the gentle art of procrastination at which dealers, as well as manufacturers, are too often adept.

The ninth cause is the failure to sell dealers on the local advertising program. One or two letters will not do the trick. The merchant must be kept after continually. Here the road force can do some valuáble work.

And ominously, *in our italics:*

Each of these nine reasons is sufficient by itself to make the best-laid dealer campaign go wrong.

That all these efforts to interest local merchants are, at least, not lost in the mails is easily proved by several interesting check-ups from the receiving end:

"For about a year, I have kept accurate check by weight on this third-class mail, month by month," writes a college man who runs a hardware store in a small New York town—a target more brilliant than large. "I find with little variation that it averages from ten to twelve pounds per month." [1] From a store not much larger, which changes its window once a week, we have heard of three window displays a day arriving for months in succession. So that seventeen complete window displays a week go to waste on this one store alone. The manager of a bigger store in a city found that he received at least twenty pieces of direct mail every day, and on some busy days as high as fifty pieces. An informal inquiry among a dozen dealers with ratings of from $10,000 to $40,000 in a city of some 25,000 indicated that even three years ago most of them received an average of about 150 pieces of direct mail advertising a week. [2] A more recent report indicates that the

[1] "Van Voris Checks on Direct-mail Advertising," *Printers' Ink,* June, 1924.

[2] D. M. Hubbard in *Printers' Ink,* May, 1924.

average drug store receives 102 pieces of circular mail *a day!* And one irate jobber writes: "If I paid the postage necessary to send out all the material that comes to me from manufacturers, I would use up all my firm's profits. If I read all the advertising that is addressed to me as an individual, I would spend 60 per cent of my time on that job."

In contrast to this tremendous bombardment of dealers with expensive printed matter, we may find it worth while to inquire the fortunes of the prospective customer—the man who wants to buy? The next chapter inquires.

CHAPTER XXV

The Follow Through

We have just seen half a million retail merchants getting every day from twenty to eighty pieces of mail they didn't ask for. How about the prospect—the probable customer—who *asks* for information? No executive should allow much advertising until he personally has checked up how politely, promptly, completely, and competently his establishment is taking care of the correspondence that results. Shiftless handling of inquiries does more than toss away sure sales revenue. It becomes a canker sore in good will.

Follow through in advertising is more important than in golf. And properly to follow through requires one of two things: either a smaller selling field than the ordinary advertiser will accept, or more money and attention than he wants to give. So the average business man splashes on the edge of his advertising like a child on the edge of the ocean.[1] Many an unsuccessful advertiser of the past would have been a prosperous bank director today had he known how to take care of his advertising returns.

"Just clip the coupon" has long been a favorite method of bringing an advertisement gracefully to

[1] Of 472 advertisers in New England surveyed by the Tolman Print, Inc., only 28 per cent follow up the wholesaler by mail, and 30 per cent use mail to follow up the consumer.

an end. As early as 1923 we find curious writers for business publications inquiring into the fortunes of a prospect who accepts the invitation so lightly given. Here is the experience of one of the first to write and watchfully wait:[1]

Company addressed	Type of reply	Days to receipt of reply	Follow-up
Health service.........	Booklet	18	0
Correspondence school..	Booklet	6	5
Book company........	Specimen	6	1
Paint company........	Color card	6	0
Lumber service........	Letter	19	0
Furniture.............	Booklet	10	1
Furniture.............	Catalogue	4	5
Dry goods............		No reply	
Varnish..............	Booklet	14	0
Meat-packer..........	Book	6	1

And here is Mr. Reiss's advice to advertisers as a result of that experience:

There are more potential sales in these "special" inquiries than most folks realize—that's why it will pay to put some one on them who has brains enough to write a comprehensive letter giving complete data on the proposition before him.

Next year, 1924, Frank Farrington carried on the same experiment with thirty-six coupons clipped from the *Ladies' Home Journal*.

Mr. Farrington found[2] that a third of his replies came within a week, another third in the second

[1] A. J. Reiss, "Some Advertising Misses Fire," *Sales Management*, April, 1923.

[2] Frank Farrington, "I Answer All the Coupons," *Advertising and Selling*, November 19, 1924.

week, while the third scattered from twelve days to never. His conclusion was that the promptness and form of the first response was not bad; but that the follow-up as a serious business-getting factor was generally negligible.

Nearly two years later, in 1926, two others took up the burden of inquiry.

Miss Marie C. Chomel was instructed by the editor of *The Mailbag* to pick out forty or fifty prominent national advertisers, answer them, and see what happened.

Miss Chomel's experience, in 1926, was much the same as Mr. Farrington's in 1924, except that her answers seemed to average a little slower. Two-thirds of his 1924 replies were received within two weeks; in 1925, only one-half of hers came within that time.

Mr. Farrington's inquiry in 1924 was followed up by 8 out of 35 advertisers; two years later Miss Chomel received that honor from only 1 in 45. Her report, moreover, was that such literature as was sent her by national advertisers, viewed in the light of professional direct mail standards, "ranges downward from very ordinary to absolutely poor."

Mr. Edgar H. Felix was next. As a country gentleman desiring material for his new house, he wrote to twenty-one manufacturers of lumber, millwork, plumbing, hardware, garden tools, etc. He explains:[1]

[1] Edgar H. Felix, "Killing the Sale by Direct Mail," *Printers' Ink*, August 5, 1926.

I had hoped to be able to select and purchase a water-pumping system, a lighting plant, an iceless refrigerator, an oil burner, inside and outside paint, plumbing supplies, and garden tools. I sought just the information which any inquirer who takes the trouble to write a letter replying to an attractive advertisement has the right to expect.

By courtesy of *Printers' Ink,* we give in a footnote [1] well worth the attention of any advertiser the

[1] "One manufacturer sent a complete descriptive catalogue with prices, the name of the local dealer, and also informed the local dealer of my inquiry.

"Two sent catalogues and prices and offered to take my order direct. One of these got an immediate order, but has not made delivery in twenty-seven days. *None* of the others gave *all* the essential information to secure an order—descriptive material, price, and definite information as to local distribution! One sent a catalogue of plumbing materials with prices but neglected to tell me where they could be bought locally, although I found, through other sources, that he has live local representation. *None* of the remainder gave any information as to *prices!* Only four out of twenty-one thought price information necessary to hold consumer interest.

"Seven wrote me that they had informed distributors (not local dealers) in cities from 55 to 1,200 miles away. Of these seven, three gave me the names and addresses of these distributors and each of these sent salesmen sooner or later. Four advised me their territorial representatives were being informed, but did not give their names; of these, two were heard from, the other two lost out through distributor neglect.

"Four offered to furnish prices to me directly if I would fill out extensive questionnaires. The briefest required twenty-one answers of discouraging technicality before I could be let in on their sacred price information. Two others advised me that they had informed local dealers, but who they were I never learned because they did not respond to the manufacturer's lead. Two sent expensive catalogues, but ignored entirely the subject of price or distribution. Two referred me to distributors and suggested I write them; one sent a list of 100 or more distributors with this accommodating suggestion. I suspect its canny sales manager wears both belt and suspenders, for he also wrote some of the distributors. So far nine have written me from four states east detailed report. Here we simply summarize Mr. Felix's findings:

It is easy to declare, as a result of this experience, that consumer inquiries are grossly manhandled by large manufacturing organizations; that half of most $1,000,000 advertising appropriations are deliberately sunk in a maze of grotesque sales stupidity; that the goose which lays the golden eggs is ruthlessly driven from the sales manager's grasp.

As late as May 12, 1927, the same condition goes merrily on. *Printers' Ink* prints the story of a California rancher who made a serious effort to buy from advertisers. Mr. Gibbs concludes:[1]

Offhand, I should say that about 50 per cent of the replies are what might be termed "sloppy." If a few executives were to address inquiries to their own firms I think some of them would see a great light in the heavens.

Combining three tests including 81 different advertisers, we find 12½ days the average time. We find 26 responding within the first week, 20 others in the second week, 18 in the third week; 16 requiring a month, and three never answering. So much for consumer inquiries. In spite of the ever-increasing use of coupons, inquiries from the public seem still to be regarded as a sort of necessary nuisance, an unimportant by-product of advertising. And, there-

---

of the Mississippi, offering quotations in car-load lots and sending me one or more additional copies of the expensive catalogue.

"Yet not a single one has sent me a price on any quantity of this product. The largest hardware store in town handles this product and remains in ignorance of my inquiry."

[1] Warren R. Gibbs, "Why Don't You Pay More Attention to My Inquiries?" *Printers' Ink*, May 12, 1927, p. 58.

fore, not taken overseriously. In inquiries that come from *dealers,* surely we shall find a different story. Read, then, of an experiment made not on miscellaneous inquiries from the public, but on leads from dealers themselves:

One of our staff replied to a number of ads. appearing in trade publications. In each case a coupon was filled out asking for some definite piece of literature describing the product. The booklets came. Some with and some without letters. In most cases but one letter was written. Some said a representative would call in a few days and supply additional information. Out of twenty-five written to, only three had any real plan back of their campaign. All the others died out in the second or third round.[1]

With some such experience in mind, one letter expert argues emphatically:

No sane, sensible business man would expect his salesman to land big business continually with the few words that can be typewritten on a sheet of letter paper. He expects his salesmen to talk volumes.

He doesn't care how much they say if they land the business. But that same well-balanced business man will send out one SINGLE letter, that could be spoken orally in three minutes, and expect it to bring results that hours of sales talk could not get.

That "hours of talk" to make a sale is not merely a bit of rhetoric is evident from the figures of a retail drygoods association, which once checked up the number of calls a salesman takes to secure an order. They discovered that:

Out of every 100 salesmen who called—

[1] *The Mailbag*

Forty-eight made one call only—and quit;

Twenty-five made two calls—and quit;

Fifteen made three calls—and quit;

Twelve made four or more calls.

These twelve salesmen who made at least four calls got 80 per cent of the sales.

No matter how many calls it takes a salesman, you may answer, these advertising men surely know what they are doing. If so many good companies, you naturally ask, handle their inquiries this way it may be the right way to handle them. No doubt, you say, they have found that most of the inquiries are from children and inquisitive idlers. Fair enough! But, before too blindly pinning faith to any such justification of palpable negligence, consider two bits of evidence: First, the experience of one company enterprising enough to investigate; and then, the corroborating testimony of experts.

Look first at one company that took its advertising inquiries seriously. It ran regularly a coupon whereon customers asked prices for weather strips. According to the common practice, inquiries were referred through district offices to salesmen. But unlike most advertisers, this company insisted on keeping track of these leads for which they had paid several dollars apiece. Here, in the words of the general sales manager, is what happened:

The replies from the sales force were slow in coming. Invariably they were unsatisfactory. The salesmen reporting on the inquiries wrote as they felt about inquiries in general, rather than on a partciular inquiry sent them. One salesman

in reporting thirty or forty inquiries, would report them all
curiosity seekers.   Another stated that the majority of inquiries were from people who couldn't afford to buy, and none
of them came from people with good homes only.   Occasionally we found a salesman who actually believed these inquiries
disclosed good prospects.

Finding it impossible to get any real spark from
the salesmen, Mr. Glaser wrote personally to the
whole list who had sent in coupons the previous year
asking *them,* instead of the salesmen, what had happened.   Out of the 1,500 answers the following facts
crystallized:

354 of 1,500 had bought the Chamberlin goods (23½ per cent)
450 "   "   " never got any answering call (30 per cent)
525 "   "   " postponed purchase (35 per cent)
 12 "   "   " bought competitor's lower price (¾ per cent)
 16 "   "   " bought from competitors because of neglected
                     inquiry (1 per cent)
 97 "   "   " bought from competitor without giving reason
                     (6½ per cent)

The Armstrong Linoleum experience was a striking corroboration of Chamberlin's. They sent out
1,832 letters to women to whom their Bureau of
Interior Decoration had given its special service.
625 of these women, or more than 34 per cent, replied.   Out of those 625 replies, 280 women reported
they had purchased Armstrong's linoleum floors.
On account of the favoring element in all questionnaires mentioned in Chapter XXV, this 44 per cent
maximum wouldn't hold throughout the whole list.
Yet these 280 buyers in themselves represent a minimum of 16 per cent on the entire 1,832 inquirers.

We may safely guess, therefore, that the actual conversion was astonishingly close to the Chamberlin 23½ per cent.

In so far as the 1,500 Chamberlin inquiries were not too far above the average, Mr. Glaser's investigation seems about to indicate that of every 100 people seriously answering an advertisement, about

> 33 out of every 100 are ready to buy
> 36 " " " " " not ready to buy
> 31 " " " " " uncertain

Even if none of the 31 "uncertainties" ever turned out a saleable prospect, the figures still seem to show that where the response is properly gauged one advertisement answerer in every three can be turned into a ready sale.

Now assuming the ordinary sales department handles its inquiries with about the same interest, speed, and determination as the Chamberlin Company, we find that of every 100 people who seriously answer an advertisement—

> 31 out of every 100 never get called on
> 24 " " " " buy from inquiry
> 9 " " " " buy from competitors
> 36 " " " " remain fair prospects

Turn now to expert testimony as to sales and money value of lists built of exactly such names as those 36 that remain "fair prospects." But stop one moment first to check up the conversion results of Chamberlin and Armstrong with those from similar inquiries by professional correspondents of a great mail-order house. The Chamberlin salesmen sold 24 per cent of their inquiries. Competitors' salesmen sold another 9 per cent—a total conversion of 33 per cent. Armstrong ranged somewhere between a minimum of 16 per cent and a maximum of 44 per cent— indicated average, say, 30 per cent. In six months' ordinary routine handling of 8,000 farm-implements inquiries, the mail-order correspondents converted 25 per cent.[1] In one three-month period they converted 30 per cent, and in one special ten-day period, 43 per cent. A Pittsburgh heating unit company in the space of five months converted 40 per cent of mail inquiries from their trade-paper advertising. As an incidental check, we are told Hoover Vacuum Cleaner gets 3.6 sales from every ten demonstrations —a 36 per cent conversion. So the assumption that at least 25 per cent of all serious inquiries to advertisements can and should be sold by salesmen seems thoroughly conservative.

Carry on a few steps further and see how this fits into even more general experience. Experts on advertising results are practically unanimous that more good business is lost through feeble handling of inquiries than through any other single cause. Careful study of several hundred direct-mail campaigns abandoned as non-productive showed they might have been made entirely successful by intel-

[1] A. O. Hurja, "How a Mail-Order House Turns Inquiries into Sales," *Printers' Ink,* December 2, 1926.

ligent use of an adequate order-blank inclosure.
Years ago Edwin B. Lord said: [1]

Beyond a doubt, the most important part of a direct advertising campaign is the follow-up.   There is no question but
that thousands of dollars are wasted annually, the results of
which could have been turned from inglorious failure to a
wonderful success, had the inquiries been properly developed
by follow-up that had been planned and edited in an intelligent manner.

Another authority claims that 75 per cent of all
advertising failures may be traced back to an in-
adequate or worthless follow-up.

As a glaring example, take the case reported by a
business engineer who was asked a few years ago to
investigate some unsuccessful selling.   The advertising had brought inquiries beyond reasonable expectation.   But those inquiries were finally found in
old fruit boxes under a counter.   Although they cost
$30,000, they had been shoved aside.   Properly fol-
lowed up, they should have brought in at least
$250,000 worth of business.

Robert C. Fay, another letter expert, was called
upon by a correspondence school.   He rescued 15,000
inquiries stacked in shoe boxes on their way to the
furnace.   From them, with a single circular at a
cost of $320, he produced $8,000 worth of business.

George Metzger, of Columbia phonograph fame,
had much the same experience.   As he was rummag-
ing around one day in a mail-order book business, a

[1] Charles W. Mears, "From Inquiries to Sales," *Sales Promotion by
Mail.*

bushel basket full of inquiry coupons, covered with dust, came under his eagle eye. Some of them were years old—the story says—and all were thought to have been worked to the limit. But Metzger started the right kind of a follow-up and sold $25,000 worth of books to these abandoned names.

Every person who answers an advertisement is entitled to a prompt, clean-cut, adequate reply. Then, whatever may be your sales plan, that name should go on your mailing list for additional attention. Just to the degree that his mailing list (the heart of a business) and the follow-up (its arteries) are skillfully handled, any advertiser can count on full returns from his advertising expenditures. The mail-order houses find it profitable to spend ten dollars to get a new customer on their books. Unless —and until—they *get* that customer, however, they consider the money poorly spent.

Many businesses that intelligently follow up their inquiries find written selling much the same as personal selling by salesmen. A prospect buys when *he* is ready. Whoever keeps after him, in person or by letter, until that time gets the business. The aim of follow-up is not "cumulative," nor even piecemeal breaking down of resistance. It is simply a persistent attack, one argument after another, trying for the exact moment when the right appeal and the prospect's own attitude will join together to tip him into action. Since this moment is almost as likely to occur one year as another, the age of any inquiry makes surprisingly little difference so long as the address remains correct. For that reason leads received from the very first advertisement, no matter how old, when followed up every month or so, right along with the newer prospects, will keep yielding returns for years.

If any advertiser now neglecting his inquiries feels this too good to be true, let him take the words of S. Roland Hall,[1] who says:

After an inquiry is received in our office, we follow it up quite extensively for about forty days with specially prepared literature, and we continue to follow up the inquiry periodically at least three times each year for two or three years with direct-mail literature.

Oftentimes sales are made from inquiries that are three or four years old. We figure the cost of an inquiry, with the follow-up, is approximately $2.50. The average sale is $70 each.

Or Edwin B. Lord, who says: [2]

Publication A, for example, brought 1,050 replies at a cost of six and three-tenths cents each. By the end of twelve months these 1,050 inquiries had been sold at a total of $916.90 worth of goods. . . . During the second year the average sale resulting from $212 worth of additional follow-up was $4.01, or a total of $4,203.20, which, with $916.90 for the first year, makes the two-year total $5,120.10.

Or Louis Victor Eytinge, who says: [3]

A certain series of five collection letters pulled respectively 11 per cent, 16 per cent, 34 per cent, and 43 per cent, and the

[1] S. Roland Hall, *Theory and Practice of Advertising*, p. 486.

[2] Charles W. Mears, "Inquiries to Sales," *Sales Promotion by Mail*, p. 176.

[3] Louis Victor Eytinge, "Follow-Up Letters," *Sales Promotion by Mail*, p. 83.

last letter 96 per cent of remainder—a clean sweep of 100 per cent of all who could be reached. A textile manufacturer who kept careful records on a long list of prospects addressed a series of follow-up letters, found that the eighth and the seventeenth letters brought the best returns of his whole series, the seventeenth pulling above all the others!

And lastly of one radical who insists:

The old method of expecting the periodical to exert such an influence that any old kind of follow-up will do, has been relegated to the scrap heap as a result of our actual experience. That is why I now insist upon a larger appropriation for the follow-up than for periodical advertising, and in such cases as the present one establish the ratio of two dollars for follow-up to one dollar for the publicity.

To appropriate "two dollars for follow-up to one dollar for advertising" is a bit too revolutionary for our present state of mind. Moreover, it is the shrill battle cry of a minority enthusiast who has unearthed to his proper delight a vital principle recklessly disregarded by the great majority. Nevertheless, it proclaims a basic truth the wise advertiser no longer ignores.

CHAPTER XXVI

The Almost Perfect Campaign

THE best asset for any business—next to gold—is good will. Marshall Field's, the Waldorf Astoria, the New England Conservatory of Music, burning overnight, could start next morning with millions of dollars in their empty hands. Good advertising creates good will. But so do good service and good goods. Any store that isn't reselling 50 per cent of its old customers is wrong somewhere. A healthy business should count satisfied old customers 80 in every 100.

Having your name known is good will. But having your goods used is better will. Truly enough, sales of certain products have dropped disastrously when advertising was discontinued, but equally true, hundreds of other brands, once safely started, have kept right on selling. The Department of Agriculture found a woman with a favorite butter almost certain to use it two years. Makers of tooth powders find people faithful to their old brands; in one famous case, the average continued use was nearly seven years. Even as "Soapine" is—quite properly—held up as a classic example of baleful effects of discontinued advertising, we hear of scattered spots of concentrated demand still glowing embers of Soapine buying established forty years ago.

Advertising that doesn't pay as it goes may turn out an investment in good will. Or it may not. On the other hand, advertising can be self-supporting—and still make good will. Once in a couple of moons it may even make *profits* as well. You expect your salesmen to build good will while selling. Why not ask your advertising to sell while building good will? By taking advertising seriously as a primary selling force, Pepsodent, practically without salesmen, has not only cleaved its way to the top of the crowded dentifrice field, but has in nine years distinctly disturbed ninety years of more leisurely and less scientific advertising by an able competitor.

A few chapters back we spoke of certain professionals who got a magazine 1½ per cent subscription returns with a single cheap letterhead, while a famous publicity expert got only three-eighths of 1 per cent from an expensive mailing. Before some spacious thinker nobly damns our narrowness, we grant that the costly circular had more publicity value. On the other hand, every thousand of the cheap letterheads put immediately into action twelve *more* yearly subscriptions. Long after letter and circular were equally forgotten, the result of the letter still lives, like a 12-ball Roman candle, shooting each month into thousands of additional homes a dozen additional samples of the commodity itself.

Take two more cases: A single five-inch advertisement of Peppie Posters brought 2,947 orders to the manufacturers. They thus got $294 in cash, distributed 2,947 samples, and approached retailers with proof their stuff would sell. And still had exactly as much publicity as if their advertisement hadn't paid them a cent. The same principle works as well with a $1,800 machinery unit as with a ten-cent novelty. A certain machine for filtering steam-boiler water is used only for plants with at least 200 horsepower. For four years a mailing list of 20,000 names brought good inquiries for this machine around $2.50 apiece. One out of three of those inquiries was converted into a sale within six months. The average advertising cost per sale was only about $25. And all advertising incident to the selling was, as with Peppie Posters, just so much velvet.

Does it pay better to try to snow the public into "acceptance" with millions of printed descriptions, or to distribute the articles as far, as fast, as widely as possible to do the selling themselves? Remembering that the direct effect of an advertisement lasts only about seven days in a daily, seven weeks in a weekly, seven months in a monthly, one sees the necessity of implanting some more enduring effect. A large part of the success of the chain stores is due to the fact that they put the merchandise out where the woman who buys can see and handle freely. The United Cigar Stores figure $700 out of every $1,000 rent goes for the big windows that everlastingly flaunt merchandise in the face of the passer-by. A tested window display in three cities for one week brought a 394 per cent increase in sales. An average drug store window—well handled—can show its own net profits of $50 a day.

As further argument for samples, we can't do better than borrow Bruce Barton's statement: [1]

Today twenty million automobiles on the road are their own most powerful advertisement.

Or S. Roland Hall's eloquent eulogium: [2]

When the newspaper has been thrown aside, the poster has ceased clamoring, and the magazine is closed, the package carries on the work of advertising, blazoning the name of cigarettes in clubs and restaurants, announcing the names of chocolates in theaters, and giving to many things names that are literally, and not merely figuratively, household names. . . . The package is nearly always the climax of a sale that was begun by an advertisement.

The real answer, however, is neither printed descriptions nor samples. It is both!

If the package is really the "climax" of an advertisement, why shouldn't every advertisement put as many packages as possible into active circulation? George Washington was one of the world's strategists. In brilliant coups like his retreat from Long Island, the General would allow no American soldier to suspect any movement was intended merely to deceive the enemy. Not fear of spies. Rather he felt that only the most serious belief by his own men that every operation was real would make it look real enough thoroughly to deceive a vigilant enemy.

[1] Bruce Barton, "Is Your Business in the Doldrums?" *Postage*, March, 1927.

[2] S. Roland Hall, *Theory and Practice of Advertising*.

One doesn't always sense this earnestness in advertising copy. Why shouldn't every piece of advertising make an honest effort to *sell* at full price one full-sized unit, at least, of whatever it advertises— be it cold cream, concrete canal boats, breakfast bananas, or railway bridges?

The difficulties are many. In most cases, however, they will be found objections to the idea rather than obstacles to carrying it out. The chief handicap is a habit of thought that still splits advertising into two classes by a boundary quite as arbitrary but far less definite than the Mason-Dixon line. Suppose, for example, you suggest to your advertising counselors that your new electro-thermo advertising help pay for itself by selling a furnace or two on the side. Somebody will look at you reproachfully and say: "Oh, you mean *mail-order* advertising!" You don't mean mail-order advertising, of course: you mean simply you would like the fun of selling in any fashion a few furnaces as a direct, traceable result to the honor and glory of advertising.

How much the advertisement sells may be more or less immaterial. The true value comes in the test of its sincerity. Again summoning to our assistance the sound eloquence of Mr. Benson:

Advertising does not command as yet sufficiently serious confidence to become effective as a buying guide. There is not enough information and helpful suggestion. Most advertising is too partisan; it tells too many half-truths; it does not look through the eyes of the consumer. It does not seek to help him buy; it seeks to sell him.

People certainly do not use advertising as they use the catalogue of a great mail-order house. In it every item is openly described. If a blanket has shoddy or cotton in it, the fact is made known. For certain uses it may be all right; for other uses it might prove disappointing. The reader is properly informed.

Why should not the same sincerity prevail in national advertising?

In these days of economic stress, any advertisement not trying to sell may be viewed as an able-bodied man at tea in wartime. Both may prove all right, but first appearances are against them. Nevertheless, your request to have your advertisement sell furnaces implies a middle ground that few advertising authorities are yet willing to admit. The orthodox recognize no compromise between direct orders and indirect influences. Advertisements must either cossack roughshod over sales resistance or stoop like a pushcart peddler to pull in passing nickels. The idea of a Wanamaker's among advertisements, dignified, colorful, institutional, and luxurious—yet unblushingly selling safety pins right across the counter—remains still to be developed from ashes of our outworn traditions.

So when you get a revised layout, you will hardly recognize your original advertisement. Instead of a picture of a prize electro-thermo furnace with a selling story, your new furnace advertisement now contains a half-page photograph of a booklet seemingly about the thickness of a dictionary, with the title, "Balmy Bermuda in your Bathroom," and a big headline, "This Valuable Booklet FREE."

"That," says your advertising man, still a bit re-proachfully, "will bring the answers you want."

As a matter of fact it will do precisely the opposite. You are selling furnaces. Not Bermuda. Nor bathrooms. Nor even booklets. If your advertising had the nerve to meet the issue squarely and at least try to sell, you might have got twenty letters. And sold, maybe, six furnaces. With the copy turned to giving away booklets, instead of to selling furnaces, you might get 2,000 inquiries. And still sell only six furnaces. There are two differences, however: In one case you have only twenty inquiries to handle perfectly. In the other, two thousand less interested inquiries to handle at considerable expense. And, more important still, you would, in the first case, have full effect of an advertisement devoting its whole soul to selling furnaces. In the other, you have only indirect benefits from an advertisement devoted primarily to giving away booklets.

All traditions to the contrary notwithstanding, orders are not incompatible with "general" publicity.

An advertisement powerful enough to start people telegraphing for immediate delivery doesn't, on that account, lose power with those who merely read. On the contrary, the best possible promise of indirect results in the future is direct results in the present.

A few advertisers are so definitely limited that they can solicit neither inquiries nor orders; they are competent to work out their own salvation, each in his special way. For the vast majority, however, the ideal order of attack is pretty clearly indicated:

1. *Direct Sales:* not necessarily by mail, but a complete and immediate sale as a direct result of reading the advertisement.

2. *Approval Sales:* once in an inquirer's hands, an article is 80 per cent sold. The loss on returns seldom even approaches the saving in the cost of getting such orders.

3. *Samples at full price:* not miniatures at cut prices; but as nearly as possible full size at full price.

4. *Inquiries without inducements:* businesslike correspondence from interested people.

5. *Requests for free samples, booklets:* A method of collecting quickly a large-size mailing list. Value of response depends almost entirely on conservatism of copy.

Begin at the bottom with the broadest and easiest. There are two reasons for samples. The most important is to get your products out into the market to help sell themselves. The other is to induce prospects to register interest so you may send them the complete selling story. A free offer ought to bring five replies where an approval offer brings three. If your tests show that the leads can profitably be turned into sales you will naturally want as many answers as can be had. In his *Scientific Advertising* Mr. Hopkins argues against a man who charges ten cents for a sample:

With samples free he gets replies from his advertisement at the cost of 20 cents, perhaps. Where he requires 10 cents payment, the cost of replies averages $1 or more. He is getting his dime, but on the face of things he is paying 80 cents for that dime. Still, that is not his major loss. He is getting one-fifth as many interested inquiries as he would without that dime. Figuring all losses on trivial inquiries, he is probably paying four times as much as necessary to get into close contact with his interested prospects.

Some figures strongly bearing out Mr. Hopkins come from an advertiser who puts out 16,000 or 18,000 samples a year. He offers a choice between a small sample free and a regular full-size package at ten cents. Not more than one in ten bought the full-size package. Without the free sample, therefore, his inquiries would have been only 1,000 or 1,800. We ourselves can't help feeling that a serious effort concentrated entirely on selling the full-size package at full price might work out best of all.

One thing to keep in mind is, an unknown product is almost as easy to sell at full price as at a bargain. Money—in small sums—doesn't matter so much as bother of answering. People really interested would as soon spend fifty cents at their store for a full-size package as to take the trouble to mail ten cents for a small sample. Furthermore, anyone who cuts a coupon, fills, addresses, stamps, and mails it, has done quite a little toward showing a real interest. The danger of being despoiled through too generous an offer is always within your own control. Where no money is paid you have no obligation to forward to any whose handwriting or address doesn't suit. Moreover, the average advertisement reader today is no longer an idler sponging free samples. The cost of weeding out the comparatively small number of irresponsibles may, therefore, turn out more than it is worth.[1]

Better than the free sample, in most cases, is the inquiry without inducement. Next to direct sales these inquiries, or "leads," are most valuable. Imagine yourself, for example, maker of an electric dishwasher. Get the name of every woman in America with electricity in her house. Scratch off every woman not immediately in the market for a dishwasher. The names remaining would be worth their weight in gold! Inquiries from the right kind of advertisement are exactly that. All the tedious and expensive list gathering is done by your advertisement. The women themselves write you of their interest. And tell you where to find them for sales interviews. All the details of your proposition laid before the whole uninterested world—heating all outdoors, so to speak—might be a costly matter. It may pay you better simply to ask those interested literally to register that interest by sending their names and addresses. Even with an institutional story a coupon doesn't interfere. On the contrary, it snaps the copy up to concert pitch. And backs it up by getting leads for intensive follow-up. Since this puts goods and promotion literature directly into the hands of the people most interested, one

[1] At one time I was offering a 50-cent sample free; I sent an order on the dealer for it. People told me that I would be robbed. So in one of our offices—in Canada—we carefully checked up on the inquiries. The frauds amounted to just 2½ per cent. The cost of checking against them was four times the cost of the fraud—Claude C. Hopkins, "Why I Do Not Charge for Samples," *Printers' Ink*, February 24, 1927.

watches with amazement great advertisers abandon it, even temporarily, to their more earnest little brethren.

Ordinarily, a booklet of no particular value apart from the prospect's own interest will bring in only about half as many answers as the free sample. In fact, as you continue upward toward *bona fide* sales, the mailing list gathered will sharply decrease in size. And more sharply increase in value. Sooner or later, in these days of high-priced space, the chief business of any serious advertising must come to sifting out the real prospects and listing them for further treatment. Ability to get interested inquiries at reasonable cost might, therefore, be a fair efficiency test for any copy not distinctly aimed at some other equally definite job. In fact, one way to clarify the exact intentions of any advertisement might be to propose its carrying just such a lead coupon. The perfection of advertising is maximum response with minimum waste. The serious advertiser must, therefore, reconcile himself to paying real money for the right kind of inquiry. And, consequently, be prepared to follow them vigorously for sales. Experience shows an inquiry costing around two dollars is generally likely to prove most satisfactory. A direct sale by mail is likely to cost at least twice as much as an inquiry.

Inquiries are the butterflies of advertising. Actual sales are governed by average human action. Inquiries, on the other hand, reflect far more largely the skill of the advertiser. Direct sales, in all ordinary circumstances, run much the same. They vary only 10 per cent, 25 per cent, maybe 50 per cent, according to the attractiveness of the *terms* of the offer itself, without too much regard for anything else. Inquiries, on the other hand, will swing up and down 50 per cent, 100 per cent, 500 per cent, even 1,000 per cent, varying with the copy, the coupon, the position, inducement, the season, and all the other incidental factors. Such fluctuations must be watched with a vigilant, and interpreted with a keenly suspicious, eye. Taken at face value, inquiry statistics are as dangerous as a molasses jug to a small boy. Inquiries, in themselves, may mean a fortune. Or they may mean only trouble and expense. The sales you can "convert" out of inquiries tell the real story. A school owner up in Boston advertised in one of the "Quality Group." He had only three inquiries. But he sold two of them. He corresponded with sixty inquiries he got from a great fiction magazine, and sold only three. So never decide finally the value of copy and space and mediums until your sales reports are closed.

The most fascinating game in advertising is to try to beat down the cost-per-*sale*. When the medium is unsuitable or the copy flamboyant the cost-per-inquiry will drop. But the percentage of sales will drop even faster. Conversely, when either copy or medium is conservative, the number of inquiries will drop. But so will the cost of selling them.

Mr. G. Lynn Sumner tells about an advertisement

that produced so many inquiries as nearly to put him out of business. Twenty-six thousand replies came in at a space expense of $1,750. They cost less than 7 cents each, when Mr. Sumner was willing to go as high as a dollar. But spending 50 cents follow-up on each of these 26,000 inquiries brought his total investment up from $1,750 to $14,750. Unfortunately, says Mr. Sumner, the percentage of sales turned out so low that the actual business from the advertisement which pulled too well was the most costly of the whole year. Looking at the other side of another picture, we recall a firm that willingly paid $333 for 132 inquiries. And sold them $34,000 worth of goods!

This varying value of inquiries is one of the strongest arguments in favor of paid-for samples, our third step-up toward more sales from fewer answers. For any advertiser whose business permits, nothing can be more satisfactory than selling a full-size sample. This can be done by mail. Or through dealers. Mr. Hopkins found inquiries that cost him 70 cents apiece by mail could be obtained for 18 to 22 cents by having coupons presented at local stores. People would rather pay car fare than write a letter and wait. His conclusions naturally favor local delivery, with a leaning toward paying the dealer full price for the sample and letting him deliver to the bearer of a free coupon. But authorities differ widely and vigorously on the whole sample question.

Our fourth step-up rises to actual goods on approval. To ask a person bluntly to send in an order

with cash inclosed is far better than not asking him
to do anything.   But with higher-priced articles,
modern advertising uses more finesse.   It baits the
sales hook with "service."   Or sends the article itself
for inspection.   In such cases the coupon is found
practically a necessity.   Just as "on-approval" seems,
these days, the natural method of delivering, and
"easy-payments" the natural method of paying, so
the "inspection-free" coupon seems the natural
method of advertising.   With installment payments
it is already the accepted method for books, radios,
vacuum cleaners, etc.   Increased competition will,
no doubt, soon make it practically universal for any
advertised article between $10 and $100, particularly where the advertiser's own salesman or a local
dealer must go out and find the prospect.   Advertisements of articles on approval should get almost
two-thirds as large response as the free sample offer.

This brings us to the fifth and highest step: selling direct at full price from the advertisement,
allowing the orders to route themselves back through
dealers.   Or by mail.   Or whatever way they will.
The coupon will, in this case, be found not alone
useful in delivering goods to a prospect.   It will
deliver the prospect to the goods.   Dr. Walter Dill
Scott once counted in a current magazine 65 advertisements.   Of these 65 advertisements he found
only 22 that stated fully the exact way to get the
goods.   Seven gave no suggestion whatever—no
price, no address, not even a hint at local dealers.
The remaining 38 had more information, but not

enough to encourage Dr. Scott to explore his home town. Few products are so familiar that all possible buyers know the easiest way to get them. So, where your advertisement doesn't personally deliver the goods to the interested reader, be sure it delivers him—still warm and throbbing—safely alongside the goods.

Direct selling is done oftener than anyone supposes. And far more easily than most people believe. But even where the direct orders are not many, the advertisement itself becomes much more effective on account of the directness of its attack. Some of us can remember when a baseball catcher stood halfway to the backstop until he put on his mask to catch the third strike on the fly. And when every pass from a football center was personally handled by the quarterback. Advertising is still suffering from a complexity complex that makes it afraid to play close behind the bat. Or take the ball on a direct pass.

Although the road to advertising success is strewn with skeletons, like the Old Oregon Trail, there is no need to establish the habit of martyrdom. In pioneer days Daniel Boone risked his life scouting around Kentucky. Today everybody visits Louisville with pleasure and safety. Great enthusiasm is felt, often rightly, in the power of advertising to accomplish miracles, but, even after fifty years of practice, there seems astonishingly little confidence in its ability to make good on simple, everyday selling. Nevertheless, advertising men as a body never seem squarely to face the fact that every advertisement stands on its individual merits, with odds against it, in savage competition for existence. Until we all frankly recognize the possibility that the average present-day advertisement does not pay, we cannot expect much progress toward evolving one that will. If any reader, intent on his own problems, feels we have dwelt overlong on advertising's faults, we beg him to remember that *he* pays for the failures. The "replenishment" necessary to keep always full the quotas of publications and of advertising agencies, is not alone one of advertising's major activities, but is one of advertising's major expenses. And every advertiser is taxed his share.

Would it be too unreasonable to ask every advertisement to pay its own cost in recognizable returns: With the price of the advertising thus recovered in immediate returns, your only gamble on future results would be the manufacturing costs of the goods thus distributed. This plan, when successful, amounts practically to securing a regular advertising campaign at your cost of giving samples free to as many people as will send in full price for them.

Nobody claims that an advertisement can always pay for itself. There are too many varying elements. Every advertisement, however, might at least try to pay its own way. And any advertisement that falls too far short of such self-support might profitably be thrust into the observation ward, even while admired for its literary and artistic beauty.

This, we realize, will sound silly to many who regard advertising as too magnificent a force to be harnessed to petty selling. Nevertheless, as an example of what we mean, here is a brief outline of one tiny campaign. The ideal of the sales manager happens to be directly along the lines we have just indicated: to pay in goods at wholesale rates for all his space, and so obtain as much national advertising as possible without involving capital he can't spare.

The articles not being cakes, we will so designate them. And, lest anyone sneer overtly at the advertiser's modest ambitions as we have outlined them, we may say he pays regular rates for space, taking cash discounts.

His objects, in order of importance, are to:

1. Acquaint the public with his cakes.
2. Induce dealers to stock of their own volition to meet actual public demand.
3. To get back *from his advertising* enough cash orders, direct:
    a. to pay for the advertisement (thus obliging him to pay only the manufacturing cost of the cakes);
    or
    b. to pay for the advertisement AND the cakes (thus getting his advertising for nothing);
    or
    c. to pay for the advertisement and the cakes AND make a profit!

He has allowed us to analyze the direct-mail sales from his most recent advertisements to see how nearly each advertisement run has come to reaching the several objectives.

Of 64 advertisements, so far, used:

All reached the public. It was first-class space in the best newspapers and magazines.

"*X*" reached the dealers. (Impossible to answer.) Orders come in from dealers in constantly increasing numbers. More than 200 of the best retailers and jobbers order and reorder.

Of the 64 advertisements:

44 failed to sell enough cakes, direct-by-mail, to pay for the advertising.

11 sold enough cakes, direct-by-mail, to pay for the advertising and the cakes.

9 sold enough cakes, direct-by-mail, to pay for the advertising and the cakes AND a profit.

Critics may justly point out that having two-thirds of the advertisements fail to pay for themselves is hardly a triumph. The sales manager's only rebuttal is that all came so near to paying for themselves that cash from direct orders fell only seven hundred dollars short of paying completely for the whole list of 64 advertisements in the *New York Times, Brooklyn Daily Eagle, Youth's Companion, American Magazine, Collier's* and *Woman's Home Companion*. Except that his method is successful, so far as it goes, he makes no claims. Spending altogether less money in a year than most advertisers would in a couple of months, he nevertheless keeps on spending. And he keeps on selling more and more cakes. And those cakes keep on selling still other cakes, thus making possible more and more advertising. The Almost Perfect Campaign will hardly be found a gorgeous inspiration. A tiny tortoise among giant hares, it plods along. But it may at least serve as our inspiration and a model for some who think they cannot afford to advertise at all.

And anyone who feels that this Almost Perfect Campaign is either visionary or altogether unique may compare it with the record of a bigger success along the same lines made by Fandango Auto Seat Covers. A *Printers' Ink* story, entitled "Won Dealers Through Mail-Order Copy," tells how the Durant Company started with a forty-seven-line mail-order advertisement in a national weekly. In eighteen months they had dealer representatives covering the United States—all as a result of this same advertising. We have room to quote only the few paragraphs that bear directly on our Almost Perfect Campaign:

A striking feature of the company's growth is that each advertisement paid for itself.

The orders received direct from the public have paid for all advertising space, covered the merchandise, and left a substantial profit besides.

Dealers have written in to say that they have been compelled to stock Durant seat covers because customers have asked for them by name.

And as the writer of the article observes with a simple truthfulness that would credit good old John Bunyan:

Advertising that will do this places a manufacturer in a very enviable position.

CHAPTER XXVII

QUESTION THE QUESTIONNAIRE

IN 1917 our nation divided. The young men went to war. Those too old to fight sent out questionnaires. The war ended. But not the questionnaire. It became our national substitute for thought. Honestly handled by an impartial expert, the questionnaire prevents advertising mistakes. Even a few simple questions to the people you meet at dinner tonight may avert disaster. But in careless or stupid hands, posing as impartial testimony from a cloud of disinterested witnesses, the questionnaire often furnishes information less accurate than the ouija board.

Let's assume that John Dodo blows up the New York Public Library. He is about to hang. Our good Governor leaves the question of a reprieve to a mail vote of the first thousand names chosen alphabetically from the New York Telephone Book. The first name is a lawyer; the second, a carpenter; the third, a stenographer; the fourth, an aviator; the fifth, a manicurist; the sixth, an advertising writer; the seventh, a chauffeur; the eighth, a clergyman; the ninth, an editor; the tenth, a subway guard. And so on down the whole list.

Now it is only reasonable to suppose that John Dodo's crime against literature has particularly prejudiced all who write for a living. Therefore, let us divide the names picked into those with desks and those without desks.

(A)	(B)
Desks	*No desks*
Lawyer	Carpenter
Stenographer	Aviator
Advertising writer	Manicurist
Clergyman	Chauffeur
Editor	Subway guard

Not alone the Governor's questionnaire, but any good letter on any subject, ought easily to draw two replies from every ten people in Group A. But in Group B the most skilled letter on any imaginable subject could hardly hope to average more than one reply from every twenty. To the clergyman at his sermon—the lawyer at his brief—the editor at his proof—answering letters is just part of the day's job. To a sailor, civil engineer, cowboy, writing is an adventure. Chauffeurs and subway guards are as glad to write as you are to put in half an hour with a crowbar. A stenographer and a manicurist in adjoining offices are at different ends of the earth when it comes to filling out a questionnaire.

So friend John is hung—as he no doubt deserves— by a large and enthusiastic majority of those who write easily. But when some editor claims that the mail returns, showing, say, 360 votes for hanging to only 40 votes against it, indicate that all New York strongly favored Dodo's execution, he is talking rot. And one good reporter from the *New York Evening Post* might in one day's investigation prove a vast majority favored a reprieve, if not a pardon! All the mail questionnaire shows is the biased opinion of a small special group to whom Dodo's hanging was important enough to offset their respective difficulties in writing a letter about it. Somewhat the same way, all questionnaires tend sharply away from the average. Very seldom indeed do enough people answer to be representative. And, secondly, those who do answer are not representative people. On the contrary, they are the minority who, for one reason or another, are particularly interested.[1] The opinion, therefore, represents only their opinion. A farm paper included in an editorial

---

[1] As this chapter is about to be typed there appears in *Printers' Ink* (December 23, 1926) a startlingly exact corroboration that one of the writers has been seeking for years. *"Of the housewives who answered the questionnaire, 92 per cent were found to be users of our product, and only 8 per cent were non-users.* Of those who did not answer, 40 per cent were found to be users and 60 per cent non-users." This is the report of Mr. William J. Reilly of the Research Staff of Procter & Gamble, who sent personal interviewers into three cities carefully to check up those who had answered his mail questionnaire. In other words, Mr. Reilly found that, out of every 100 women whose opinion on, say, Ivory Soap was asked, 61 were Ivory Soap users. Out of these 61 users—presumably from the most friendly—*came 36 out of the entire 40 answers.* Of the other 39, who didn't use Ivory Soap, only 3, or 1 in 13, took the trouble to write.

As to remedies for this distortion of information at the source, Mr. Reilly suggests: "The remedies are usually quite simple. If, as in our case, experience shows that the information by mail comes from a group of people who are prejudiced in favor of the product, an examination of actual conditions may permit the use of a discount figure to be applied to all such mail information. Or, if it is found that the questionnaire is not securing replies from enough non-users, such changes as a more careful selection of the mailing list, great emphasis on an appeal inviting suggestions and objections, or an offer of some little reward to those who answer are often used."

coupon a question as to what make clothing its men readers wore. Some 3,000 answers indicated that at least one in ten wore "Styleplus" or "Hart Schaffner & Marx." Only half admitted no special preference. A personal canvass in a fine farming section showed —by way of contrast—that fewer than one in eight farmers really had any knowledge or preference as to the make of his suit. Both investigations, no doubt, were correct. In the first case, the fact that farmers wrote for "publication" brought even into that pale and diffused limelight the human desire to pose. The personal canvass, on the other hand, escaped this error, and, in so far as those interviewed were representative socially and geographically, came nearer the real facts. Two questionnaires can thus be equally accurate and still not agree. Every day the five-hundred-mile front in France saw minor victories for both armies. Each, naturally, reported its own.

To say a certain "cross-section" questionnaire is absolutely false when universally extended doesn't mean it isn't true as it stands. Nor *vice versa*. Nevertheless, we repeat, not one questionnaire in a hundred represents a true cross-section of any greater group. And, unless extraordinary care is taken against this fallacy, any argument adduced from a questionnaire is likely to be altogether fantastic, especially expressed in percentages. A loaded shotgun in the hands of a seven-year-old cowboy is safer than the questionnaire recklessly turned into a testimonial. Or worse yet, used as proof of facts.

Therefore, in judging any information announced as a result of any questionnaire—in fact, in judging any advertisement or news article—an outsider does well to keep in mind the improbability of spontaneous unselfish action on a large scale. There are two sides to every question. All advertising, and a lot else, consists in stating one side so plausibly that the other is forgotten. As some one has said, "Figures don't lie; but they lick the hand that feeds them." Just as anybody can get plenty of signatures on a petition to hang his most popular friend, so a smart statistician can—quite honestly—make his researches prove whatever he has in mind. Says Professor Franken: [1]

One can, for example, *prove* that people drink lemonade for breakfast. Let the investigator go out and ask a hundred women, "Do you drink lemonade for breakfast?" Ninety of the women will probably slam the door in the investigator's face without replying, and ten may think him a fool and answer, "Yes." Thus a tabulation of the results will read, Ninety did not answer and ten said "lemonade," making a perfect advertising case for a fruit growers' association.

Again let us specifically except all surveys made for information only by impartial outside experts who have nothing to gain from the results.

Far too few advertising researches, unfortunately, can be thus undertaken purely in interests of science. Somebody must spend money. If intended for pub-

[1] Richard B. Franken, "How to Get Unprejudiced Market Data," *Printers' Ink*, April 21, 1927.

lication, the only profitable return for that money is distinctly favorable testimony. In these circumstances no intelligent person could be expected to investigate a poor locality or frame a set of questions that would fail to bring in favorable answers. And if anything slips—so that the answer turns out less favorable than expected—the results, naturally enough, are never published. The man who intelligently consults public opinion before committing himself to a single move may get lots of bad news —and die a millionaire.

But, the advertiser using a questionnaire to dig up favorable evidence is in the fortunate position of the young man who tossed up Sunday morning to see whether he should play golf or go to church. And had to flip the coin sixteen times in succession.

On the other hand, it follows with equal force that anyone who wants real facts—for his own information—must never disclose who might be helped by any answers. One has only to recollect how utterly lax people are giving references to departing cooks or stenographers to appreciate how readily they will do a good turn to anybody, especially to him who flatters them by asking an opinion in an important matter. A certain newspaper found that return postal cards addressed to the paper brought in a far more flattering return than the anonymous check-up which it was wise enough to add.

Says Professor Poffenberger on the matter of care in selecting questions: [1]

[1] Albert T. Poffenberger, *Psychology in Advertising.*

In general, it may be expected that questions concerning one's intimate affairs, his morals, his religion, his financial status, and many of his personal habits, are likely to remain unanswered, receive evasive answers, or be answered falsely.

"Do you do your own washing?" as a question, failed to bring forth a single washlady among thousands of homes where there were known to be no servants. On the other hand, when asked what magazine they like best, hundreds of men and women regularly name expensive publications they see only on news stands or in doctors' waiting rooms. That a good proportion of those who answer questionnaires will seize every opportunity to register superior intelligence, wealth or culture is only to be expected. One magazine, some years ago, had to abandon an elaborate questionnaire because it proved conclusively that its readers alone owned more Rolls-Royce cars than a factory had ever turned out. Even in personal interviews, the Cimaline company found three families in ten reported using their product— a situation quite beyond their fondest expectation!

Face it frankly. People always like to seem more important, more educated, richer, wiser than they really are. An enthusiastic collector of "statistics" for the *Atlantic Monthly* proved, beyond the shadow of doubt, that its readers own nearly $100,000 worth *more* Steinway Pianos than Mr. Steinway has so far manufactured. It is all very simple. The first 1,000 subscribers reported ownership of so many pianos. Multiply the whole number of readers and there you are! Honestly, now, wouldn't you feel it your duty as a gentleman to tell a stranger at your doorbell that your wife sent the washing out to a laundry rather than that she bent over the tub herself? So would everybody else. And they do!

Hundred-per-cent truth-telling about your circumstances and your motives is as rare in a questionnaire as it is in an autobiography. Mark Twain tried once to prove that it could be done. His brother Orion was a hopelessly unsuccessful, impractical, and yet honest-minded man. "I've invented books about queer characters," thought Mark, "but Orion has *lived* a more extraordinary book than I could invent. He has nothing to conceal. All he has to do is to tell the truth about himself, and it will be the funniest, most pathetic, and greatest book in the world." Orion fell into the idea. He was honest, and he struggled hard. But before long he began to "cover up." He just couldn't confess himself a dumb-bell on every page. He tried to bare his soul, and his soul kept running to cover. Before long, if the book had been continued, Orion would have dramatized himself as a fine fellow—an earnest, splendid character only defeated by conditions that he could not control.

Question the questionnaire. Question the "facts" it brings in. No normal person will fail to "prefer" a Cadillac car to a Ford; nobody will plead guilty to pimples, wife-beating, lack of linoleum on the kitchen floor, cruelty to children, or disregard of the great virtues of life insurance or good bonds. People always dramatize themselves, just as Orion did, even when he knew he could grow rich and immortal by telling the plain truth. It won't make any farmer rich and famous to tell your investigator that he has bad breath and your prophylactic didn't cure it. Ten to one, he will work a high-class miracle right into your statistics.

And question the questionnaire before you send it out. Answer it honestly. See if *you* feel like running downstairs to look at the label in your refrigerator, and then out to the garage and find out what make of carburetor you use? Or who made your hat? Or your socks? Or what publisher issued the novel you finished last Saturday? If you can't pump up any true enthusiasm for these manufacturers, who are outside your own business, the folks who get your questionnaire probably won't feel any more interested in you.

Questions, therefore, must be more than easily understood. They must look very, very easy to answer. And they should in fact be as simple as possible. Only vital questions should be asked. Unless you catch people off guard or flatter them into an undeserved interest, most whose opinions are worth anything won't bother. To get the greatest practical value questions should bring answers lending themselves to simple statistical treatment. Ask a question or two such as "What do you like best about your kitchen stove?" on which anybody may exhaust a little self-expression. The answers need not be tabulated, and among them may drift in valuable suggestions. All other answers should be such as may be counted. And added: so many "Yes"; so many "No"; so many "in winter only." Extra care must, therefore, be taken that no question requires several facts in one answer.[1]

It is important, too, in conducting any questionnaire—or in fact any investigation—to make a sharp division between established facts and mere opinions. On simple statistics, such as how many pairs of shoes a year an American family wears, the questionnaire will be found surprisingly accurate. On matters of opinion, it is dangerous beyond words. Weight of numbers has, of course, no relation to truth. Mr. E. V. Shepard tells us that out of 807 answers to the first auction-bridge problem sent over the radio, 804 were wrong. Facts continue to be facts regardless of how many people believe them. One intelligent, trained judgment is worth more than a million guesses. And piled up prejudice means absolutely nothing except a hazard that has to be reckoned with.

All trade is transacted in the human mind. No-

[1] The following formula to introduce a questionnaire appears in an article in *Advertising & Selling*. That it is effective most persons can testify from their own experience and susceptibility to the device.

"A symposium is being conducted among a few of the country's leading . . . (insert here citizens, dry-goods merchants, importers, exporters, etc., etc.) to determine their opinion on a matter of great importance and public interest. The question on which we wish to secure your opinion is . . . (insert here the question or questions to which an answer is desired.)"

In spite of what our strictly rational attitude towards such an appeal might be, it does tickle our fancy to be classed among the leading. . . . Our pride, our self-assertiveness, our ambition, are all aroused and we do not apply our logic too strenuously.—ALBERT T. POFFENBERGER, *Psychology in Advertising*.

where else!   That fact will some day explode into
business consciousness. Then every worth-while advertising agency will boast its own trained psychologist to check up the dynamic potentiality of every
proposed advertisement. Trade psychologist will
rank alongside our statistical economist. The fluctuations of the public mind will be studied as carefully as is the weather today. "Bad" business will
thereby be diagnosed in advance rather than two
months too late. And a new generation of advertising men instead of freezing up in the frost of hard
times will turn on the proper amount of sales power
with all the accuracy of trained engineers.

The first aim of any advertising survey, therefore,
today should be toward a study of minds. But, like
everything else in the advertising field, research still
devotes itself almost entirely to markets. Advertising men have done wonders in organizing retailing.
If advertising never did another thing beyond what
it has already done to put modern merchandise into
packages, the world would always owe it a debt of
gratitude. But advertising as advertising—the real
power—hasn't, perhaps, gained as much as the various stepchildren it now supports. The advertisement itself seems sometimes sunk about to the importance of the king in a modern monarchy. A new
school of practical distributors has pushed goods into
the public hands faster than old-school advertisers
could ever pull them. Consequently, we are fairly
flooded with the working sheets of the new school;
statistical studies and market surveys, facts of circu-

lation, facts of wealth, facts of buying power, a magnificent array all showing *where* to apply advertising.

Compared with these data on where to apply it, we have practically no facts worth mentioning as to what advertising to apply.

Or just how to apply it.

Circulation figures, marketing analyses, or merchandising statistics, submitted *as such* to any business ripe for them, are valuable and important. But as a part of a preliminary plan for the average advertiser, detailed studies of a market's buying ability are about as useful as road maps of upper Mongolia to a Ford owner in Oklahoma. Before any advertiser can profitably discuss distribution as an advertising *result,* he ought, obviously, to be fairly certain he will have that result. Wherever possibilities of the market are allowed to precede probabilities of the advertising, somebody's cart is running away with his horse.

Monumental works of masterly analysis, like those of J. Walter Thompson, Curtis, Richards, Barton, Durstine & Osborn, Crowell, and the *Chicago Tribune,* the *Milwaukee Journal,* would be a credit to any industry. To any advertiser qualified to use them, statistics are infinitely valuable. If, however, they distract him from his real problem which is primarily psychological, they may to the average advertiser prove dangerous exactly in proportion to their excellence. Army officers tell us that troops are not expected to do any execution with their rifles; small arms are merely to keep rank-and-file occupied while the greater strategy rolls over their heads. Some of our master advertising salesmen may, perhaps, have found an equally simple expedient in talking about markets and taking for granted the efficiency of the advertising.

At any rate, whenever long columns of figures spread before you the magnificent markets you are to *reach*, make certain you have, in parallel columns, equally definite figures as to just what you will do for yourself when you reach them.

Any advertiser who wishes to test the practical utility of any market or circulation statistics submitted to him, need only to ask their sponsor to boil down his whole plan to answer broadly six simple questions:

1. How many people will have the chance to read my advertisement.
2. How many of them *will* read it?
3. How many of those who read will *buy?*
4. How much will they buy apiece?
5. In what localities will these sales come?
6. How soon?

That accurate answers to these six questions are impossible, we realize as clearly as the most ardent advocate of easy advertising. But, because it is absurd to expect exact answers, we can't agree the questions are absurd. On the contrary, every advertiser who insists on cool millions of general purchasing power being translated into warm dollars itching to buy his own particular goods, does a real favor to the nation's business. Without some mutual agreement, in each case, as to some sort of answer to our six questions, advertising must continue a kind of commercial White Magic. For a wealthy man to waste money, socially or personally, is no longer considered good taste. Similarly, the best business practice begins to frown on unproved expenditures. Today, more than ever before, current business and general industrial welfare, as well, demand that advertising throw its full force directly into the greatest and most immediate distribution of goods the nation can possibly contrive.

There are 500 experimental laboratories at work in the United States, seeking more efficient ways to make things. The paper industry alone has spent $2,000,000 within the past few years to eliminate manufacturing waste. Selling waste is America's *real* problem. Research laboratories on scientific selling are few and feebly supported. Even so, there is no excuse for waste in advertising. Advertising can prove its own puddings. Every advertiser is his own laboratory. He needs no complicated apparatus, nor, indeed, any formula at all. All he need do is ask the man on the street.

CHAPTER XXVIII

PROVE YOUR OWN PUDDING

"*Hard* selling doesn't pay. It is the avoidance of selling obstacles that pays," says Mr. John A. MacMillan of the Dayton Rubber Company. "This means plenty of brain work, study and engineering, long before the selling begins."

In opera, if anywhere, professional critics still reign. Yet Vienna last January experimented an opera première over the radio. Kienzl's "Hassan der Chwaermer" was tried out on the aërial dog. Austrian newspapers favor this radio first night, which not only puts new operas strictly on their musical merits, but gives the composer a direct appeal to the public before risking money on scenery or costumes.

Nearer home, take "Abie's Irish Rose." Here is what the *New York Times* English dramatic critic cabled of its London opening:

It is desperately ingenuous and unsophisticated. You are not allowed to perceive or discover its humor; its humor is, on the contrary, thrown at you with both hands from the beginning of the evening to the end. Its appeals to sentimental maids, the wedding march and Christmas trees, twin babies and grandfather's toys—are stale beyond the nightmare of farcical melodrama. . . . I confess that by few quite harmless pieces have I ever been so bored.

New York critics had also been bored. They

ranged from coldly unenthusiastic to emphatically bitter. None of us blame them! Yet Miss Nichols' shrewdly calculated appeal carried far beyond the public she built for. It created its own new public. In New York, where five months is good, it ran six years; in Cleveland, where one week is rare, it ran six months; in Erie, Pa., where one night is a long stand, "Abie," ran a month. Ten companies carry it to tank towns like Bucharest and Budapest. On July 6, 1927, "Rose" beat "Chu Chin Chow's" five-year run in London. The play that critics high-hatted now spreads out, without precedent or competition, into an apparently endless string of world's records.

Few people, however, will ever realize the advantage ingenuous Ann Nichols had over the critics. Not only did she carve every character and situation out of time-tested, sure-fire, professional vaudeville, but, before coming East, had seasoned her show for months on California small-town audiences!

In lack of sympathy for dumb little man, man with his dirty dollar bill, dramatic critics are by no means alone. Ten literary critics were asked by the *International Book Review,* a few years ago, to name the best books published since 1900. The *Review* then put the same question to the public. Eighteen hundred readers responded, naming 2,164 books. When these titles were arranged in order of poularity, not one book named by the critics was found among the first ten. On only one book did the two lists in any way agree: John Galsworthy's *Forsyte Saga* was about twelfth in both. The first book in the critics' list was thirty-fourth in the popular list. And Wells' *Outline of History*, overwhelmingly first choice on the popular list, was not noticed by the critics.

At the advertising exhibition held under the enterprising auspices of the New York Advertising Club in 1925, some 13,000 people took their choice among many advertisements. The advertisement voted best by artists and advertising men was placed *ninth* by the housewives for whom it was particularly intended. This is no reflection on the men with artistic training. Their choice was correct. The women were wrong. Nevertheless, it reminds that the most artistic advertisement is not always the most effective. Also, that experts, as such, are seldom good judges of public taste.

Ten years later Snow repeated the Hollingworth experiment described in Chapter XVI. He got opinions from 227 men and 528 women, with emphasis on the selling value of the various appeals. Then Professor Snow turned to five prominent sales managers and asked each to rank in order of selling value the same appeals according to his own judgment. The first six appeals in the combined choice of Snow's 755 men and women ran in this order:

1. Time saved
2. Appetizing
3. Cleanliness
4. Safety
5. Efficiency
6. Scientifically made

The five sales managers' first six choices were:

1. Durability
2. Family affection
3. Sympathy
4. Sport
5. Appetizing
6. Hospitality

These two lists, you will notice, do not coincide at any point: "Appetizing" alone appears on both: it ranks second on the people's list and fifth on the sales managers'. The people's first choice is the sales managers' eleventh. The first choice of the sales managers is fourteenth on the people's list. "Family affection," considered a very close second by the sales managers, is held only tenth in importance by those to whom it is supposed to appeal. "Sympathy" ran eighth, and "Sport" seventh in people's minds, instead of third and fourth as in the sales managers' estimate.

"Cleanliness" caused the greatest disagreement: Snow's 528 women placed it third; Snow's 227 men placed it second; Hollingworth's 40 men and women placed it third. But the sales experts placed it twenty-second. This disagreement as to cleanliness shows how dangerous it is for any of us to jump at general conclusions. In Dr. Starch's similar test, men put "Time saved" tenth; women put it first. Men put "Sympathy" seventh, while women put it twenty-third!

Mr. S. H. Giellerup carried these tests still further.[1]

[1] S. H. Giellerup, "Let's Stop Guessing About Copy," *Advertising and Selling*, September 23, 1925.

A difference of opinion arose as to the best of four types of copy for a famous toilet article. All agreed to leave final decision to a test by actual selling. In the meantime, to get a guess from other advertising men. Also to get an advance judgment from the public itself. The jury for the public was selected at random out of Albany and Syracuse telephone books. Sixty-nine strangers were affable enough to return written ballots expressing opinions as to the probable selling powers of the several advertisements. Their first choice was the advertisement put last by the advertising men. As usual, the middle choices were nearest alike. But careful records of actual sales made by the several advertisements proved the 69 samples of public opinion absolutely right on their first three choices. And proved the advertising men absolutely wrong on their strongest two dislikes.

In his book, *Advertising Response,* Mr. H. M. Donovan sets up eight factors that he feels make for ideal conditions in advertising. They are:

1. Primacy—first in its field
2. Continuity—running without break
3. Large space
4. Frequency
5. Recent appearance
6. Appearance in leading local newspapers
7. Appearance in important national publications
8. Extension—backing up in direct mail, car cards, etc.

Most of us will give his factors a high and enthusiastic vote of approval. But when Mr. Donovan begins to match up actual facts in the Philadelphia high schools with his ideal conditions, something seems to slip. Franklyn Sugar, first on Mr. Donovan's list with 84.7 per cent results, shows only a 69 per cent fulfillment of his ideal conditions. Colgate, with a 99 per cent fulfillment of these ideal conditions, comes eighth on his list. Gillette, with 89 per cent ideal fulfillment, comes sixth; while Underwood, with 61 per cent fulfillment, comes third. The fourteenth on Mr. Donovan's list of results stands sixth on his list of theoretical perfection. And Underwood, eleventh in theoretical perfection, stands third in results. Incidentally, of the eighteen products which lead Mr. Donovan's test, nine had no national advertising at all. Once more we find the only safe reasoning in advertising is the record of results.

Two towns across the Mississippi River are 600 yards apart as the ferry drifts. On the map of the inexperienced sales manager they are tweedledee-and-tweedledum. But old salesmen know that anything which sells in one town will not sell in the other. Some racial difference in early settlers set those two neighbors as far apart as Tampa and Duluth. Radios, magazines, and Sunday newspapers are making the country think—or stop thinking, if you prefer—as one man. But there are still belts of buying that must be respected. The South won't take black cough drops; the rest of the country doesn't want yellow. Boston likes its asparagus and rubber white, and its eggs brown; Philadelphia votes with Boston on brunette eggs. The rest of the country prefers red rubber and white eggs. Chicago stands out for green asparagus. New England likes dark rubber-stemmed pipes and light cheese. The South prefers light celluloid pipestems and dark cheese. None of these preferences need cause serious economic concern. But they show how people make up their minds as to what they want. Therefore, we continue respectfully to urge that the antennæ of an insect, or the famous cat's whiskers, are no more serviceable to their respective owners than are tests to the alert advertiser. The best way to find out what people will buy is to make them an offer. The quickest way to find out whether an advertisement is good is to test it.

There is the case of Mrs. S————. Her husband died and left a candy store. It was a prosperous candy store with lots of excellent advertising. Any practical man would have recognized the relationship. And let well enough alone.

But, being a woman, she was curious. Also unafraid.[1] She saw money coming in for candy. She saw money going out for advertising. Like Pandora, she longed to lift the lid. Finally she couldn't resist the temptation to tilt it just a little.

She took out one advertisement!

Then she stood anxiously by, ready to jam it back in again if anything happened.

[1] "Because of woman's newness and inexperience, the phrase, 'It's never been done before,' with its insidious assumption that therefore it can't be done, holds for her none of the restraint that it frequently exerts over the masculine element of the community, sobered and rendered ultraconservative by a long past of up-and-down business experience. She has no such past, therefore she is unafraid."—MISS ANNE MORGAN in an address delivered over WEAF, February 28, 1927.

Nothing happened. Sales went right on. So she kept that advertisement out permanently. Then she took out another. Business fell off. So she rushed that advertisement back to stay. And so she went patiently through the whole list, in all possible combinations. Finally she found exactly the advertising that kept the business going at the same level with the least expense.

In the meantime, her husband's hard-boiled half-brother, head of a great company with an appropriation around a quarter of a million a year, told his friends:

I spend $100,000 a year on magazines, and $100,000 on posters. I don't know which brings in business. But business keeps coming in, so I keep advertising.

He was president of an advertising club or two, and made an informal speech at Denver. Although his half-sister in candy doesn't even suspect the meaning of a milline, she is advertisingwise, on a somewhat sounder basis than he. For she, at least, paid advertising the compliment of demanding from it the same cause-and-effect that he demands from everything except advertising. Advertising needs no such exemption. We should ask no such odds. Contrast with the gentleman just quoted the alertness of the advertising manager who reports:

We have made mailings of 450,000 on one list this fall, simply on the information we got from a test of 2,000. The big mailing of 450,000 is coming through all right, that is, it was up to the time I left the office, on practically the same ratio as the 2,000 test.

To advertise at a profit, as we have already said, is within the power of any man likely to read this book. No radical change of method is necessarily involved. Merely a change in mental attitude. As soon as vulgar curiosity as to advertising's effect takes the place of academic discussion as to appearance and expression, the problem becomes much simpler.

Advertising, to be sure, hasn't quite the fresh appeal of its early days. People are distracted toward newer things. At the same time, we have found human motives still flowing smoothly along the same channels, centuries deep. And, like the little Japanese policeman who jiu-jitsus his opponents with their own force, we have found many professional advertisers keenly utilizing these motives to make advertising pay handsomely. That opportunity is open to any advertiser not too proud to learn as he goes. Often there is difficulty checking results. But never is there a question as to the formula:

Any advertising that is an exact extension of any already profitable activity will always pay—provided it does not cost too much for the amount of extension it actually brings.

Let us examine this formula in practice.

You sell fresh eggs at low prices. A big sign saying just that will unquestionably pay. In fact, as many such signs as you can find room for. In your spare time, moreover, you might profitably make a selling call on your next-door neighbor—and your next—and next—right around the block. And even the block beyond. But, sooner or later, the amount of time you and your customers take going back and forth becomes a distinct factor. As distance increases, your selling cost increases, while your chances of trade decrease. Finally, at some one block, this extra expenditure of time and energy will exactly cancel all possible benefits. And, from that point on, every block farther you carry your extra selling simply cuts that much deeper into the large easy profits out of your own immediate neighbors.

So long as you keep walking, this is easy enough to realize. Now, telephone. To telephone is far easier than to call personally. Yet the element of distance —in terms of added time and expense—still enters your problem. Let's suppose you have bought some delivery wagons. Up to ten, twenty, thirty miles you find you can sell by telephone and deliver at a profit. But at some point—probably as you get into toll-line telephoning and long-haul delivery—you strike the same snag you did in your personal visits. Every bit of business done beyond the boundaries of a certain rough circle so many miles from your plant must be financed out of the profits of the easier and less spectacular trade from just around the corner.

This naturally leads to branch establishments. So you reach national advertising. Here, though not so easily detected, precisely the same problem confronts you. Your advertising, if checked as carefully as the woman in the candy store checked her advertising, will repeat your two earlier experiences. Your best advertisement in your best publication will bring business at a jolly profit. The same advertisement in the next best publication or the next best advertisement in the same publication will do almost as well. But down the profit line they gently slide, until —as in your personal and telephone calls—you reach the one advertisement and one publication which barely pay. That is your danger point. From there on, every less effective advertisement must be financed out of the profits of your better advertisements. And if you go too far, the tail of your advertising list may cost you more than its head is making.

Every advertiser can use all the information he can get as to what each of his advertisements does for him. Comparison of publications, carelessly considered the chief reason for "keying," is one of the least important. If all elements of advertising were as steady, standard, and stabilized as the average 10,000 circulation of any high-grade magazine, leading newspapers, standard theater programs, first-class billboards, or recognized radio broadcasts, advertising would be far simpler. In fact, the extraordinary pains these mediums take to prove their admittedly ample buying power suggests Gertrude Ederle sending a small boat ahead to prove the Channel deep enough.

The test tube, scales, and stop watch—engineering and laboratory methods—extended to every aspect of your advertising, may do far more than save you money. They might save your business life. In a strategic crisis, three months wasted on the wrong sales tack means more than mere money cost.

One manufacturer advertising entirely to women was surprised to find his orders chiefly from men. Another, a maker of talcum powder, spent thousands of dollars on literature glorifying purity, smoothness, and antiseptic qualities. Then he made an investigation. He found 95 per cent of the women buying his talc because they liked the odor, and the other 5 per cent because they liked the little can. Still another advertiser spent hundreds of thousands of dollars exalting the healthful iron in raisins before he took the trouble to discover that he was interesting only 8 in every 100 customers. The other 92 were buying raisins because they "taste good." Two companies, independently, had elaborate investigations among 5,000 women checking up advertising appeals for soap and dishwashers. Both made the same discovery. Only one thing really mattered:—women don't want to spoil their hands in dirty hot water. One food advertiser tried out fifty different plans in five years, constantly improving his method. In the fifth year he found the one he sought. It cut his selling costs 75 per cent. Another great company is said to have spent $40,000—and been satisfied—to prove through tests in a sample territory that a certain new product could not be marketed.

Advertising accounting is still in swaddling clothes because of a theory that *any* advertising can win by keeping everlastingly at it. Advertising, true enough, is like a nettle. Grasp it firmly or let alone! Nor is there any doubt that a man who hammers resolutely away with only a fair campaign will go further than the man who jumps in and out with a fine one. Nevertheless, in advertising as surely as in the great Mojave Desert, any traveler not sure of his way had better sit still rather than walk in the wrong direction.

For example, one firm mailed a selected list of dealers 50,000 copies of its spring announcement. The firm counted confidently on at least 1,000 replies. Only three came in. Then it was too late to start afresh. A small test mailing would have saved the entire season. A certain double-page spread, with coupon, brought in about 500 answers. This cost nearly $400 apiece to give away a free booklet. $200 worth of circular letter tests might have saved that $20,000 for an advertisement of proved effectiveness. A bank sent out 33,000 letters to especially desirable clients. Only 1 in 3,000 answered. Think of the bad effect of so weak a letter on the other 32,989 prospects. Not every letter or advertisement can be a world beater. But there is no excuse for failure. By testing separately, attention, headline, and text, Dr. Starch found he could, with the help of a small group of people, indicate around 80 per cent of perfect accuracy the relative strength of various advertisements. With 113 advertisements in 20 different series, he demonstrated that the prophetic accuracy indicated by the 69 strangers out of the Albany and Troy telephone book was no accident.

One handicap to accurate advertising is an unwillingness to test and a complete willingness—an anxiety—to compromise. Instead of stopping to prove, once and for all, which of several opposing ideas is right, everybody joins in one advertisement to include them all. Mr. Black, president, insists the best appeal is quality; Mr. White, vice-president, that it is price, not quality; Mr. Browne, second vice-president, that it is neither price nor quality, but terms; Mr. Green, sales manager, that, regardless of price, quality, or terms, we really sell through unique service. Now they all can't be right. There can't be four chief appeals. One of the lot would certainly prove better than the other three put together. What do Black, White, Browne, and Green do? Before spending real money on advertising, do they sit down and prove the best appeal? They do not. They give-and-take until all are satisfied—and none pleased. The public gets an advertisement that blurs four personalities as well as four appeals. And advertising gets blamed for the failure!

Unlike other courts of last resort, the public will nearly always give a clear intimation as to its final judgment. You can test groups of human beings almost as accurately as you sample wheat or measure the heat value of coal. When a chemist wants a mixture for any special purpose, he does not guess a thousand gallons together for shipment. Instead, he mixes a few drops in a test tube and tries it out. He keeps on this miniature scale until he finds exactly what he is looking for. Just as the chemist's test tube prevents costly failure, so wise advertisers, by solving their problems in miniature, avoid waste. And confidently invest their money in proved propositions.

For there is nothing mysterious about an advertisement. No golden Minerva to burst full panoplied from a godlike brain. No metaphysical unearned increment that suddenly flowers into unexpected spring. The inexplicable power that never fails was an excellent fancy back in the days when advertising managers brought their whiskers to business on tall bicycles. Since then, less poetic young men in department stores and mail-order houses have pulled advertisements apart to find what makes them go. Cold-blooded psychologists too have added a good many very enlightening facts.

There is, therefore, no more excuse for advertising without a barbed idea than for fishing without a hook. Less! We can't ask the fish how they like the bait. But we can always find out how people like the idea. Ask them! Fifty opinions will give you a safe start; five hundred will prove your case.

In a little lunch room on Forty-sixth Street—ably conducted by a business woman—a bright-eyed girl in the cashier's cage tabulates your cup of coffee the moment you pay your check. A Boston grocer tabulates all his sales every day. He catches instantly growing popularity of some articles and slowing down in others. This gives a sure hold on everyday staples that leaves him free to experiment with profitable novelties. He demonstrates every day the truth of somebody's shrewd suggestion that the worries of retail stores would disappear if they would only work as hard to buy the goods their customers want as to sell them goods they don't. If grocers and lunch rooms find fresh facts worth this trouble, what about great advertisers who can lose more in a day than these little establishments make in a year? One advertiser, spending $5,000 a month on dealers' display signs, awoke after ten years to the fact he didn't know which style paid best. All he needed was a record of each display sent out and a comparison of that dealer's subsequent selling. Lest this talk about small details seem to show no very vast vision, we hasten to quote an advertiser large enough to test whole cities against each other.[1]

Here is the way we work out a test campaign. One, two or sometimes three medium-sized cities are chosen. . . . .

. . . We've found St Louis very satisfactory for a metropolitan district. For test cities of smaller size, we used Grand Rapids, Michigan, Peoria and Decatur, Illinois, and Des Moines, Iowa.

. . . In one of these cities chosen for tryout, we may test out a plan for sampling through the dealer. In another, a house-to-house method. In the third, sampling may be done through mail. . . . We have had as many as six test campaigns running at once in twenty different cities.

If, within a month or so, a campaign in a certain city shows signs of being a productive one, we may put the same campaign into other cities, just to make the test more thorough. Some tests run only two or three months; others run as long as a year. They may run ever longer than that. . . . Not

[1] Harlow P. Roberts, "What We Have Learned from Seven Years of Advertising," *Sales Management*, February 20, 1926.

until every plan has been tested in this fashion does it become a part of our nation-wide campaign.

The question naturally arises, then, whether a campaign tested locally in this manner can be expected to produce in other territories with equal satisfaction. The answer is, "yes." . . . So far as our particular problem is concerned, people are much the same from Maine to California. *A campaign that pulls in Delaware will pull about the same results in Illinois or Washington.*

What's true in the test tube is true in the vat. Prompt, accurate records are vitally important to any business, large or small, that lives through selling. Advertising returns—whether on cities or sandwiches—are important enough to deserve checking at the cashier's desk along with the actual money. To key returns is, of course, not always easy. Neither is it ever so difficult. Whether it be a matter only of different colored inks or of vital selling policy, a quick test can always be made with two sets of circulars identical at every point but the one in question, or by advertisements published in any carefully matched pair of states, counties, or towns. These tests will, moreover, often help out on more than the single decision. Watching the responses, reading carefully all the answers—besides settling the main point at issue—may tip you off as to what portion of your advertising is carrying the highest voltage. Every effort should be made to find the reason for any particularly strong runner-up. Try to crowd into the winner—the circular or campaign finally chosen as best—*all* the good selling points developed in the less successful copy and follow-up correspondence.

Advertising suffers a frightful handicap. Under that gorgeous ubiquity "It pays to advertise" it is given—*as is nothing else in the artistic or business world*—an unqualified blanket guarantee of success.

A man may write a poem, put on a play, paint a picture, sing a solo. As soon as he attempts to make it "pay," clarion critics warn him of weakness. If, as often happens, the public agrees with the critic, our unfortunate author, painter, or singer swiftly slides into silence. In advertising, on the contrary, no matter how ignominiously he may be failing, he is still assured by all our sacred traditions that he is bound to win if only he has the courage to keep at it.

No rule will guarantee advertising results any more than any rule will guarantee a needed invention. But the good old "trial-and-error" system works in advertising quite as accurately as in Edison's laboratory or Luther Burbank's garden. When you screw an electric bulb into a new socket and get no light, you don't know first whether the bulb is defective or the current turned off. But it doesn't take long to find out. And once you get a trusted bulb or an established current, you can proceed with absolute certainty. As a friend in a great Chicago department store once told us: "I used to be *afraid* to check my advertising, item by item, against actual sales. But when I once began to know what I really sold, the whole position of advertising in the store was changed. The merchandise buyers looked to me for help and advice. As advertising manager, I became a sales director, not a clerk."

The editor of the *Mailbag* tells of a new machine to make a simple product. The machine he saw was sixteenth in a series which represented already an investment of $198,000. How many advertising men are there, asks the editor, who would try out sixteen successive experimental sales campaigns before making a final recommendation? How many advertising campaigns involving $198,000, asks the editor, get even sixteen weeks of really exacting preliminary rehearsal before being turned loose on the public?

The elderly man and the established business both find a terrific temptation to substitute experience for experiment. The corporation that hires Nestor for sales manager—with Pandora as his first assistant—will live forever. Opinions keep advertising a game. Tests make it a business. Unless you are warming up for the Royal Academy, or have an ambition to write the great American advertisement, test as you go. Test before you go. Most of all, test before you stop. Don't cut loose from good money you have already spent until you are certain it is doing you no good. Don't play with your advertising. Find out what is right—and make it a man's job. Don't depend on appearance. Or *a priori* reasoning. Or technical excellence. Prove your own pudding!

CHAPTER XXIX

Your Advertising Dollar

If advertising could, of itself, make money, we were all rich long ago. Advertising makes money only in the sense that the moon makes marriages. It brings two parties together in the most favorable light. That done—all is done. Nature must take its course. The intrinsic attractiveness of the proposition and the potential public response are, strictly speaking, entirely outside advertising's jurisdiction. Advertising, as a friend of the court, can only advise the advertiser what the public will probably like, and then beg the public please to like it.

The U. S. Parcel Post is a wonderful convenience. Radio is a wonderful invention. The motion picture is a wonderful institution. Advertising is all three —it is a convenience—an invention—an institution. Nevertheless, like each of the others, it can do only certain definite things. And it can do these only when properly used. You don't expect your parcel-post package to reach more than one person, nor your radio to deliver a parcel. So don't begin by expecting too much of advertising.

Advertising is, as we have said, only an extension of an idea. Is your idea really worth extending? Unless you have an idea you are sure will extend to your profit, you have no more use for advertising

384

than you have for a drum-major's full-dress uniform. A railroad train doesn't interest you until you want to go somewhere. A telephone is more or less nuisance unless you want to talk to somebody. Advertising is the same. Don't let it waste your time until you know how you want to use it. Advertising merely for the sake of advertising is the world's most expensive luxury.

There is, however, one man more extravagant than he who advertises when he shouldn't. That is the man who doesn't advertise when he should. He walks rather than rides. He delivers his packages on foot. He draws his water in the old oaken bucket and walks up the Woolworth Building stairway rather than bother with an elevator.

The man who can advertise and does not, advertises, nevertheless. He advertises himself as one unable to utilize one of the greatest of modern forces. On the other hand, perhaps, he is not always to blame. Possibly he doesn't know how simple and practical the right kind of advertising can be. If more men realized how simple it is to wade gamely into profitable advertising, fewer maybe would splash around the shallows. Or plunge headlong into deep water before they can swim.

Our generation will probably never live down the idea of an advertising man as somebody called in only to move goods out of the storeroom. Therefore, we find difficulty today in visualizing our advertising man's coming successor—the psychological engineer! This 1930 model publicity expert will crowd into the picture long before goods ever reach the storeroom. In fact, until this psychological engineer knows how any proposed new line is going to strike the public fancy, he won't even allow raw material to be ordered, except for experimental purposes. And, once a line of goods is decided on, he will have full power to see that popularity and publicity are manufactured into these goods at every stage of production.

What have you already in your goods that people like habitually? "Always remember," says Q. E. D., "that the bulk of advertised products are bought by people who drive Ford cars and who, therefore, can think faster with their feet than they can with their minds." What can you say about your business that people who think with their feet will all want to know? Find out. Try it on clerks and customers. Test it on your friends. If they seem more than merely politely interested, extend your idea a step further to your public. Try a window display, a circular letter, or a small newspaper advertisement. If you don't get a sharp gleam of interest from the first few people at hand, go back and start the attack from another angle. If your proposition doesn't flicker in a little test, it will never flare in a big one, no matter how much more power you put behind it. A little spark will show you are on the right track. Even champion marksmen fire sighting shots. Tilden warms up before he plays. Thomas A. Edison begins with small preliminary experiments.

But, you say, all this is petty nonsense for some peanut peddler! We do great institutional publicity.

We advertise nationally. We sustain thousands of retail merchants. What interest have we in your tests and flickers? On the contrary, dear sirs, the more important your mission, the greater your institution, the broader your appeal, the more money you spend—the more vitally you are concerned as to whether people favor the proposition you propose. Beautiful big institutional advertisements are the easiest of all advertisements to do—and the most dangerous. General publicity, you will find, is a battleship chugging along in a dull gray fog compounded of hypothesis, of theory, of persuasiveness of the advertising agent, and of the wisdom of the men who approve the copy and pay the bills. Mail-order advertising, on the other hand, is like a torpedo boat dashing to the attack under the blinding glare of a searchlight. If copy writers and publishers were paid only for what an advertisement *does*, instead of what it costs, you might wake up some morning and not recognize your own campaign.

The little advertiser takes small risks. But the man who spends really large sums of money must test. He must prove his response at every step from the simple idea to the finished advertisement. All trade is enacted in the human mind and nowhere else. The kitchen in which Molière read plays to his cook differed less than one might suppose from the magnificent experimental laboratory of the General Electric Company.

As soon as you have decided what you want to do, and satisfied yourself that the public is likely to take a lively interest, call in an advertising agent. Show him how far you have gone. Tell him you need all his skill and experience to help you carry on. A good agent approached in this way won't need to be told that you want to develop step by step.

But take pains to show your advertising agent the bright side of the picture. Guarantee him, in consideration for his patient testing—first for direction, and then for results—that you will stick to advertising as long as it makes good. And stick to him as long as he does. On no other basis can any intelligent advertising man afford to handle your advertising in a way you can afford to have it handled.

Remember the old Scotch proverb: "You get naething for naething and mickle for ha'penny." If advertising were anything more magic than sound business practice, inspired by imagination, ingenuity, and enterprise, there would be 200,000 steady national advertisers instead of 20,000 in-and-outers. Measure your advertising plan to the money you have to spend, and you will soon have more of both. And remember, for every advertiser who has failed through going too slow, a full hundred have flung their money so far and so fast they have starved to death waiting for it to come back.

Be patient as well as practical. Every advertisement costs money. It either brings that money back with a profit, or it doesn't. There is no more excuse for an unprofitable advertisement than for an unprofitable branch office. Or an unprofitable salesman. Remember, too, your advertising is an expense only when it is a gamble. Backed with enough common sense, time and testing, it becomes an investment. Even so, prompt returns are always desirable. A quick turnover is as necessary in your advertising as in your merchandise. The better the advertisement, the more quickly you need to repeat it over and over again. Prompt results keep your advertising dollar working harder with less risk. At any rate, don't tie up a lot of money waiting for something later on. If nothing at all happens in the beginning, you might as well make up your mind the fireworks are wet. No advertisement—whether good or bad— single or part of a series—will, in four months, four years, or four centuries, acquire, directly or indirectly, any more strength than it has the day it reaches its peak circulation.

On the other hand, the people who still believe that advertising is some sort of a cumulative Santa Claus are perfect Solomons in wisdom compared with those who think they can turn advertising on and off like an electric light without throwing away money in tragic sums.

Neither good will nor money in the bank vanishes the minute one stops adding to it. Unlike money in the bank, however, good will starts spending itself the moment you stop adding to it. The fact that one can't see good will dissipate doesn't alter the fact. The things we can't see are almost always the most dangerous.

So keep hammering away. But in order to keep hammering, you will have to keep simple. Don't get entangled in the extraneous trappings and trimmings advertising has so painfully accumulated. Any really good golfer can make an excellent score with only one club, while a dub can't help his score no matter how many clubs he uses. Keep away from statistics until you actually use them. Then get only the figures you *know* you need.

Weight of circulation is one thing, effective copy quite another. Yet the two are constantly confused. Wilbur Wright used to say that he could fly on a kitchen table if he could get a powerful enough engine. So, regardless of how bad the copy may be, you might make some sort of a success of any advertising campaign if you spend enough money in a small enough territory. So any South Sea Islander might thrash a golf ball completely around the golf course with his war club. But the youngest caddy would know better than to call it golf!

Copy, in one form or another, is the heart and soul of advertising. Except as an aid to the preparation of copy, or its extension, everything else is more or less meaningless. In fact, much of the unnecessary complication in modern advertising thought is due to straying away from that one simple fundamental.

Research develops facts that may help sell goods; but a hundred men in a hundred Fords, filling out questionnaires all day long, wouldn't, of themselves, sell enough goods to pay for their gasoline. Wise choosing of places to publish advertising copy unquestionably enables that copy to sell more goods; but you could sit and choose mediums until you were black in the face, and thereby never move a boy's express wagon full of toy balloons. Mechanical departments help copy find favorable expression, but the most meticulously artful piece of typography that ever lulled a roving eye will never turn a nickel, unless it eases home a message some copy writer has cut and hammered until it starts something personal in the man who reads it.

Avoid complications of every kind. Stick to one simple idea. Extend it always. Vary it slightly now and then, but never change it. Shun all extra expenditure for supplementary advertising schemes of all kinds except inexpensive logical, exact extensions of the same idea you have already proved profitable. Remember that if your basic idea is good enough, your advertising will succeed without a dollar spent on anything except the space to put it in. If your idea is unattractive or your copy wrong, the most elaborate marketing and merchandising plans will only pile up the possibilities of failure. But there is little excuse for failure if you only use a bit of imagination and a lot of ordinary common sense.

Don't worry about buying power; if your advertisement and your proposition are right, you can shut your eyes and choose any good recognized medium. It will give you all the buying power you can reasonably ask for. Try the livest smaller publications first, because you tie up less money and run less risk. As your returns check up, work slowly and steadily into the biggest and very best circulations you can find.

A market survey is a means to an end and never an end in itself. If it does not immediately serve to improve the effectiveness of your sales and advertising, it is worthless. Any statistical study, whether a straw vote or a monumental market analysis, depends on:

The WISDOM of the man who plans it
The HONESTY of the man who takes it
The ACCURACY of the man who compiles it
The SOUND IMAGINATION and JUDGMENT of the man who interprets it.

When you are sure of all these elements, put full faith in a questionnaire, summary, or investigation. Straws tell which way the wind blows. It is a waste of time and money to hire a man by the year to toss a bale of hay. One intelligent, live judgment—tested under careful observation—is worth a library of dead statistics, no matter what you paid for them.

The quickest test of your advertising idea is to try it on somebody. So get started! Start testing with anybody, and work promptly into more scientific investigation. Battleships don't wait to fire broadsides to get the range. They let loose one or two experimental guns. And spot the hits. Get going somehow, and increase or modify as the check-ups prove you are right. A start this January is worth a dozen perfect plans next June.

INDEX

393

*The following pages
contain advertisements
of other Harper
business books*

T-162